CW00470911

Modern-Day
Salvation
Encounters

Modern-Day
Salvation
Encounters

40 True Stories of Highly Dramatic, Incredibly Astonishing & Riveting Salvation Conversion Testimonies

ALLISON C. RESTAGNO

© Copyright August 2016 - Allison C. Restagno of Restagno Developments, Inc. All rights reserved.

All rights reserved. This book is protected by international copyright laws. This book may not be copied or reprinted for commercial gain or profit. The use of short quotations or occasional page copying for personal or group study is permitted and encouraged. Permission may be granted upon request. Scripture quotations are taken from the King James Version of the Holy Bible. All material included in this book which was excerpted or derived from the books and writings of other authors are included with the expressed permission of the original author/publisher to whom the copyright belongs.

This book, *Modern-Day Salvation Encounters*, along with *Modern-Day Miracles*, both by Author Allison C. Restagno, are available at bookstores and distributors worldwide.

To place an order for either *Modern-Day Miracles*, or *Modern-Day Salvation Encounters*, by Allison C. Restagno, please go to Amazon.com, Google "purchase books by Allison C. Restagno," or visit the websites for these books:

www.moderndaysalvationencounters.com
www.moderndaymiraclesbook.com

*Modern-Day Salvation Encounters is also available in e-book format.

Disclaimer: Please note that both the publisher and Allison Restagno assume no liability either directly or indirectly for the selection, use, printing, and distribution of these aforementioned personal testimonies, nor assume any other liability in any other way in part or in whole. While to the best of Allison Restagno's knowledge, these stories are believed to be true, and testimony contributors have all signed legal documents attesting to that fact, neither the publisher nor Allison Restagno (RESTAGNO DEVELOPMENTS, INC.) assumes any liability whatsoever either directly or indirectly from the use of these stories. Complete responsibility for the truth and integrity, content and form, as well as any liabilities for these aforementioned testimonies, is held in full by each of the individual story contributors separately.

Soft Cover ISBN: 978-0-9952843-0-2

Audio Book ISBN: 978-0-9952843-1-9

Ebook ISBN: 978-0-9952843-2-6

For Worldwide Distribution, Printed in the U.S.A.

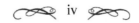

Dedication

This book is dedicated to the glory of the Lord
and in accordance with the "Great Commission"
(see Matthew 28:18-20).

Acknowledgments

I am utterly overwhelmed with gratitude to so many persons and ministries that have helped in varying roles to take this book through to publication, so that you, the Reader, would be able to read these 40 incredible, amazing and awe-inspiring personal salvation encounters.

As such, I would like to take this opportunity to sincerely thank all of my 40 new testimony contributors for this, my second book in print; you so generously volunteered your stories for inclusion into Modern-Day Salvation Encounters for the glory and purposes of the Lord.

I would very much like to extend a special thank you to all of those contributors who have provided me with referrals for this book including Mr. Sid Roth and the staff at Messianic Vision, Mr. Jack Olson, Mr. Bruce Van Natta, Mrs. Audra Rose Haney, Rev. Cecil Murphey, Stan Cottrell, Sammy Maloof Ministries and staff, and Ms. GiGi Erneta. Thank you all so incredibly much!

Thank you also to Holly Anderson of Nico Hill Ministries, Dave Alley of Katie Souza Ministries, Katelyn Rose Gondell referred by Janeen at Sammy Maloof Ministries, and Mr. Jack Olson who have each done some special writing for a story in this book. Also, I want to thank Mark Virkler, President of Communion with God Ministries, for allowing me to include his concise and well thought out Four Steps to Salvation Prayer and very insightful commentary.

A special thanks goes out to my mother, Carolyn Curran-Fyckes, for writing a few of these stories out and her highly valued editorial input into this book for the Lord. May the Lord reward your faithfulness accordingly! You have blessed the work of the Lord! Thank you.

To all of those persons who have supplied books, CDs, DVDs, pictures and other resource materials to help with putting this book forth to printing — a very big thank you goes out to you, too. Your assistance was invaluable and most timely. Thank you so very much!

To Stan Cottrell, who wrote the foreword for this book: Thank you for blessing this book with such a wonderful foreword! You are so amazingly talented, and such an incredible person. You have not only gifted me with this foreword, but also with your friendship! Your invaluable support of this project, along with your highly insightful suggestions, have served to greatly enhance this work of the Lord.

To Rev. Bruce Van Natta, who wrote such a special word for this book: Thank you for listening to the Lord, obeying His leading, and choosing to give your recommendation for this book. Your spiritual friendship and words of wisdom over the years are very highly valued! You are a willing and faithful servant of the Lord. It is a great pleasure to see the Lord working through you, your incredible ministry, and to be able to appreciate you as a good Christian friend.

To a very special team of book endorsers and friends: Audra Rose Haney, producer of *THE 700 CLUB* from the North Star, Tennessee, office; Evangelist Rev. Dr. Jerry Spencer of Jerry Spencer Ministries; Mr. Daniel Fazzina, author and host of *Divine Intervention* syndicated radio show; Evangelist Rev. Bruce Van Natta of Sweet Bread Ministries; Ben Robinson of the Toronto Christian Business Directory; Dr. Jerry Horner; Mrs. Javetta Saunders; Olympian Chris Brown; Mrs. Glenda Pettey of R&G Ministries; Mr. J. D. Smith; and Mr. Ed Epp. I cannot thank you enough for your wonderfully encouraging words. You have all been such a blessing to this book project for the Lord's glory, honor and purposes! Thank you all so very much!

Additionally, I would be remiss if I did not thank a very special testimony contributor, Mr. Tommy Woods, for his amazing assistance with this project. Without knowing that I was being called by the Lord to compile this book of 40 salvation testimonies, Mr. Woods heard the voice of the Lord speak to his spirit and prompt him to send me his personal salvation testimony. Included along with his testimony was a note granting me permission to use his salvation story in my book if ever I should need it someday. Most interestingly, Mr. Woods's testimony along with his note arrived precisely on the day that I had been asking the Lord for a confirmation as to whether or not I was indeed to compile this book comprised of 40 salvation testimonies by faith. Thank you so very much for sending in your story first!

Next, I would like to take this opportunity to thank Dr. Jerry Horner, Mr. Jack Olson, Mrs. Javetta Saunders, and a publisher who has requested anonymity, who all have selflessly granted permission for use and inclusion of a few testimonies to be included into this book. Thank you all again. Only the Lord knows your reward in eternity for this! Bless you all abundantly!

Now, a word of great thanks to two outstanding individuals who have worked "behind the scenes" to support this book coming together: Mrs. Marissa Hale, who has edited this book with a wonderfully light edit so that we can "hear the voices from each individual testimony contributor"; and Ms. Margaret Hampton, my publishing assistant and my publicist, who was sent by the Lord for the purposes of finalizing this book and releasing it far and wide for the Lord's glory and purposes. Thank you both so very much. You were instrumental in the success of this book! Thank you for putting your time and your talents into this book. ~ An incredibly tremendous thank you also goes out to Stan Cottrell of The Global Friendship Run, who orchestrated this divine "set up" in the first place. You are indeed a very special "Specialer." Thank you for pouring your time and energy into this book as well!

Finally, thank you to all of my family and my amazing friends whom the Lord has blessed me with! These include, of course, my wonderful testimony contributors and so many others who have most graciously lent support to this book from the inception to the finale for the Lord's sovereign purposes! I couldn't have done it without you. I pray that the Lord greatly blesses every one of you through His sovereignty! I love you in the Lord and I am so eternally grateful to each of you (named and unnamed).

May you be blessed "exceedingly above measure" for all you have so graciously given to this book for the Lord's total honor, glory and purposes!

In His Name & In His Love,

~Allison

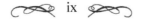

Endorsements

As one of the contributors in her previous book, *Modern-Day Miracles*, I know Allison Restagno's amazing drive and persistence in following the Lord's mandate to carry out His will. *Modern-Day Salvation Encounters* is divinely ordained to be game-changer in the real world where heaven meets earth. The 40 stories from such a wide spectrum of the global population are a foretaste of many more to come. Each testimony uniquely declares the glory of the Lord and that His Kingdom will have no end. Thank you, Allison, for using your talent and moreover, for your prophetic insight to encourage Christians with these examples which will make a way for others to come to the saving grace of our Lord and Savior, Jesus Christ.

Glenda Pettey
Author of *Heaven is Real, One Man's Story to Heaven and Back*,
and Chapter 21 in *Modern-Day Miracles*
www.rgministries.org

We all have a story. Personally, I love to pick up a magazine and read true-life stories about others, as well as autobiographies. I really don't have time for fiction any more. I want to learn something from someone else and I am quite interested in why people choose what they do. I love to see the results of their choices.

This book is a collection of amazing stories. The interesting thing is they are "God Stories." In every situation, something happened, and God showed up in a real and practical way. When you read these true-life situations, you think things like, *That could have been me*; *I have been right there in my life;* and *If God did that for him, then He can do that for me*. This is an important and easy book to read. You will pick it up many times and reread the stories. Perhaps one of them you will really relate to, and you will encounter God, and it will change your life forever.

J. D. Smith
Business Owner, Toronto, Ontario

A compelling book that reassures us again and again that God's promise to protect His children from the storms of life is everlasting.

Ben Robinson
The Toronto Christian Business Directory

Wow! Allison Restagno has given us another life-changer! What a terrific book. She shares with us authentic faith encounters from 40 fascinating individuals. Each one uses powerful words in describing their grace experience with Christ — Salvation, Regeneration, Transformation, Redemption and New Birth. This dynamic collection of personal testimonies will excite, entertain, enlighten, encourage, inspire and influence every reader! This unique book is surely destined to be a bestseller.

Dr. Jerry L. Spencer
Jerry Spencer Ministries

The testimonies in this book prove that people's encounters with God are as varied as people are themselves, but the net result is always the same: God making himself real, and an intimate relationship growing out of that. I encourage you to read this book and judge for yourself if what we see is all there is, or is there much more to life than meets the eye? I guarantee you won't be disappointed.

Bruce Van Natta
Author, Speaker and Founder of Sweet Bread Ministries

Allison Restagno is a tenacious warrior for the kingdom of God. The powerful testimonies she has compiled for this book are a clear sign that the God of the Bible is alive and still working in the lives of everyday people today — changing the world, one heart at a time. I know you will be blessed and encouraged by reading this collection of inspiring stories.

Daniel Fazzina
Author, *Divine Intervention - 50 True Stories of God's Miracles Today*
Host, *Divine Intervention Radio* - www.divineinterventionradio.com

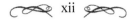

If you haven't dared read *Modern-Day Salvation Encounters*, you've missed out on your own "Golden Moment." There is FIRE in these testimonies! This is a "GOTTA READ!!!" Five Olympic Thumbs Up!

Chris "Fireman" Brown
Multi-Medal Winning Bahamian Olympian

Many people think that they are so evil, or have done things so bad, that God would never save them. One of the most effective means in bringing people to salvation is a convicting personal testimony, and the ones included in this book provide ample evidence that God can and will save anyone who comes to Him by faith. If you are concerned about the salvation of lost friends or loved ones, I encourage you to give this book to them.

Dr. Jerry Horner
Former Dean of Oral Roberts University School of Theology
Founding Dean of Regent University School of Divinity

The people whose testimonies are recorded in this inspiring book are trophies of God's limitless grace — demonstrating the great love and kindness of God in renewing lives, broken and shattered by sin. Their stories glorify Christ and will encourage the faith of those who are witnessing to others.

Javetta Saunders
Christian Businesswoman, Singer/Composer, Author, Speaker

We live in a dark and discouraging world, but the Bible tells us that our enemy is overcome by "the blood of the Lamb, and by the word of their testimony (Revelation 12:11a)." Therefore, I think this collection of dramatic salvation testimonies is so vital for our generation. I'm excited to applaud Allison for her relentless efforts to bring God's amazing stories to the world in this format, and I'm excited to see how our great, miracle-working Savior uses them all to bring souls into His Kingdom.

Audra Haney
Writer and Producer for *The 700 Club*

We are called to be part of God's miracles in this world — through acts of generosity and healing and hope.

Ed Epp
Executive Director, cbm Canada

Seek ye the Lord while he may be found,

call ye upon him while he is near:

~Isaiah 55:6, KJV.

Contents

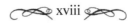

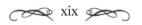

FOREWORD BY STAN COTTRELL

Marvelous! Splendid! Brilliant milestone!

These were the precise words which came to mind after reviewing the writings in Allison Restagno's new book, the one you are holding in your hands right now. I believe this work will surely be touted as a major addition to inspire people who are hurting or are disillusioned, those who have gone astray from their faith, and all who find themselves bankrupt morally, financially, ethically and spiritually.

I applaud Allison for her tenacity and vision, for stepping out of the boat and taking a giant leap of faith into the exciting world of seeing her work go into the marketplace. Each chapter of *Modern-Day Salvation Encounters* has a different author. A strong attribute which bred creativity amongst her authors was her non-threatening style, allowing her authors to share their authentic story.

The world wants and needs "real" people sharing their hearts with a minimum amount of threat. We live in a vastly exaggerated, technological world. We, in America, take more medications, sedatives and resort to mind-altering drugs over all other nations. The world has physiological nearness — as evidenced by growing populations, blending cultures, redefining and shaking apart values of God, Country, and The American Way of Life — but where are honesty, friendship and genuine care? Humankind is screaming, "Help!"

Modern-Day Salvation Encounters provides a perfect forum to fit your specific situation, regardless of where you may be in your life right now. All of these authors represent all of the scenarios that you frequently hear about on the 24-hour news stations. In addition, all of these authors have dealt with their own unique dragons — whether it was financial, physical, relational, moral, ethical, boredom, loss of aspiration, anger, bitterness, aggression, loneliness, emptiness, apathy… and you can add your own subject line to this list.

Here's great reading. *Real people* with *real stories*. Do you wish you could get off this endless merry-go-round of going nowhere? Do you feel that you are a fraud? That if people really knew you, they would never have anything to do with you? Do things never seem to work out for you? What messages are you sending to yourself? Are you wounding yourself with labels that God never intended for you to have?

Allison's fantastic compilation of 40 powerful testimonies as discovered in this book, *Modern-Day Salvation Encounters*, is designed specifically for you. God's Hand is upon this work. Each chapter is easy to read, invigorating, inspiring and thought-provoking.

The most appealing thing to me was that I realized I am not alone by any stretch of the imagination. Here are people who have dealt with the same struggles, have gone through the same parade of the seasons… and just look at how similar we all are.

Each author comes to an amazing conclusion, regardless of their circumstances. Each one arrives at the same location, regardless of the circuitous routes, winding roads, dark valleys, depths of despair or even temporary successes, from a worldly point of view.

Somewhere in my journey, I heard it once said, "Out of the presses of tears comes the soul's finest wine." I further remember some old man who had never gone to school say to me, "A brook can't sing its song without the rocks."

We all have a song to sing. All of creation has been waiting for our arrival with our own unique message of faith, hope and love. These abide.

Here's to you, Allison, and to the willing servants who answered your sweet, wistful, tender call to share their story with the world. I believe this book will be a classic in Christian lore, sermon illustrations, Biblical counseling courses, and that it will also serve as a wonderful, non-religious but highly spiritual book, which is must reading for all who seek Truth.

After all, truth is beauty, and beauty truth. That's all we know and all we need to know.

Stan Cottrell
Catalytic Influencer, People-to-People Goodwill Ambassador,
Inspirational Speaker, Author, Founder: The Global Friendship Run,
Former Guinness World Record Holder for Trans-USA Run
Nobel Peace Prize Nominee 2017
RealStanCottrell.wordpress.com
FriendshipSports.org

A Word from Bruce Van Natta

I first met Allison Restagno several years ago when she coordinated my appearance on a major Christian television show in Canada. Later she asked me to be one of the contributors for her first book, *Modern-Day Miracles*. Throughout the years, we have stayed in contact through ministry opportunities and as prayer support for each other's ministries.

I can say after knowing her this long that she has a heart for God and for ministry. She is able to hear God speak clearly and communicate His heart and love for people. As an example, I am aware of one time when she was talking to a complete stranger and went on to tell him the name of the place he worked, what shift he worked, and what was going on at his job that was troubling him. In the end, her words proved to this man that God was clearly real. Better yet, God was paying attention to him and his circumstances.

There are many other instances I could share like this, but they all end with the same result — people having an awareness of the reality of God, and specifically His love for them. The testimonies printed in this book accomplish that same thing. I personally know a couple of the people whose stories are in this book and can vouch that they are people whose lives have been changed forever by the knowledge of a living God who loves them.

In 2006, I had a semi-truck fall on top of me while I was working underneath it. The front axle crushed my body in half like a blunt guillotine. Arteries were severed in five places and I was "bleeding out."

I called out for God to help me and ended up having an out of body/near death experience. I then watched the accident scene from above and saw two huge angels the Lord sent to save me. A Christian woman showed up who prayed me back to life. With the benefit of extensive medical documentation, I have shared my story on over 45 television shows, over 100 radio programs, nearly 1,000 speaking events and in several books, including two that I wrote called *Saved by Angels* and *A Miraculous Life*.

I am now in full time ministry, travelling the world and sharing what God did for me — even though I didn't deserve it. As I travel and tell my story, we often pray for people and see God make Himself real to them through a miraculous physical or emotional healing, bondages being broken, or a touch of His presence.

My hope, prayer and belief for you, the Reader, is that after reading this book, you will have the same kind of experience — a realization that the Creator of the universe is alive and well, that He loves you, and that He wants to have an intimate relationship with you!

Sincerely,
Bruce Van Natta
Author/Speaker and Founder of Sweet Bread Ministries
questions@sweetbreadministries.com

FROM THE DESK OF ALLISON

Smiling thoughts abound.

Here I sit. All the stories are finished. The enormous amount of phone calls, e-mails, skype calls…the coordination, the hands-on time with each author, working with my wonderful editors, the business people…multi-tasking, running a music studio while juggling this book, and a myriad of other duties are now behind me and we enter a new phase — getting this book to You.

I am literally visualizing you reading our book. All I feel is joy.

Oops! There goes another smile.

I find myself tempted to ask "why and how" all this has happened; then I conclude those answers aren't the important issue. Almost a year ago, I felt this "nudge" to put together a collection of stories from people who have real-life messages of overcoming brokenness, failure, bankruptcy and other heart-breaking challenges common to humankind.

When I started this mission by saying, "Yes Lord," I had no idea where it would lead. I was armed with only a burning desire to be obedient to the calling. I quickly learned obedience is the key which unlocks the heart of God. It mattered not that, at this juncture of my life, in the world's classroom, I would have been voted "The Most Unlikely Candidate" to undertake such a mission.

A thought just rushed across my mind. *Noah did not have a college degree in structural engineering when God commissioned him to build an Ark.*

So what did I do? I started talking and sharing my book idea with a few close friends. It was amazing. So many times I heard the reply, "I know someone who has a story you need to know."

My formal training is in music. In a very real sense during this project, I became the orchestra director. In a short period of time, 40

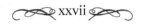

contributing Authors accepted the invitation to participate. I know you will find our Cast to be truly amazing people.

Sweet tears well up as I think of how all this has been divinely orchestrated. I know, I know, we have all heard stories of well-known celebrity-types throwing temper tantrums with overbearing, unrealistic agents. I experienced, to the person, a dimension of "selfless love" which I know you will sense from the first page. So, I'm a bit dramatic. Our book is made up of 40 love letters orchestrated to opening your eyes to truth and light perhaps in your own times of darkness.

Our book to You is bathed in such cooperation, selfless spirits and dynamic people with riveting, compelling adventures in thought, heart and spirit. I know, *I know*, as you visit with each one of my new best friends forever, you, too, will be smiling. What a beautiful experience.

It has been said, "When the Lord ordains and sanctions an endeavor everything falls into place." I saw and experienced this firsthand. To illustrate, I never called a thousand people with the hopes of getting to the number to create this manuscript. Hmm, there's something dynamic about the number 40!

I have exceeding joy and a heart filled with gratitude that you have chosen *Modern-Day Salvation Encounters* as part of your reading experience. I am a bit prejudiced, but I know you will be inspired. I know you will find answers and you will feel God's love vicariously flowing into your life. Your time of reading will be a life-changing, life-altering, significant milestone. Oh my, I hear a symphony.

These are my thoughts and I am standing by them. Oh, my goodness, there goes another smile!

With love, respect and awe of this great adventure called life,

To God be the Glory forever and ever…

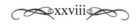

INTRODUCTION

When I look back over all of the miracles that have happened as a result of putting this second book together, I am again truly and utterly amazed! God is so good all of the time! He never fails us, nor forsakes us (Hebrews 13:5). Although it may not feel like it sometimes, the Bible says there are angels standing charge over us to keep us in all our ways (Psalm 91:11).

Much of this world is unseen. Every day, scientists are making new and often life-changing discoveries. There are so many mysteries waiting to be solved. Where did we come from? When did the earth take form? How did the earth take shape? Was there a Creator — Someone with far more intelligence than us — who designed our world, our universe? Did this just happen or did it evolve coincidentally over time? While there are many theories out there — some say already proven; some say they are not — I would like to leave those theories for time to reveal the truth.

This book, you'll find, is not at all about theories or one's idea pitted against another person's or another group's idea. This is a book filled with wonder; a book filled with excitement; a book brimming over with 40 highly incredible, astonishing and captivating real-life stories from real people just like you and me.

Some of the people sharing their stories have dared God, desired God, even run from God, but God had a different order of plans waiting for them. God had an astonishing adventure awaiting them to their utter amazement — and in some cases near disbelief — when first faced with their "God encounters."

I hope and believe you will note while pouring through these wonderfully amazing pages that life is to be cherished, enjoyed and loved. Most of all, life is a gift to be revered and respected, never taken for granted.

Many people wander through life often wondering what their purpose is and why they are here. If you are one of those people, please let me share with you, right now, that you are not alone. Many great and scholarly minds have contemplated life's purpose and why they were put here on this earth. Let me assure you that you are among "the greats" as you, perhaps, contemplate *your* life's purpose.

What will set you aside and propel you toward finding and achieving your special place in life? I believe, with my entire being, that this simple book is going to "lift the veil" for you and give you a little foretaste of the divine — of Jesus, of God, of Heaven. I say this not out of arrogance or in a "puffed up" way, but humbly, as one who has experienced the joy of coming to have glimpses of the divine as well.

This book, I believe, will encourage and feed your soul, your spirit, your mind, your will, even your intellect. This book is set apart from most other books on the subject in that these are personal stories written about real people. Some story contributors have been willing to include their first and last names and often the city, state or region and country in which they reside. Other contributors have included their personal contact information — including their cell phones.

Who would do that unless they really believed what they were going to share with you? Not many, I assure you.

For those of you wondering if perhaps these contributors were somehow "crazy" or "off their rocker," I want to share with you that there are highly intelligent people from all walks of life and widely diverse backgrounds in this book. Specifically included are persons such as John Elliott, a former CIA/INTERPOL agent; international caliber Olympic medalists and prominent sports figures such as Chris Brown, Bill Renje, Stan Cottrell and others. In this book are scientists, pastors, evangelists and even an ambassador to the United Nations.

You will recognize names of those who have accomplished outstanding achievements, received numerous presidential accolades and recognition, and other tremendously high achievers, some of whom hold doctorates. One outstanding story contributor is a current Nobel Peace Prize Nominee. How's that just for a start?

Now, let's throw in some Hollywood. There are acclaimed movie stars, stunt drivers, former television show hosts, directors, producers and screenwriters included in this book.

All story contributors have come together for one common purpose: they want to share their incredible, true "God stories" with you in the hopes you will be assured there is a God, and you, too, will come to know Him on a personal and intimate level. In essence, these wonderfully amazing testimony contributors want you to have the same opportunity as they have had in coming to know God, learning more about Jesus and experiencing the realm of the "impossible" with God.

All things truly are possible with God. When you place your trust in Him, He will never fail you nor forsake you, and He will bring you through — just in time — as he did with all of these highly-valued story contributors in *Modern-Day Salvation Encounters*.

Will you walk along with me, journeying through these stories with an open heart and an open mind, and allow His spirit to fall so freshly and most marvelously upon you?

I hope so. I believe that you're really going to enjoy the ride.

Please come with me on an adventure...one that you are likely never to forget.

PART I

But God commendeth his love toward us, in that,
while we were yet sinners, Christ died for us.

(Romans 5:8, KJV).

CHAPTER 1

"I WILL SHOW YOU, I AM"

(included by permission from
Walk With Me, 2nd edition, by Mark Lynch)

Mark R. Lynch

*Howbeit when he, the Spirit of truth, is come, he will guide you
into all truth: for he shall not speak of himself; but whatsoever
he shall hear, that shall he speak: and he will show you things
to come*
(John 16:13, KJV).

The first time I had really had the privilege of being in front of God
was in my wooded backyard. I was very angry, screaming out, calling
Him all sorts of nasty words that I'm truly ashamed of now. He then
came to me in an amazing way; this invisible Being suspended me
above the ground. Instead of being completely crushed by Him after
what I had said, and having my full attention as I could feel the
immense power radiating from Him, He spoke to me. It was a quiet
peaceful voice and He said these words that I will never forget.

"I Am," He said. "I will guide you."

Then I was let go and He was gone.

This is my testimony as I lived it and how I believe it. I have
actually experienced death twice and if the same thing that happened to
me happened to you, how would it affect you? Would you share your
experience with others or keep it to yourself? Please allow me to share
just a few things I have experienced.

I grew up in a family of nine. We were on the poor side but we survived. You don't miss what you never had. I was the oldest son of five boys. I grew up knowing how bad rejection and abuse feels like. Growing up in certain environments affects our outlook on how we look at life. What was normal then is now known as extremely dysfunctional.

I know through my experiences that I have had (and somehow miraculously recovered from) that God really does exist. I have had three personal experiences where I have been directly in His presence. I can testify to the truth that God is very much alive. He is very real, very alive and He does have a plan for all of us. For me this is a fact, not fiction.

Like a lot of people I also had thoughts of, *Why does He allow certain things?* Only in seeing it all play out can you see how life works out as sort of an interlocking puzzle. Certain people and events are put in each of our lives to see how we choose. Our motive and actions are mostly what God is watching for.

Do we choose the quickly gotten pleasure of sin that always comes with payback or choose a different path? Are you the "what's-in-it-for-me", more of a "selfie" type person? Or are you someone looking out for the benefit of doing good to others and expecting nothing in return type of person? Guess which of the two are the God type persons?

Following God does not always make sense to us. God allows "bad" for our benefit, even if you can't wrap your head around this, someday you will understand. He knows all the answers and it is all for good; the evil must exist for good to triumph.

Let me share a true story. Back in 1975, I was living in Bridgewater with my wife and our twin daughters. I couldn't find a job and yet I needed to provide for my family. I was looking for a solution to our money problems when I came across an ad for a new business. It involved chemically cleaning brick and stone surfaces. I was so hoping that this new business would be the solution to all our problems.

I borrowed $5000 from my in-laws to buy a franchise. By now, the bill collectors were even calling us in the middle of the night. I knew if this new business didn't work we would probably lose our house.

Instead of paying the mortgage, I spent the remaining money we had and bought this old van. I needed the van to get the chemicals and a high pressure washer to the job sites. The van was a junk box and I was not a mechanic.

It was a mild spring afternoon around two or 3 o'clock. I had driven this van around to my back yard and had painted the van by hand with a paint brush and a gallon of bright orange paint that a friend gave me. It looked better than it did before the paint job.

When I finished painting I jumped in and was planning to drive the van to the front of my house. I couldn't get the van to start. I tried everything including kicking it. This was the last straw! I didn't know what I was going to do.

Here I was, 24-years-old, with a wife and two young babies. I had no job. We were in debt beyond repayment and the bill collectors wouldn't just go away. I didn't know what to do. I had gone to my in-laws to borrow the money I needed to get this business going and I had no other source I could turn to for help. I was at the bottom, or breaking point, of my life.

I don't know why, but out of nowhere a thought crossed my mind. *Maybe I could pray.*

I couldn't believe a thought like this would ever cross my mind! Me, of all people! *Me, pray? To who? To what? To God?* I really wasn't even sure there was a God!

Then I thought, *If there really was a God, why would a superior Being even gave a damn?* I thought I was being ridiculous. If there was a God, He must be blind. Or he just didn't care! Why, if there was a God and He was this all-powerful Being, doesn't He notice what's going on down here? Where has He been hiding all my life? Or was it that He just doesn't care, not just about me?

Doesn't He see all the suffering in the world? If He was this all-compassionate Being, how can He face a crippled child? How can He allow babies to have birth defects? How does He allow evil to go unpunished? Maybe He just wasn't that powerful after all!

(Just a note here; He eventually did answer all of those questions and now I understand. I truly was blind then, though I thought I could see.)

The more I thought about it the angrier I became. At the time I was wrestling with this in my mind I also was noticing my neighbor mowing his lawn and the children of another neighbor playing on their swing set. My thoughts were racing, thinking of how much was wrong with this world; how the corrupt seemed to prosper while the good seemed to get crushed.

How could there ever be a God? I was becoming furious! If there was a God, He was totally insensitive and removed!

Then I did something I would not recommend anyone do. From the bottom of my soul, with every ounce of emotion I could muster, I challenged God. I guess I did this just to really see if anything would happen. I meant business, though.

I screamed to Him, "If You are there, if You exist, I say that You are a coward and no God!"

I spat on the ground and stated that I had more respect for the spit than for any blind, self-proclaimed God! I was furious! I screamed out that even *I* would do a better job than He ever could! I wouldn't allow all the suffering and injustice to continue as was so prevalently seen in the world He supposedly created.

"I challenge You, God, right here, right now, You coward. If You exist, You show me! You prove to me that You exist! ...or are you afraid of me?"

In an instant everything became very quiet. I looked at my neighbor mowing the lawn, but now I couldn't hear the mower or hear the children playing on the swing set anymore. I could see, but I could no longer hear. Now, I was getting alarmed.

My back yard was mainly comprised of dense woods. As I faced the woods, I looked in amazement. Though it was quiet, the trees started parting. Not like they were being blown by a gust of wind, but more like something big was coming and pushing them aside like they were twigs. It was as though a giant creature or a bull dozer was moving and pushing the trees aside that were in its path as it plowed straight through them and towards me.

At first I tried to blame it on the wind, but there was no wind and the trees were not bending in the same direction. I could clearly see rows of trees being parted to the left and right at the same time. These were big trees. Whatever it was that was doing this was also heading towards me, and I started getting nervous.

Then the most amazing thing happened. I can only describe it as a presence that came right up to me from between the trees. This invisible Being — yes, I said Being — surrounded me and held me frozen just slightly off the ground!

There was no mistaking His awesome power as He held me tightly. It was like a powerful energy field that held me as its captive. I could turn my head but my body wasn't able to move!

I looked at my neighbor and the children on the swings. I could still see them clearly, but I couldn't hear anything. Though I could clearly see all around me, I couldn't see who held me captive.

I felt the presence facing me. There was no question what was happening to me was real. This was no illusion. I was not asleep or in any hypnotic trance. I was not on any medication either, prescribed or otherwise, and I don't drink.

Now I was a lot more than nervous. I was scared...really scared! I felt like I was an insignificant nothing under the pressure of this Being's power. I felt the power intensely and knew He, yes, He, could easily crush me in a blink of an eye. His power was immense, so indescribable. The presence was unmistakable!

It was similar to an experience where you are in a completely dark room and someone is standing right in front of you. You feel their presence; you know they're there even though you can't see them.

There was no mistaking what this Being wanted. He made sure that He had my full attention. I was in total awe and wondering in my mind what or who this Being was. In answer to the question in my mind, I heard a quiet, calm voice speaking directly to me. He wasn't angry, though I felt He had every right to be after what I had said. It was a quiet, still voice, not excited or forceful, just perfectly calming.

He said, "I will show you, I am."

He could have crushed me like an ant; instead, He took pity on me.

Then, I was let go. I fell to the ground and He was gone.

I immediately heard my neighbor's lawnmower and the children playing. I was left in total shock and awe. This was no PTSD zoning. This was not a hallucination. This was frightening, exciting and beyond bizarre all in one experience! I was trembling and my mind was racing. *What had just happened?*

I knew what I had just experienced was God. God communicated with me! Why was I allowed this? Why couldn't someone have been with me to witness this event? Regardless, it happened. I wasn't given any new miraculous words, no new golden tablets or tablets of stone, no new hidden secrets and no big "poof," or "now I'm an angel" or some holy being. It was just a miraculous experience and the words, "I will show you, I am," that I will never forget.

Something else happened, although I didn't know it at the time. This Being "was and is God." He planted a seed in me that in time would take root, grow and change me. As I stated, I did not instantly become some perfect being, nor did all of my problems just disappear. But now something was definitely different and I could not get what I experienced, or Him, off my mind. Now I knew God really did exist. Now I wondered who or what *was I*?

His creation? His creature? I didn't know at the time that God knew me. He knew everything about me. He knew every thought and experience I had ever had. He also knew then everything that I would experience in the future. Hindsight is very clear. I know in the present what I did not know in the past. God calls himself "I am."

I know through my life experiences the worst pain you could ever experience and really not have any chance of recovery from, but I did. I know how that actually feels and how the shock wave aftermath of horrible emotion that comes with it feels like as well. I did not have an easy road down this life, but I can testify that Jesus was with me every step of the way even when I didn't have a clue. God was my guide through all the twists and turns and events in my life.

He takes you through the thorn bushes, not down the fluffy path roads. He is the author of all of us and all of everything around us. God is Spirit and God seeks those who seriously would love to have a serious relationship with Him.

Trust me here; you cannot fool God. You need to be serious about it and decide to live life His way. It will most likely not be a rosy life, but you cannot even come anywhere near close to imagining the reward that awaits you in Paradise for eternity. Emotions so spectacular they do not exist here on this plain. There is so much more to gain.

What is God really asking for you to do? To live life His way. Just think this through; God is stating that if you want to live forever in a state of total bliss you have to live by His rules here and now. If you want to live for eternity in His house you need to live by his rule.

Even growing up on the streets we recognized boundaries and why boundaries must exist. God wants you to give up doing it your way (which most likely wasn't very good up to this point) and really be sincere with Him. Decide to live life His way by following His way as outlined in the Bible.

Do the best you can to make good choices, not bad. Does what you do benefit others or just what's in it for you? He knows everything about you already. He is willing to take away your sin penalty for your very sincere trust in Jesus to save your sorry ass.

This means you need to build a personal relationship with an invisible-to-the-eye, loving Jesus. Even when you can't see Him, He is there and He will be in you. If God the Holy Spirit is not in you, then take this as a warning that you are in great danger of a most horrible eternity, my friend. But if you ever want to reach that empty part of you and find what you have always really craved, then I strongly urge you to check it all out for yourself with an open mind. Just get a copy of the Holy Bible that is easy to read or it's also available in audio. My life turned all around when I really, with all my heart, put all my trust in Him to save me.

None of us can save even ourselves. I choose to live the way that it is explained in the Bible. I understand that if I am to live with Him in His house, certain behavior is expected. I was serious with God. He knows my heart and your heart; you can't fool God. He knows every thought in your head and even what you are going to choose to follow: His way or do it like Sinatra, your way? Everything we do is being recorded behind the scenes that you don't get to see until the end.

I truly did experience paradise and I begged Him to let me stay. But it really is His will and it always has turned out for the best, down the road, following His advice. It was the best thing I did in my life.

I was in the real estate business and I met all kinds of folks with all kinds of ways they see things, but the only thing that really matters is how God sees it. Even if you stomp your feet and tap the heels of your ruby slippers and actually believe He doesn't exist, He still *does* exist. You will see this for yourself someday, this I can guarantee with a personal promise!

Let me share just a little more from my book, *Walk With Me, 2nd edition.*

The Second Time I Died

I was in the hospital for three weeks. While there, I felt totally depressed and angry. *Why me?* I felt betrayed by who I thought was my most beloved friend, God. I didn't understand it.

Had I done something that really had Him angry with me? I knew the Bible. I knew His words and I knew His promises. I still had no answers. I was starting to lose hope and starting to become bitter. How many times did my faith need to be tested? How much pain had I needed to experience?

I was told the swelling in my neck should have gone down enough that the doctors could place a smaller trachea in my throat; that would eventually allow me to speak and eat. The doctor explained the procedure. It did not sound like it was going to be fun and I didn't really trust the doctors that much anymore. I was not too thrilled at the prospect of any more pain, but I knew this had to be done before I could ever leave the hospital. I had to be awake for this procedure, too.

It involved deflating the balloon that was placed down my throat that held the large trachea or tube in place. The balloon also helped in keeping the swollen area open.

They explained to me anything could happen when they deflated that balloon.

My wife was with me this time, holding my hand. They deflated the balloon in my trachea, quickly removed it and tried to shove another trachea down my throat, but my throat closed up immediately before they could get the smaller trachea in. My wife states when they deflated the balloon, she saw my entire body thrash, then drain and turn pale as my body collapsed in her arms.

I, on the other hand, had experienced something much different! At first, I remember not being able to breathe again with the excruciating pain that happens when you are suffocating to death. I died, again, and felt myself leave my body.

I floated up past the ceiling to a level plain. When I floated to this plain all of my pain disappeared in an instant and at the same instant my whole being was filled with the most wonderful feelings that I can't even begin to put into words. I felt this utter peace and the most wonderful feelings. I can't begin to describe how far beyond blissful this all felt. I was of the "Woodstock" generation and, contrary to Mr. Clinton, I have to admit that I did inhale.

In fact, if Mr. Jimmy Hendrix were to ask me, "Are you experienced?"

I would have to answer, "Yes, I am very experienced."

I was no angel. I tried many drugs back in the day.

I have also had kidney stones before, which produces serious pain, and was given three consecutive injections of morphine to try to kill the pain. The morphine did not eliminate the pain. Pain medication or any medication only deadens the pain experience, but you still feel dull pain and you don't get to go where I was now. This time it was different; all of my pain was completely gone! All worry, anxiety, fear and concerns were gone. This experience was far greater than anything I could ever have even imagined. It's frustrating because it is so difficult to explain.

While experiencing this unexplainable bliss of feelings and emotions that do not exist here on earth, I was also engulfed in this beautiful, peaceful light. It feels fantastic being out of the body. (It is amazing how much our bodies weigh us down and block us from experiencing things.) I was lighter than a feather as before, and this time I was traveling upward toward the source of this beautiful light that engulfed me.

I was not aware of being in a tunnel with white lights going past me as I traveled upward, as reported by other people who have had out of body experiences. My focus was completely on the light source. The closer I came to the light source, the better I could see it.

As I got closer, I could see that the light source was actually three separate lights. There was one light off to my left that was very bright and flashed with color. There was a huge golden light as big as the sky that also sparkled with various colors. Then there was what appeared as this long, horizontal, white light with flashes of golden light running through all of it.

As I approached, I saw that the horizontal light was a multitude of people. Each person was as white as a florescent light bulb. They appeared transparent, somewhat like jellyfish, or like a black and white negative. They were all individually outlined in what appeared to be a brilliant, gold light that somewhat resembled gold-lit garland.

They were all facing this bright, golden wall that was the second light. I looked but couldn't see where the wall ended in any direction. To me the wall looked like it was made of semi-transparent gold and was very thick. The wall was filled with the most beautiful sparkling jewels that would change the color appearance of the wall. It was like a certain paint I have seen on some cars. If I looked at it from one angle it appeared as a metallic maroon color, then it would appear as a metallic green or blue.

As for the multitude of people, at first all the people had their backs toward me and I could not recognize anyone as a relative. I couldn't see all of their faces. Every once in a while one of these people would turn around and smile at me, but no one was approaching me or communicating with me.

I do remember this one man. He was around my height, had a wonderful smile, a black beard, a black sailor's hat like a scully cap with his black hair all curled up around the hat. He had an outfit on that appeared to be like what you would find back in *The Three Musketeers'* day: a puffy shirt tucked into his puffed-up-but-slimming-down-at-the-knees pants, high boots and a vest. He would look at me but he did not approach me or say anything. He would nod his head up and down in an approving manner and then just smile at me. I didn't get it and to this day I wonder, *what was that all about?*

I was in such a wonderful state just taking this all in that I did not see Jesus at first, but felt that wonderful presence. I suspected He was standing near me. Then I heard my name being called. It was not an audible voice; it was telepathic.

I turned to my left and there was the third light, shining brighter than the other lights. It was Jesus. He was slowly levitating. His body was a very bright, white light. His head and feet shone like the sun and encompassing His entire body was a rainbow like I have never seen. He was too bright for me to be able to stare at him and I had to turn away with my head down. I saw Him as Lord of Lords in His glory and He was beyond mere words.

Other people may have had a similar experience and may have even seen Him differently. Remember what is recorded in the Bible when He was first seen by Mary, Peter and John, and others? Even though they were with Him and saw Him probably every day for years--they even ate with Him--but after His resurrection, they all did not recognize him at first?

That is because Jesus can manifest himself in any form He pleases. His abilities are infinite as ours are limited. I tried to see details of his face and clothing but I couldn't, as He was far too bright. It was like trying to look into the sun.

The energy force that He emitted was the same as I felt with God the Holy Spirit and God the Father. The rainbow that encompassed Jesus must have had around 150 different, beautiful colors that I never saw before on earth. *(I think these may be His crowns?)* Each color was alive and filled with a different emotion. They radiated off of Him in waves and as they hit me, each color had a new and different feeling. It was beyond anything I could have ever imagined. It was so wonderful; my words cannot do it justice.

As I was trying to stand before Him (and it was very hard to stand) I had thoughts, but before I could ask, He would answer each thought in my mind telepathically. It was mind-blowing! I wondered if I was in Heaven and He explained to me that I was not in Heaven; I was in "paradise." He noted the golden wall and told me that was a wall of Heaven. Only the truly innocent, mainly children, were in Heaven for now. The rest of His chosen must wait for the great wedding feast in heaven of the bridegroom to His church, the bride.

Paradise is the reception area and Heaven is the main banquet hall where the great feast is to take place. When Jesus died on the cross He said to the man being crucified beside him, *"... Verily I say unto thee, Today shalt thou be with me in paradise"* (Luke 23:43b, KJV). Jesus meant exactly what He said. That's why all of those people were looking towards the wall as they were waiting for this event to take place. All I know is that it sure did not matter to me; I could be a zillion years in paradise and be perfectly content with that.

Then He told me what I didn't want to hear. He said I was only allowed a brief stay in Paradise. I was only allowed to experience and see what I was allowed, and that I must go back; what I am to do back on earth was not yet finished. He never told me exactly what I was to do when I was sent back.

I remember reading in the Bible where it's written to be absent in the body is to be present with the Lord (2 Corinthians 5:8). Well, that was right on the money!

I understand what Jesus meant when He stated everything hidden in darkness will be brought into the light (Matthew 10:26). God has telepathic ability. You can't hide your thoughts, motives or actions from Him. He alone creates and sustains all life. Nothing that exists is hidden from Him. Whether on Earth, in Paradise or in Heaven, you can't hide your thoughts as everything is exposed to Him. Even if you could try to hide a thought, it still comes to the surface and is exposed.

I was only allowed to hear God and no one else, and He heard all my thoughts. It was not explained to me why it was this way. I guess it's because that is also all that I would be allowed for now.

I understand that we are here on earth for a reason. Everyone and everything that exists has a purpose, a reason for existing. God uses good and bad to accomplish His plan.

There had to be somewhere where God our Father could teach us and prepare us for an eternity together. That place is here on earth. We have to learn how we are expected to live in His house. We all start out here on earth. Then, when we leave our bodies behind (or put another way, when we die here) we go on to live an eternal life. What you did or did not do while here on earth will determine where you spend this eternity.

If you are a true, chosen, child of God, you will be linked together with God and all of His children, all living of one mind in an eternal bliss. So, we need to know how we are expected to behave in order to live with Him.

If you can't learn to obey His rules here on earth, how do you expect to stay with Him for eternity? If we do not experience bad things here on earth for a short period in time, how would we ever understand and appreciate the good He has for us? Or how can you ever learn to appreciate all that God does for us?

As Jesus said in Matthew 23:11, *"But he that is greatest among you shall be your servant."* God provides everything for us; God is serving us and taking care of us. He truly is the greatest of all as no one else could ever possibly do this for us. You can't live apart from God. It would be like disconnecting from the power supply that allows us to live.

I did not want to leave Paradise, but you can't argue with God and win. No one would want to come back here after being there. Trust me; here on earth it is basically hell when comparing it to paradise, but you won't know that until and if you get to paradise.

You can't take your own life and expect to get to paradise or heaven either. You have to play out this game or life adventure that He gives you and do it by His rules. That is what is authorized. You have to do it His way if you plan on living at His place for eternity.

He put in His book all that you and I are allowed to know in order to make up our minds in having free will. He is not forcing anyone to do anything. You can choose to not believe in Him or believe that He does not exist and you are a descendant of an ape. You are given free will and free choice.

Many today are trying in ignorance to distant themselves from God. If that applies to you then you are trying to unplug yourself from the only source of energy that allows you to exist. Some people want God out of the schools and everything else in society; they claim even the mention of God is offensive. When we as a society allow this, we are destroying ourselves in many ways as well as destroying our country and this planet. Whether you believe in God or not does not change anything. God exists, period, and He is in control of everything.

God has laid out everything we need to know as the truth in His Word. Nothing can or need be added to His Word, the Bible. The decisive questions of where you fit in all this depends on are where you stand with Jesus and are you living a life in being obedient to God? Or are you living a self-centered life, seeking to please yourself? Do you want to sell yourself short in indulging in the self-satisfaction of the fleeting pleasures of sin during your brief existence here on earth? Or do you want to obey God, deny yourself those pleasures and trade your life here for an eternity of pleasure far greater than anything and everything that exists here on earth?

You cannot exist without God, regardless of whether you accept this fact or not. My paraphrase of Jesus' plain statement is, "The greatest of all is the servant of all." Since God provides us everything, He is that Great Servant. In order to understand the Bible you need to have the Holy Spirit guide and teach you. Otherwise, you will never understand and miss what you do not want to miss. You have to let this sink in.

You have to have your goal in front of you and keep your focus on the goal without wavering. Then, you will finally achieve the goal.

That goal has to be God and an eternal life living with Him. You do not want the alternative and the alternative is very real! You cannot be good enough to get there on your own or through any other religious belief. Jesus said it loud and He said it clear, no one gets there but through Him (John 14:6)! From firsthand experience, where I went beats all the worlds' gold any and every day of the week. Stop selling yourself short!

My motivation for my public testimony is to lead people to the truth and not for my personal fame or fortune. I did not write my book, *Walk With Me, 2nd edition*, in seeking to establish any new religious organization, but rather to enlighten people to the truths that can only be found in God's Word, the Holy Bible, the number one selling book of all time. I stand beside my many true brothers and sisters in scattering seed.

My book, *Walk With Me, 2nd edition*, is my personal testimony. It is what I have experienced and lived. I want to share my personal witness of the experiences, knowledge, understanding and words God has shared with me. The theology in my book has been around for thousands of years.

Some of the words I have to share you may have heard preached from a pulpit, read in a book or heard from a minister or a friend. Sometimes we hear without really listening as we may choose not to. Sometimes someone will tell us something and we never hear them. Then someone else will come along and tell us the very same thing. We may not really pay attention the first time we hear something. It may have to be repeated or said differently a second or third time before we really hear and get the message loud and clear.

As long as the reader gets this message, and it helps in advancing glory to God, then my goal is achieved. I have found many people need information broken down so that they can understand it better. I have taught quite a number of people including professing "Christians" over the years who never knew a lot about what they professed to be their belief. I have also found quite a number of people who hang on to their beliefs simply out of tradition. These people have never really given any serious thought to what or why they believe as they do. It was just the way they were taught or brought up by their family.

Teaching is more than just knowing and understanding your subject matter. You have to be able explain information to others in a way that they can know, understand and apply the information. I believe the experiences of my life and the people placed in my life, along with the gifts of understanding and teaching, are all from God. The gifts I have been given are to be used to help others.

I strongly believe my most cherished Friend wanted me to write my own book and I did. His name is Jesus. I also believe that I was not allowed to remain in paradise when I died, as that book needed to be written. I firmly believe that I was to write that book, and repeat some of the stories here as a witness.

It is my intent to point as many people as possible to the right path in this life. My most treasured prayer is that one day I will hear Jesus tell me, *"Well done, thou good and faithful servant"* (Matthew 25:21). I am writing not to glorify myself, but to place all the glory where it belongs, on God alone. I am attempting to illustrate, through glimpses of my life and through personal experiences, how God has guided and changed me. How God has given me a new nature.

When I was young, I "knew of God." I now "know God," yet not completely. When I was young I lived a "me-centered" life. God has shown and taught me that to "really live" is to live a "God-centered" life. As I share parts of my stories, the reader can see how God has worked in my life. God allows certain circumstances and people to enter our lives to mold us into the person we are to become. Now, I can't even fathom living any part of life without God.

ABOUT THE CONTRIBUTOR

Mark and his wife, Agnes, have been together as soul mates for over 50 years now. On the day Mark was born, God sent Agnes; she arrived nine and one-half months later. They both grew up in different parts of Boston. God arranged for them to meet and the rest is history. They have four children and nine grandchildren. They currently reside in Braintree, Massachusetts, and Bonita Springs, Florida. Their three daughters, along with their spouses and children, all reside in Braintree. Mark and Agnes strongly believe in family and support of the family.

Mark is now retired as a military connected DAV. Mark and his family worked in Mark's real estate company for over 37 years. This allowed Agnes and Mark to start up and run the Braintree Community food pantry for over 24 years now. The pantry is Christian and all volunteer based with no paid staff. God sustains the pantry quite nicely and has kept us running in the black for 24 years and counting.

If you would like more information about Mark, you can visit his website at: www.walkwithmebook.com, or you can contact Mark at: mark@walkwithmebook.com.

Walk with Me 2nd edition by Mark Lynch is available world-wide, and can also be purchased through his website: www.walkwithmebook.com.

Mark's book is available as an e-book from Kindle and Amazon.

CHAPTER 2

NO MOUNTAIN TOO HIGH

Testimony as written by Stan Cottrell

I can do all things through Christ which strengthened me
(Philippians 4:13, KJV).

"You're dumber than an outhouse rat, Stan Cottrell."

"You're the runt of the litter."

"You can't."

I've heard phrases like these all my life. Negative voices telling me I couldn't succeed, that my dreams, hopes and aspirations were such fantasy and foolishness. When the word "potential" was discussed, no one referred to me.

I like to think every person has their own unique heart story. Every person has their own compelling stories of trials, tribulations, grief and victories. At this season of my life, I can see patterns. Suddenly, it all makes such sense.

My heart story begins in a very rural part of the State of Kentucky...on the backside of a place called, "Nowhere." I am the oldest of six children. The memories of my early years were filled with what many would call abuse in every sense of the word. Obviously, the two central characters who loomed larger than life were my Mom and Dad.

Dad stood over six feet tall and tougher than a pine knot. Unfortunately, he had some emotional dragons which hounded him most of his life. His mode of therapy was a whiskey bottle. My earliest memories centered around drunken rages, moonshine and literally a backwoods shootout. I was hiding behind our pickup truck just knowing any second I was going to get killed.

As a child, you can't reason all these things out. I couldn't understand *why so many whippings,* which made no sense at all. I knew I hurt a great deal of the time. I remember so many times Momma sounding the alarm and we (my two sisters and baby brother) would run to hide out in gullies to be safe from one of Dad's drunken rages.

Yet, I wanted desperately for Dad to be proud of me. He wanted me to grow tall and be a basketball player. Dad thought something was wrong with me. In fact, he thought I had worms and gave me a "worming" every month along with his fox hounds. He never understood the concept of heredity.

Now enters my "Momma" into my story. You talk about the difference between night and day. Mom was just the opposite of Dad. I knew she knew a lot about God. She talked a lot about "The Good Lord" and seemed to always be singing some old time Gospel song.

I remember early on I would hear her morning prayer begin with, "Lord, I'm reporting for duty."

I would ask Mom, "Why is Dad so mean to me? Why doesn't he love me?"

I vividly remember Mom putting her arms around me and saying, "I know he loves you. I reckon he doesn't know how to say the words. God didn't make a mistake with the Daddy He gave you. But I love you, God loves you and I know God is going to do something very special with your life. You are not just special, you are Specialer!"

Momma knew a lot about God. I knew a lot about hurting.

Very early in life, I began to find I had a coping mechanism. Of course, I didn't know fancy words or possess the ability to analyze what the "dang" deal was going on. When I was five, Dad would send me out to go run and bring the cows to the barn for milking. I was always running. Many times, the morning chores caused me to miss the school bus and I ran to school some six miles away.

I discovered I could run for long periods of time without getting tired or winded. In fact, one morning, a rabbit came running across the barnyard and I decided to catch it for a pet. I literally ran the rabbit for five hours before catching him. I was 7 years old.

A major "marker," or moment of discovery, came to me when I was 12. We had a social event called the "County Fair" going on. Someone announced there was going to be a 100-yard dash and anyone could participate regardless of age. I asked Dad if I could run.

He said it was foolish but, "Go ahead."

I won the blue ribbon. I had discovered there was something I could do well, and I wanted to do more of it.

Over the next six years my fame spread. Farmers seemed to be constantly coming around and asking my Dad if they could borrow me to chase after a mule or cow which had broken out of the pasture.

Dad would say, "Take him...not sure he will be able to hold up, because he's no bigger than a bar of soap after a good warshin'..."

In April of 1961, I received a letter from Western Kentucky State College offering me a one semester, partial, probationary scholarship worth $60 to run on their newly formed cross-country team. My mind was bubbling over with possibilities.

I went to my high school principal, showed him the letter and sought his counsel. I was shocked with the words which followed.

"Stanley, Jr., let's face it," he said. "You've got to be smart to go to college. Get these foolish notions out of your head. The only future you have in the world is to go join the army before the draft gets you...come back home and live on your Daddy's farm. If you try to do anything else, you will make a fool out of yourself. In fact, you're dumber than a poop house rat!"

That was my career counseling. I chose not to believe him.

Momma cried the day I left to go to college. I had one pair of Sunday church britches which were ripped out in the crotch. All she had was red thread to sew them up. Off to college I went. Long story short…five years later, I graduated. Yes, I ran track and cross country.

I held four part-time jobs, worked at a factory from 10 at night to seven in the morning. I flunked math four times and passed on the fifth time around. They changed the book three times. I took a speech class as one of the four English requirements.

At the end of the semester, the teacher called me in and asked, "Mr. Cottrell, how did you ever get in college? Watching you try to give a speech has been the most psychopathological spectacle I have ever witnessed."

She gave me a "C" out of the goodness of her heart. More career counseling.

During those times, I found solace and significance in running. I would run distances which were unheard of during those times. In 1964, I was the first southerner to run the Boston Marathon. I found a perverse pleasure in the attention which came my way. I was a man definitely on the run.

In the fullness of time, and with bulldog determination, I graduated from college. Dad had literally beat into me the message, "Cottrell's never 'mit," or "never 'sub'mit."

Someone once said to me, "Your Daddy put the iron in your soul." I wanted him to be proud of me.

Over the next few years, I definitely was an achiever by worldly standards. I was going up, up, up in the eyes of the world. I was a teacher, salesman, national product manager for a pharmaceutical company, a husband and a dad of three children. I was building a resume which society said was impressive. In the midst of all this, my long distance running drew attention and opened doors of opportunity.

During all these times, Momma would gently remind me, "Stanley, Jr., now don't forget the Good Lord."

I was an achiever and a visionary. There was a hungry horse inside me which could never seem to get enough food. In the mid-1970s, I saw "Corporate Fitness" as the next big innovation. After all, there had to be a correlation between physical fitness and fiscal fitness. I was ahead of my time.

To prove I knew something about fitness, I put together a promotional plan to run from the top of the State of Georgia to the Florida line…a distance of 405 miles. It was a media success as I ran the distance in less than five days. It was definitely a "wow," but in the eyes of business executives I was a "Nut!"

Someone came to me with a list of potential records I should go after. In those days, ultra-distance running was an odyssey and virtually unheard of. I contacted all the known regulatory bodies to find out about accreditation. My next big run was culminated in my setting a new 24-hour record. I ran 167.25 miles, or 669 times around a 440-yard track. Again, a media success, but the milestone distanced me further from the business world.

The next step in my quest for egomaniacal martyrdom was a run across the United States. I broke the old world record by six days averaging 66 miles per day. I just knew this was going to make me a "Hollywood Star" with movie offerings, endorsements, etc. *Get ready, Robert Redford, a new kid is on the block!*

What was going on? Six months passed and nothing. The only offers were what I would later call "LSD" deals. The people offering such outlandish things had to have been on dope, and had I accepted the same would have been true for me.

I went to see my attorney with a handful of new inquiries. He literally threw the folders back in my face.

His words hit home. "You don't get it! God is kicking you on the shins," he said. "Is He going to have to break your legs to get your attention? The only way I will represent you any longer is you have to be in church next Sunday with your family."

I agreed just to get out of his office.

On the drive home, I made the brilliant decision to divorce my wife. After all, it would be the best thing for her. I was a man on the run. Suddenly, I smelled smoke in my car and pulled up into a shopping mall. Within minutes the car was in flames.

I had to call my wife to come and get me. So much for the divorce plans. Echoing in my mind were my attorney's words.

I said to my wife, "I think I would like for us to go to church this coming Sunday."

She was shocked. You see, she had been in a woman's Bible study group for a year and she said they had been praying for me every week.

I was seated in the balcony with my family come Sunday morning. My attorney was looking around for me. When he saw me, he gave me a "thumbs up" in smiling approval. My life was about to change forever.

"Are you a man on the run...do things seem to never work out? Are you having financial difficulties, problems in your marriage, etc.?" the preacher asked.

The sermon was about me...uncomfortably personal.

"Have you gotten yourself out on a limb and is God going to have to saw the limb down to reach you?" he asked. "God wants to go home with you today."

I had never heard anything like this before. All my fumes of self were vaporized.

That afternoon I went out for a run. One mile later I crawled up into the woods and cried out to God.

"Whatever you want, my answer is 'Yes,'" I sobbed into the dirt. "Come into my heart...if you want me to run, I'll run...if you want me to go back to Kentucky and live on a farm with a mule and plow, my answer is 'Yes!'"

I realized a man can't run to God's own Son until he had run out of himself. One cannot find the true way until one has been lost.

God gave me back my running in a way I never expected. I now run all over the earth promoting the spirit of friendship and working with orphans. Record books? My name is in the only record book which matters: The Lamb's Book of Life.

Thus far, God has opened the doors beyond my wildest dreams. I have been privileged to have run across 40 countries including a 2,125-mile run in China about which a feature-length film was made. During that run, I fell down a mountain ledge and ran the last 1,000 miles with two broken vertebrae.

And now, at 73, I have never been stronger. What's next? I am working around the clock to start a seven year run which will take me to every country, colony and territory in the world. Lord willing, this initiative will culminate in Washington, D.C., with 1 million children.

I have learned, regardless of what God allows in your life...I am certain beyond all doubt, there is "No Mountain Too High" with the resurrected power of Christ who lives within me. I am complete and whole!

For these reasons, when you see me run, I am akin to a child at play. I now run with inexhaustible zest, because I know my life's last turn will be my very best!

ABOUT THE CONTRIBUTOR

World renowned, ultra-distance runner, award-winning inspirational speaker and international businessman, Stan Cottrell shows how he rose above discouragement and defeat to become "Friendship Ambassador to the World." With unmatched ultra-distance running feats and people-to-people diplomacy throughout the palaces and remote villages of the world, he encourages you to take on challenges and strive for achievement, too.

The inspirational story of his early life and the courage and endurance that have enabled him to accomplish such amazing feats are revealed in one of his books, *No Mountain Too High*. Raised in a poor family in the hollows of Kentucky, Stan could never quite measure up to his father's expectations. Labeled a failure by his father early in life, he nevertheless persisted in trying to please him. Then in sixth grade, Stan participated in a 100-yard dash at a county fair and finally discovered something at which he could excel — running. As his love and ambition for this sport grew, he began treading uncharted frontiers.

Stan has now run more than 250,000 miles through 40 countries, the equivalent of 10 times around the world. In 1980, he broke the prior Guinness World Record for his 3,103.5-mile Trans-USA run in 48 days. He completed a 3,500-mile run through 12 European countries; a 2,125-mile run from the Great Wall to Guangzhou in China in just 53 days (the last 1,000 miles taped up with two broken vertebrae); a 486-mile run from Hanoi to DaNang in Vietnam in 1988 (pre-Normalization); a 500-mile "Freedom Run" from the Brandenburg Gate in East Berlin to Warsaw, Poland, when the Berlin Wall fell; and runs through Korea (twice), Dominican Republic (twice), Jamaica (twice), Bulgaria (3 times), Crimea, Cambodia, Ethiopia and many others.

Stan has received over 300 awards from U.S. government agencies, foreign governments and nationally recognized service organizations for promoting international goodwill and the U.S. image abroad. Among others, these include commendations from four U.S. Presidents, 10 Senate and House Resolutions passed in his honor, and the coveted Healthy American Fitness Leaders Association Award (HALF — "The Oscar of Fitness").

Likening his momentous pursuits to mountains, Stan shows how he struggled to the summit of each one. His fascinating story will help you feel better about yourself, boost your self-confidence, and show you how you, too, can reach new heights in life.

Stan's still climbing mountains. Running strong at age 73, he is embarking on a seven-year series of Global Friendship Runs through over 200 countries, territories and colonies. Spreading the messages of Friendship and the "Power of Hope," he's showing God's love in action for the 146 million orphans and abandoned children around the world.

Learn more on http://FriendshipSports.org, then follow Stan on Facebook, and come out and join the events and fun. You can also support the Run and the children through http://give.mobi/run.

CHAPTER 3

A WAY IN A MANGER

Written for Pastor Kip Philp
by Carolyn Curran-Fyckes

*And I will give them a heart to know me, that I am the Lord:
and they shall be my people, and I will be their God: for they
shall return unto me with their whole heart*
(Jeremiah 24:7, KJV).

Let me give you some background before I plunge into my story.

I was raised in a good, loving family. We didn't go to church, but
as a child I was taught to pray a simple prayer at bedtime. So, growing
up, I had a sense of knowing that God was real.

By the time I was 12 years old, I gave little thought to God. My
family and I had moved two years prior from North Bay, Ontario, to
Holland Landing, north of Newmarket. The move brought me new
friends — friends who took drugs.

I progressed from doing drugs to dealing drugs by the age of 13.
Eventually, I was kicked out of school. I didn't need school and all
those boring rules. My life was exciting because I was important. At 17
years old, I was supplying dealers with drugs.

Money was plentiful. I was never busted by the cops. Life was
great. I thought that I was unstoppable.

Then, Halloween night, October 31, 1991, happened. In my caveman costume, I gathered up a stash of drugs to share at a party. I felt generous.

The party was well underway when I arrived. Everyone seemed to be already in the party mood. I decided that there was no need to share the drugs. I was feeling higher and higher as I indulged in my supply.

Without any warning, I started seeing demons and hearing licking flames. The atmosphere of the whole room electrified. Someone told me that I had died.

I didn't know what was real or not real. In that moment of confusion and desperation, I knew I had to call out to God.

Realizing that I had overdosed, my friends quickly grabbed me and threw me roughly into the back of the pick-up truck. They struggled to hold me down as we sped down the road.

All I knew, at this point, was that I had to escape my attackers. *Who were they? What were they planning to do with me?*

I bumped, head first, out of the side of the truck, onto the dirt road. They eyed me with disgust as I lay in a bloody, mud-covered heap in the middle of the road. I wasn't worth saving.

"Forget him," they shouted. "Let's go!"

I didn't have the strength or the wherewithal to move.

Within me, I still had a strong urgency to call on God but I didn't know how to pray anything except my childish bedtime prayer. I decided to sing a Christmas carol, *Away in a Manger*. In my wavering voice, I continued to sing as loudly as I could and to cling — desperately — to the hope that the Lord would show me mercy.

At about 5:30 am, a police car approached cautiously. I am sure I must have looked like road kill. I begged the officer to take me back home. Fortunately, he had pity on me and didn't arrest me.

I now had to make drastic changes to my life; there was no other sensible choice. As soon as I was physically able to, I sought out a church. The Pastor of the church patiently explained to me the story of salvation and the need to get right with God by saying the Sinner's Prayer.

While I was repeating that special prayer after him, the peace and joy of the Lord saturated me. I knew I was no longer the same person, nor did I have any drug addiction.

Several days later, I led a druggie friend through the Sinner's Prayer. I had a new addiction — an addiction to witnessing.

Relatives in the Muskokas invited me to move in with them. At 17, I was starting my brand new life. I became an enthusiastic member of the local church and of the high school. At every opportunity, I shared my testimony.

I didn't need drugs anymore; I was continually on a high for God. As a result of my willingness to witness to others, I was invited to preach at a Christian retreat. Doors for preaching engagements, especially in schools, swung open.

By age 18, I was travelling quite a lot due to these exciting, God-given opportunities. I had planned to enroll in a college in order to study theology. God had a different plan.

I was offered a position at church on their staff for three years. I worked at two other churches before moving to work at a church in Burlington, Ontario. The Lord was preparing me for a bigger work — church planning.

In our local newspaper, I came upon an article about a night club which had overcrowding issues. Subsequently, the club had lost its liquor license. This night club was the oldest nightclub in Canada. Ironically, the club's name was Kingdom.

I felt the compulsion to seek my senior Pastor's permission to check the club out as a potential site for a new church. I was aware that many people, especially young people, were uncomfortable in traditional churches. So that's how I came to find myself in a popular night club with its black painted walls.

While I watched the familiar party scene in front of me, the Lord spoke to me. He reminded me about the Samaritan woman whom Jesus met at the well (John 4). Jesus asked this very worldly woman for a drink of water. He said that if the woman really knew who He was, she would ask Him for living water to quench her thirst.

Suddenly, I understood why Jesus was bringing this story to mind — the people in the club were trying to quench their thirst, not literally for drink, but for the peace that was missing in their lives. They didn't know how to find peace that would always satisfy their souls. They were searching.

I felt that the Kingdom was the site for this new church. Now I needed to explore the feasibility of renting this facility with the manager.

I dragged a friend along with me for the appointment at the club. The manager informed us that we would be allowed to rent a portion of the club for Sunday services. Sheepishly, I admitted that I couldn't commit to this amount of money since the church had to rely on donations which would fluctuate throughout the year.

At that point, I was expecting to be thrown out of the club for wasting his time. When the manager countered with an offer to donate the space, I was in absolute shock. *I didn't really hear that offer, did I?*

Nothing truly is impossible for God — on Feb 4, 2007, the church was born. Within about a year from that date, the club closed down. Of course, we had to start paying rent but we were ready, thanks to the grace of God our provider.

This new church was given a very appropriate name 24/7. We need to be Christians 24 hours a day, not just when the time suits us. The act of the Apostles themselves took place anytime, not on an inflexible schedule.

Most importantly, we had assurance that the Lord would gather His people in: *'Then I will give them a heart to know me, that I am the LORD; and they shall be My people, and I will be their God, for they shall return to Me with their whole heart '"*(Jeremiah 24:7, NKJ).

God kept His promise. He brought people in who were thirsty. I often look back to that seemingly hopeless time in my life when I lay broken on a dirt road and began to sing over and over again, *Away in a Manger*.

Why did I choose that particular carol to hold on to?

The Lord gave me the answer. Jesus came and brought Grace and light into a dark world. On that deserted road, I was learning to reach out for His grace and His light to save me. In 24/7, many searching souls would come to find His grace and His light also. Praise be to God!

ABOUT THE CONTRIBUTOR

Kip Philp was born in North Bay, Ontario, where he lived until he was 10 years old. At that time his family moved to Holland Landing, Ontario, a small community north of Newmarket. Kip accepted Jesus at the age of 17 following a near-death experience with drugs and he has never looked back!

Kip has been in full-time ministry since 1993. During this time he has pastored in five different churches and served in a wide variety of ministries. His passion is to see lives transformed one step at a time as people learn to walk with Jesus in the real world.

Kip is the Lead Pastor and founder of Emmaus Church (Emmauschurch.com) in Burlington, Ontario. He believes that church should be practical, creative, fun and exciting — as the most important message deserves the most dynamic presentation. He strives to make church a place that's not only for "church people," but also for anyone who wants to see God (regardless of where they are in their spiritual journey).

Kip and his wife, Shanni, have three amazing children: two sons, Tanner and Seth, and one daughter, Kaylie.

CHAPTER 4

QUEST AND TROPHY

Jack E. Olson

*Happy is the man that findeth wisdom, and the man that getteth
understanding: For the merchandise of it is better than the
merchandise of silver, and the gain thereof than fine gold. She
is more precious than rubies: and all the things thou canst
desire are not to be compared unto her.*
(Proverbs 3:13-15, KJV).

Atheism: The Logical Way

It was a cozy evening. A soft breeze gently moved the leaves
among the cottonwood canopies above. My best friend and I lay on the
lawn of Weber College discussing scientific discoveries.

Our discussion turned to religion and how such ideas might fit into
the measurable universe. It was clear that they did not. We decided that
the idea of God was unthinkable. We resolved that integrity required
we declare ourselves atheists.

We would not be included in the company of people who danced
around fires, muttered incantations and fiddled with trinkets.

We could see no need for any god to keep the universe moving.
Stars were being born out of interstellar gasses and cycling through
predictable life courses; everything was done within the precision of
physical law.

Religion, on the other hand, was laden with mystery. There were countless ideas, endless contentions and confusion. Ministers, all claiming insight from the same God, publicly castigated each other's teachings while they called for brotherly love. They professed eternal life and spent half their time talking of death. They told the poor and hurting to trust God for their answers, then went begging to them for their own needs.

But the greatest offense was the irresponsible manipulation of science to prove their positions. Now, at last, my friend and I were free from that confusing hypocrisy, its suffocating traditions, ravings and messages of fear.

At the same time, I suspected there was more to life than the dimensions of time and space because like it or not, there were well-documented psychic experiences. Although I was sure such things also obeyed mathematical law, I hoped they might provide a shorter route to truth than physical science alone.

I began looking into psychic science and the occult, practiced psychic sight and became involved in an eastern system that appeared to be a path to knowledge. When I learned it demanded death in order to progress, I abandoned it. (I had never died before and I already hated it!) I did, however, continue my psychic dabbling which produced results. Occasionally, the outcomes were predictable, but usually not. A few were even frightening.

For instance, I had been watching a television show on individual ability to create something by power of will; it may be a vase or a cat or even a house. It looks and feels like the real article but it's really a psychic substance called ectoplasm.

That night, I was awakened about midnight by the "pressure gauge." I closed the bedroom door and proceeded to the bathroom. Returning, I paused in the hall, wishing I could "mock-up" something.

Suddenly, I knew I could, and instantly before me appeared a large vaporous white being. It filled the end of the hall. It may have been in my mind but my wife, asleep behind the door, screamed. It scared the daylights out of me. I turned it off, having no desire get properly introduced to who or whatever it was.

In another instance, my wife and I were touring an old English mansion. I told our guide I could feel a ghost in the room.

He said, "There was a ghost in the adjoining room."

I replied, "It's in here now."

He then told the story of a woman standing before the large third-story window holding her new baby. As she watched, the banker came riding up to take possession of the property. She couldn't endure the thought of her child being dispossessed, and cast him through the window onto the paving stones below. When she realized what she had done, she dove out the same window and died there with her child. Apparently, her intense desire to reverse her action created the ghost.

This confirmed another common element of many psychic occurrences; it is an intense, often insane, desire. Another element of many psychic experiences is relinquishment, which is achieved by chanting, trances and mind clearing. Some called it "getting in tune."

I had many experiences — some entertaining, some helpful, some informative — but nothing dependable. Most were spontaneous or with only a nudge from me. All this should have set off an alarm in my head. It was senseless: give *all* control, even life, to gain personal power. Nor did it make sense to accept blind guidance from something that might deceive, and even less sense to give it to something unpredictable. But I wasn't thinking.

Something to Consider

One day I overheard a unique conversation. I was working in a small electronic lab. My boss and my best friend, both devout atheists, were conversing. My boss spoke of a seminar on psychology. The leader had stated that the book of Genesis was an excellent account on the psychological development of man.

If that's true, I thought, *I've been missing something! Perhaps the Bible has hard data caged within its stories that has been overlooked?* I had criticized Christians liberally, having never read their book. I decided to give the Bible a careful read.

I found it surprising. By the time I finished the fourth book of Moses, I realized that it was not authored by men, but was indeed written under the express dictation of Someone far greater. The idea of "Cosmic Consciousness" offered no explanation. It certainly was not written by an ascended practitioner of Vedanta because they and their ilk didn't permit people to have minds or realistic understanding.

Moreover, as I read, the words were piercing into my inner being.

There was but one logical conclusion. God is real and alive, and Jesus is exactly who He says He is. I had found the foundation I had been seeking. Instead of insane desire, there was a call to love; blind relinquishment was replaced with leadership and a call to free-will obedience. In place of a weird faith in one's "gift," there was love and trust in God. In place of unreliable information and excuses, there was verifiable data.

Years later I would find out how voluminous and precise that data is. It's difficult to cast off one's views and embrace something foreign, but in this case, it was done with great delight.

A Commentary

You see the error everywhere. I erred myself in judging Christ by the acts of people. No one is immune to error. Ambition for instance, is like a false twin to faith.

Many people begin a good work in faith, and gradually lose sight of the priceless fruit under the glare of ambition. People tend to be temple builders, while love is one-on-one giving. We hate seeing Christ disgraced by those who claim special insight without testing their revelations.

I am sure God is pleased by people who listen. He has also given us minds and a mandate to be wise. Wisdom tests ideas. It is inseparable from love.

There is another important point my experience teaches and it is this: psychic phenomena do actually happen, but I have found them to be mostly deceptions geared to either generate awe and fear, or distract people under the guise of personal power or gifts. We get sucked into these falsehoods because when we think we have found answers; we either stop looking or narrow our reading to support our expectations, refusing to listen to the warnings, unaware that our lives are the trophies.

ABOUT THE CONTRIBUTOR

Jack loved philosophy; he was sure it was the seed of all science, as well as the fount of wisdom and understanding. Physical science was fascinating, from the mind boggling sizes and distances of astronomy to the bazaar findings of quantum physics, but for the single gem of the *meaning* to life, he turned to eastern wisdom and the occult for help.

At age 30, he was close to becoming a warlock because of his psychic vision and experiences. More detail and the circumstances of his salvation are presented in his testimony, titled, "Quest and Trophy," included in his book.

At the time of his conversion, Jack was working in nuclear electronics. He would later head up a consulting service managing engineers and scientists which designed 80 instruments, processes and products in a single year; he was credited with four new technologies; one of his patents was cited in the flat-screen television design — all this with only a high school diploma. Even there, about 1948, he observed microwaves, not realizing the importance of what he was seeing.

He has owned and operated three small businesses designing and manufacturing electronic and mechanical instruments and tools. During that era, Jack wrote 80 testimonies, several articles, two monthly columns, four small books, four major books and two seminars, plus studied and spoke on Creation Science and presented seminars on Applied Creativity.

He has come to the realization that the depth of the Bible is staggering, surpassed only by the love of God and the sacrifice of Jesus. The understanding of that love was the inspiration for his latest book, *Our Loving Relationship with God.*

CHAPTER 5

WELCOME HOME

A True Story from the Life of Tommy Woods

*For by grace are ye saved through faith; and that not of
yourselves:
it is the gift of God: Not of works, lest any man should boast.*
(Ephesians 2:8-9, KJV).

Life in a "crack house" is hell! I should know. I live in one. Have been living here for five years now.

A former triplex, each unit has been remodeled into four single rooms with a common area. The common area contains a refrigerator, microwave and a telephone for local calls. There is a shared bathroom in each unit.

For my own reasons, I keep the bathroom and my room clean.

The entire building is old and dingy inside and out. The floors are covered with carpet laid when the building was new. The smell requires denial to overcome. Peeling wall paper, chipped paint and unwashed walls add to the decor.

Cockroaches dwell in the closets, drawers and on counter tops. This is not a place that many would call home. However, I am fortunate. My room is the largest. I call it the "penthouse."

Tenants include nine men and three women at the moment. They come and they go. Two of them are alcoholics. The rest are drug addicts. The drug of choice is crack cocaine. We call each other "crack heads." I am one of these. I hate this, but I am.

We are full of fear, mistrust, guilt and hatred. We fear each other and we fear the police. We trust no one. We feel guilty for what we've become. We hate each other and the rest of our worlds. Suspicion inhabits every encounter, every glance and conversation. In truth, none of us want to be a drug addict, but it's a pit of slippery walls out of which we cannot climb.

Paranoia runs rampant. We lie to each other. We fight each other. We steal from each other. And then, we sit down and smoke crack together.

It is sick, sick, sick. Though none of us ever wanted to become a drug addict, now we have no choice. We speak often of quitting, but it's too late now...and so it goes.

Family? Yes, I have a family. A son, a daughter and five grandchildren. Lovely, they are. I also have brothers, sister, mom and dad, all living in other cities. I love them more than anyone could know.

But I have become an alien. I can't afford to care and they can't know of me. You see, they are Christians. They couldn't understand my hopelessness or why I have isolated myself in Phoenix.

We are separated by a far greater distance. It's called crack cocaine.

Because I've tried everything to quit, and nothing works, my mind says, *I may just die right here.* Still, there is one more option. Today, I have come to a rehab center.

They say, "We want to help you."

Now here is a reason for hope! But they also need $3500 with no guarantee, plus a commitment to six months of intensive therapy. Sounds like fools hope. I already had that! I think they only care about profit. So much for hope.

Back at home things have just become worse. My car won't start. It's parked in the alley. My fellow renters are telling me it is the computer. Too expensive to repair, I'm forced to take a bus to work.

Weeks pass.

While getting ready for work this morning, I see I'm out of coffee. Will hurry to the corner store before the bus arrives. It's just two blocks away and I will catch the bus there.

I buy the coffee and wait for my bus.

I cannot believe what I see! It's the lady from the bus. I once heard her say she overcame a problem because she had "faith in Jesus Christ." Her words affected me deeply. Now this fascinating lady is coming toward me from across the street. Maybe she will talk to me.

She didn't. But now I know where she lives. Just a couple of blocks from me. What a coincidence! From this day forward, I will use this bus stop. I must meet her.

A month later: This is ridiculous. I've been using this bus stop for a month now. She shows up here every day. I can't find the confidence to talk to her. I've got to stop playing this game.

When she gets here today, I resolve to introduce myself. Here she comes.

"Good morning, Miss, I hope you will excuse me, but do you go to church?"

I shouldn't have asked her.

She says, "Yes," and is digging through her purse. She gives me a card from a church.

She invites me to go with her and offers a ride. Her name is Marie and she's a member of nearby Parkway Community Church. She never talked to me before and now she won't shut up! I only wanted a simple yes or no.

I finally tell her, "Yeah, maybe someday, but when I do, I will walk."

Another month passes and Marie continues her invitation.

It's Sunday morning and I feel terrible, the effects of last night. But I have a strong urge to find that church today. I will clean up and see how I feel.

Better now. My mind is made up. Today, I'm going to find that church.

There it is. Nice building. But, I can't go in there. These people I see driving in are clean, well dressed and completely sober. They belong here. I don't. I am none of these. I want to go back home.

Still, something says, "Go!"

It's been 40 years since I attended a church service. I can't do this. I'm not sober. I don't know what to expect. Still, it seems, I have no choice. OK, I'm going in.

Someone in the lobby hands me a package. I'm told it's given to first time attendees. He's got that right.

I've really done it! Don't know why I came all the way down here to the fourth row. No easy escape from here. And, I'm sitting in the aisle seat. People will see my dirty tennis shoes. I'll have to push them under the pew so no one will notice.

What's in this envelope? Several things. Oh good, a free pen. And here is a beautiful glossy picture. It's a mountain scene and reminds me of Colorado. There is a message on it that says, "Welcome Home."

I feel a lump in my throat. Welcome Home? Who would welcome me here in this beautiful place? The message continues, "It is not by accident we have the joy of meeting you." My eyes are burning now and I feel tears. There is more but I can't finish. Will read it when I get home.

Why am I crying? I never cry, about anything. But I am crying. If these people only knew me they would never say, "Welcome Home."

On a platform above me I see several people with microphones. They begin to sing. It's a beautiful song. When I look around, I see some with their hands raised. I've never seen this. It's as if they are singing to God. I begin to feel warm and relaxed. I'm not singing, but I feel nice—somehow, clean.

Walking home, my eyes are filling with tears again. *Why?* I can't stop. I must be crazy. This, I do not understand.

Tomorrow is Monday. I have the week off. Exhausted, all I want to do is sleep. There will be a lot of drug use when I get home. But I don't have the usual craving. This is stranger. I just want to sleep. Maybe for the whole week.

It's Wednesday. I have little desire for drugs. This is unusual. I wonder if one day in church would do this. Impossible! I'm just tired. But, it's been a long time since going three days without crack.

It's 10:00 a.m. and someone is knocking on my door. It's the manager. She has spoken to the owner in Palm Springs. He told her to lock me out of my room at 4:00 p.m. today. I am $1000 behind in rent and he wants at least $150 now. This isn't much money, but the problem is I don't have it.

I have six hours to find some cash. If I can't, I will be on the streets and lose my job. I've seen the manager do this before. She's serious. I've got a serious problem! How am I going to handle this one?

Anger rises in me. Real anger! I can always buy drugs without money, but this is different. I know I can't put the manager off any longer. But what can I do? I must find some money, but where?

Maybe I should pray the way they did in that church. No, I don't know how to pray. Besides that, God wouldn't help someone like me. I'm on my own here.

Aha! I remember a place at Camelback Road and 7th Street. Their sign says, "Payday loan." I'll give them a call. Can't hurt to try.

They say I am qualified to receive a loan. That was easy. I'm on my way. Still angry over my situation, I begin to feel a need to drug. I may ask for a loan of $200, pay the manager, and with the extra $50 I will buy some crack. When I call my dealer, he will meet me in ten minutes. If I have cash. When I ask for a front, he will still deliver but at his convenience.

As always, stronger cravings come with anger. I need relief from this anxiety. The sooner, the better.

A five block walk, a few minutes bus ride and I'll be there. I have made up my mind to apply for extra money so I can also buy drugs. My conscience keeps saying, "Don't do it," but something else says, "Yes, go ahead, do it."

The closer I get to my destination, the stronger the cravings become. Alright, I've decided. I really need the relief the drugs will provide. I will get the extra money. Buy the drugs and get high just one...more...time.

How many times have I said that?

Completing this application is difficult. I can barely read my own handwriting. My hands are shaking now. I have this sensation in my stomach and my legs feel hollow. And my mouth is watering. I always get these feelings when I'm about to satisfy this addiction. I hate it! But I have no control.

On the application I ask for $200. Fifty of it will buy the drugs I desperately need. And the manager gets the rest.

The clerk has called me back to the window. She's finished checking my application.

She says, "Because you are a new customer, I can only authorize $150." My plans just hit a brick wall!

As she counts out the money, I'm thinking, *could this be for a reason I'm not aware of? Could it be...God?* No, I hardly think so! There is a man in the next line over applying for a loan. He's asking the clerk if she is "saved." He's telling her about Jesus Christ and has invited her to his church.

She is uncomfortable and obviously embarrassed. As I turn to leave, I stop beside him, tap him on the shoulder and say, "Just keep up the good work." What did I say that?

As I approach the exit door I hear a loud voice, "Brother, are *you* saved?"

Oh no, why did I start this? How do I answer? I'm not even sure what it means--to be saved? I feel like running.

From my mouth comes some words, "If I am, it would only be by the grace of God."

Where did I get that? What does it mean?

Here he comes walking toward me. He hugs me and says, "God bless you, brother."

Whatever I said must have been good. Everyone in this place is looking at us. I've got to get out of here!

Once, outside, I stop to gather my thoughts. What just happened? Where did I get those words? What, exactly, do they mean? I am shaking all over and now here it comes again...thoughts of this God. *Can all this have anything to do with Him?* I feel my eyes getting warm and I begin to cry. Tears again! What is this!

Over there across the street, I see a Walgreens store. On the outside wall, I also see a public telephone. I know I shouldn't do this, but I need to calm down. I'm going to call my dealer and order some crack. I'll spend fifty bucks on it and the manager will have to be satisfied with the rest. At least, she won't kick me out today. My mind *is* made up. I'm getting high today. God or no God.

I've got to dry my eyes and get to that telephone.

Whew! Seems like it has taken forever to get here. My legs are so weak. I can hardly walk. Now, to make that call. I've got coins in my pocket. Only need 50 cents. Wouldn't you know it! All I have it 47 cents. Dig deeper and you'll find it. Nope, I only have one quarter, two dimes and two pennies. Nothing is going right today! More anger!

Here comes that thought again. *Could it be possible that God is trying to stop me from buying drugs?* That's a ridiculous thought. He couldn't do that. Why should He care what I'm doing?

I've got it! I'll go into the store, buy a small package of gum and the change I receive will give me the coins I need. Oh yeah, I can always figure out a way.

Now I have the gum and soon I'll have the change to make my call. I have been turned away from one cashier and sent to another. Frustrating! There are seven elderly ladies in this line. I'm standing here 10 minutes now and the line isn't moving. Seems every one of these ladies has a problem to solve. What's taking them so long? All I need is a single quarter. Then my problem will be solved. The anger within me is building. Please, hurry up!

Finally, it's my turn. I draw a sigh of relief and hand my purchase to the cashier. He swipes it over the scanner and nothing happens. Again, he scans it. Still nothing.

After his third unsuccessful attempt, I lose what little composure I have left and say, "Just ring the d____thing up by hand!"

His response is, "Why don't you just chill out?"

He enters the transaction manually. A split second before he presses the cash button...the electricity goes off. The lights are out and the store is dark.

Someone from the back of the store is shouting, "All customers, leave your purchases and exit the front door."

As I stand there stunned, the cashier is telling me, "Leave the gum here and exit the store."

I want to hit him! An employee of the store is hand cranking the electric doors open. As I walk through and out into the hot sun, I feel defeated.

I see other customers filing out and I'm thinking, *the simple task of finding a quarter for a phone call has become an impossibility.*

By now, the need for crack cocaine has become extreme and the fact that I may not score drugs at all becomes a reality. This thought is frightening. But it's clear something is definitely working against me.

God? Maybe. It might be Him. These unusual happenings are not coincidence. *But why Why would He care if I use drugs or not?* I'm beginning to feel a powerful assurance it is Him! I'm convinced, and this scares me.

Where are these thoughts coming from? I am so confused. If it is Him preventing me from calling for drugs, why? I believe it and now, I've become furious — at Him. I need drugs and He says, No! *What now?* Deep inside I feel somehow it's over. I think I'll go back home.

Will wait right here for the bus to arrive. So, I'll go home...then what? I'm still shaking. I am more desperate now than I've ever been. Waiting for the bus I begin to pace. Desperately trying to decide what to do and in utter desperation, I look up at the sky in anger and I challenge God.

"God, I believe You *are* doing this to me...and if it is *really You*, why don't You come down here and take this out of me?"

Suddenly, I feel something inside me begin to stir. I'm stunned! I begin to feel this vile "stuff" being pulled out of me. It feels like standing at the edge of the ocean as the tide recedes and a magnetic pull toward the open sea is felt. This is how I feel now! As this "stuff" leaves me, a breeze is blowing it away. Although this is frightening, it is incredible! I know what is happening, but I don't understand it.

Some time goes by. I don't know how long I've been here. I feel different now. Oh, yes, my legs feel strong as I test them standing in place. My stomach is empty of the butterflies and knots. My mouth no longer waters. And my hands! I hold them up and look at both sides. They are granite steady. No shakes. As I inspect my hands I notice a man on the sidewalk watching me. His face is a sight. He is staring at me as if I need a strait jacket. I can't care less. I'm in a new world all my own — not his. I feel new and clean. I feel free!

I'm still breathless and unable to think clearly. I have just asked this God whom I've never known to do the impossible. And He did it! There is no doctor, no clinic or drug rehab facility in the world that can do this. But, He just did! Now I know for sure. This is God! The anger has left me. The cravings and desire for drugs are gone.

But something else is happening. I feel like I am being filled with ice cold water. I begin to chill and it's a hot day.

I am frightened again. *What have I done now?*

Did I hear someone speak from behind me? Not audible, almost a whisper. I turn to see and no one is there. A few moments have passed and I hear it again. A little louder this time. The words...I don't understand...and still no one is there. A third time. I heard that! An insistent voice from somewhere has just said, "Thank Him!" Immediately, I recall last Sunday. The pastor's sermon was giving thanks to God for all things. It was his Thanksgiving message.

I turn around, raise my hand, (I had seen them do that in church), and I say out loud, "Oh, yeah, Jesus, thank you!"

Immediately, just below my shoulders, I feel movement again. This time, something is coming into my body instead of leaving it. It feels thick like honey. It's very warm...swirling and rolling around inside. It's accompanied by an unusual taste of sweetness...pushing downward; the cold is leaving...it is now gone. As I stand here, I feel total relaxation and a pure peace I've never known.

As I savor this new indescribable emotion, I want to stay here forever.

My thoughts turn back to God and I hear myself say, again out loud, "God, now I believe! You are real. You are alive and here with me." The realization of what He has done causes an immeasurable love to surround me. A love for Him.

How much time has passed? I do not know. I see the bus coming. I'm going back to what I call home. The fare will be $1.25. I take a dollar from my wallet and reach into my pocket for the quarter I know is there.

As I take the change from my pocket, I see the two pennies, the two dimes, but what's this? Here are two quarters! I could have made that call after all! But, where, oh, where did this second quarter come from?

I will always believe that God, being comical, was saying, "That was Me, too."

I am thankful He patiently watched me go my own way and make my own choices until I fell into desperation so that He could pick me up. I am uncertain what my future is, but I do know one thing: today is the beginning of a new life.

I board the bus and return home. Right away I go to the manager's office and give her the $150.

She asks me, "Where did you get the money? I thought you were broke?"

And I respond, "Sit down, I have a story to tell you..."

***

The story you have just read evolved between the years 1996-2001. I continue to attend Parkway Community Church, the very place I was so afraid of years ago. I have found a lasting and loving relationship with God and the people of my church. Here, there is no fear, mistrust, guilt or hatred. Only love. Love for God and love for each other.

"For I am persuaded, that neither death, nor life, nor angels, nor principalities, nor powers, nor things present, nor things to come, nor height, nor depth, nor any other creature, shall be able to separate us from the love of God, which is in Christ Jesus our Lord" (Rom 8:38-39, KJV).

ABOUT THE CONTRIBUTOR

Tommy Woods was born and raised in Colorado. He is the father of one son and one daughter, and is the proud grandfather of five. A large part of his adult life as a non-believer was spent living, working and playing abroad. His employment took him to the Republic of Congo, Iran, Saudi Arabia, Panama and Colombia. He lived a life of consuming alcohol and six years of crack cocaine before calling on God for help. God heard him and delivered him in such a way as only God can do as his testimony reveals.

Tommy lives in Phoenix, Arizona, where he attends Parkway Community Church of God and was honored to serve five years on Pastor Jeff McAfee's council. He can be reached at woodstommy86@yahoo.com or 602-279-5181.

This story is courtesy of both Pastor Tommy Woods and Pastor Jack Olson. This testimony was formerly published under: www.olsonhouse.org, a testimony site created by Jack Olson. You may contact Jack for more information about his testimonies at: yukonjack1931@gmail.com.

CHAPTER 6

AN EARLY MORNING VISIT WITH JESUS IN MY BEDROOM – MORE AND MORE OF HIM

Aaron Arakaki

For we walk by faith, not by sight
(2 Corinthians 5:7, KJV).

There is nothing better than to walk with God.

The more you get to know Him, the better it gets. He is truly the way, the truth and the life. He is loving, full of mercy and grace, and no words can fully describe Him. He is God. He is the great "I AM." He is our everything.

My mother took me to church as a child. When I was about 8 years old, one Sunday the Holy Spirit's presence was so strong that most of the congregation was in tears. I asked our pastor why that happened and he explained very simply.

He said, "When God's love flows through you, it overflows and comes out in tears."

I use this explanation whenever new believers start crying for no reason at all and ask, "Why is this happening?"

During my early teenage years my parents moved and I no longer had my Christian friends. I quickly denied Christ and adapted to my new surroundings. For the next 35 years I lived for myself.

Nine years after my first marriage ended, I remarried. About five years into that marriage I started to see change in my wife. Good change. She was walking with the Jesus I knew when I was young, and she didn't do anything to make me change. She was, without knowing it, living 1 Peter 3:1, which says, *"Likewise, ye wives, be in subjection to your own husbands; that, if any obey not the word, they also may without the word by won by the conversation of the wives."*

She put a *Daily Bread* devotional reading in the bathroom. She knew I would read it if she left it there. Little did I know I was being spiritually fed every day. I was won without a word from her. All glory to God.

I soon joined the men's ministry at our church and attended a three day retreat. After three days in God's presence, I broke down and cried. I was used to only one hour of His presence every Sunday, not three days, 24 hours a day in a row. I truly realized I was neglecting my God and my wife.

Before the camp I was drinking 12-20 beers a day, followed by shots of whiskey or tequila. That weekend, the Lord delivered me from drinking, cold turkey, no withdrawal symptoms. Whom the son sets free is free indeed! (John 8:36)

With that bondage removed, I could think clearly. I received the baptism in the Holy Spirit and started praying in tongues. I started to have boldness to share Jesus with others.

For one year I didn't work. I had no desire to. I only read my Bible. I read a book each week and spent much time in prayer. This time of learning was also a time of discipline which continues still today.

Although we attended church, gave tithes and offerings, and were involved in small devotional groups and different ministries, we struggled financially. We didn't know it but money was our god. The one true God helped us to realize it. The Lord taught us how to steward money and put us through a series of tests that helped us build a sure foundation over a four year period. It was hard but worth it. We started speaking each morning, saying, "We're out of debt, our needs are met, and there's plenty more to give away."

While we made good money, we had much debt: $550,000 in mortgage; $45,000 in credit cards, lawyer debt, and we even owed a friend money. We kept on tithing and giving offerings, followed by paying all the bills and living simply. Toward the end of that four year period, some progress was made in bringing down the debt but most remained. We wondered if we had enough money to pay for half of our youngest child's graduation party and the upcoming college expenses.

Then came our breakthrough! We thought this only happened to other people.

Over the next six months, we saw multiplication as only the Lord can do. We didn't have any big jobs, but as the Lord multiplied, guess what? The graduation party got funded. All remaining credit cards got paid off. The lawyer debt got paid. Money owed to a friend was repaid. We fixed our rental house enough to move in *and* had enough for our daughter's college *and* were giving large amounts in offerings to different ministries every week.

We're out of debt, our needs are met, and there's plenty more to give away. We thought we had to sell our house first to do any of this but God showed us nothing is impossible with Him.

As soon as our rental was fixed enough to move in, our main house sold for what we expected. After improvements, we now live in a better house than our old house and we are completely out of debt. All glory to God. I can't explain it. We seek first the kingdom of God and His righteousness and everything falls into place (Matthew 6:33).

The Lord has shown us many healings and miracles. I've come to learn that there's more to the healing than the healing itself. In one instance, I called a customer to tell him I was coming to check the repairs needed on his house.

He asked me if I had a cold because he had cancer and didn't want to be exposed.

I replied that I didn't and came to check his house.

After the inspection, we stood outside the house by a sliding glass door. I asked if we could pray for his condition.

He said, "Yes."

I put my hand on his shoulder and he put his hand on my shoulder. I had just started to say, "Thank you, Jesus. Thank you, Jesus." Right then, a profile image of Jesus with a crown of thorns appeared in the reflection of the sliding glass door. Immediately, electricity went through my arm and he grasped my shoulder in response.

A few weeks later he talked to me and said, "I've been wanting to talk to you!"

His tests revealed no traces of cancer. The miracle was amazing, but even more amazing was the message from the miracle. The reflection of Jesus in the sliding glass door showed me that Christ is truly in us! Normally, you see yourself in a glass reflection, but seeing Jesus was proof that He is in us.

I can't even make up the things the Lord shows us. He is truly amazing and fun to be with.

Another thing the Lord does is speak to us in many ways. Hearing His voice excites me all the time. I'll share one instance. I was away from home for a couple of weeks in obedience to God. One evening as I talked to my wife on the phone, I heard the words "full time ministry" from the Lord. I told my wife what I heard.

She replied, "I hope we don't have to move since we just settled down in our new home."

Early the next morning as I was doing my devotions, I got the full revelation from Him.

He said, "You are in full time ministry. Full time ministry is not a position or a title but a condition of the heart. You are to be ready to speak or share my love with others 24 hours a day, seven days a week."

I then told him I knew it was Him speaking to me but I still wanted a scripture to confirm this. I heard, "1 Thessalonians 4," and quickly went to that scripture not knowing what it was. Not knowing what verse He meant, I just read from verse one.

I read and heard the Lord say, "I am pleased with what you are doing. You will do so more and more." Truly the living word of God.

That was two years ago. He is truly doing much through us, more and more, as we yield to Him. His word does not return void. Many more speaking doors have been opened from radio, in other ministries, to youth, for missions and even in care homes. We used to tell the Lord at the end of each year, "I don't know how you can beat last year." But he does, year after year. We expect it, because He is a great God who loves us more than we could ever imagine.

I'd like to end with a dramatic experience that had an undramatic result. Early one morning Jesus appeared to me in my bedroom. He stood at the corner of the room, lifted off the ground a few feet. He looked like He was about 6 feet tall. He had a white robe on and light was shining brightly off Him, but the brightest light came from His face.

Descriptions in Matthew 17:2 and Revelation 1:16 are pretty close. I could actually see the rays of light coming off His face. The light was so bright I could see only the outline and shape of His face. He didn't speak a word but I knew, immediately knew, it was Jesus.

The room was warm and the only thing I could feel was pure, pure love. It's love that you could almost touch; it's hard to explain in words. I've heard others who have encountered Jesus say it felt like liquid love. I told Him I didn't want this to stop and that I wanted to leave this place and go with Him. When He left the room I went back to sleep.

I told a pastor friend who is a golfing buddy of my experience, and he said to me, "Aw, you just love Jesus so much you imagined it."

I replied, "I wasn't walking with the Lord when He appeared to me. I was living in total sin, drinking heavily, money hungry, arrogant, living in fornication…you name it."

He couldn't say a thing after that! But here's the undramatic result: the next morning when I woke up I didn't sign up for Bible school. I went right back to my sinful life. When the feeling left, so did I.

It wasn't until seven years later that I made Jesus my Lord, Savior and Friend. I often wondered why He appeared to me. Some say it was a calling, but it didn't happen right away. I do know one thing and it is one of my most repeated verses in the Bible. 2 Corinthians 5:7 says, *"For we walk by faith, not by sight."* At that time it was only the feeling that attracted me. Now, I love His presence, but I walk by faith as it is the way to please Him.

Our relationship grows as we spend every morning with Him before we do anything else. He then blesses the rest of our day like you would not believe. It's a kingdom principle that you need to get used to. By faith, we do the little things, and watch Him do the big things. I share this because I want everyone to see how beautiful He is. How great is our God!

ABOUT THE CONTRIBUTOR

Aaron Arakaki and his wife, Min, live on a farm in the countryside of Honolulu, Hawaii, USA. They have three grown children living in New York, Oregon and Honolulu. They are partners with the Korean church, and are involved in a homeless ministry at the Ala Moana Beach Park in Honolulu, Hawaii, which has a service starting at 11 o'clock a. m. on Mondays. Aaron and his wife, Min, invite you to join them if you are in the area. Their phone number is (808)223-5130.

Aaron is also retired from the federal government after 29 years at the Pearl Harbor Naval Shipyard. Currently, Aaron and Min have a workplace ministry that arises from being a general contractor. The Arakaki's often go on Christian mission's trips where they meet wonderful people and get to see God doing amazing things, wherever God leads them to go.

CHAPTER 7

CHASING MONEY – FINDING GOD

Doug Collins

He that believeth on me, as the scripture hath said, out of his
belly shall flow rivers of living water
(John 7:38, KJV).

Motivated by Insecurities

When I was young I always felt like I didn't fit in. I felt other people looked down on me. I was never that popular. Most girls avoided me.

I had a few "Geek" friends who were not popular either. I had very low self-esteem. I spent much of my time in high school programming computer games.

I started my first computer company before the advent of the internet and would travel southern Ontario selling computer games to various user's groups. I got a taste of a little notoriety and popularity as a "whiz kid" which was exactly what I craved — some type of acceptance by others.

Because I always felt like I was less than others, in spite of loving and supportive parents, I had a strong desire to achieve. I wanted to prove myself, to make something of myself. I will never forget the day when I told my brother and sister, "Watch, I will be a millionaire when I grow up." I felt this tingly sensation all over me. I had no idea what prophecy was all about in those days. I just knew something happened when I spoke those words over myself.

My Path to Atheism

Even though I was brought up in a Pentecostal Church with believing parents, I became an atheist by the time I went to university. Even though people prayed, I never saw a miracle happen in a church that supposedly believed in such things. I thought it was all a fraud. Over time I even developed proofs why God didn't exist.

I was very hard toward God.

The Woman of my Dreams

During my third year at university I met Donna, the most captivating girl I had ever laid eyes on. She was a stunning brunette with a fun, spunky personality who had ambitions of going to medical school. Smart, fun and beautiful — what more could anyone ask for?

I met her because I was teaching a computer lab for non-computer majors. I remember one class while helping her with a question thinking to myself, *I wish I could have a girlfriend like her.* She had a bunch of guys chasing her, but she was so innocent she thought they were all just her friends.

Boy, was I lucky. Since they were all just pretending to be friends, I used the direct approach. She turned me down at first, but I was eventually able to win her heart. Every moment with her was magic. I was in love!

But God

Donna had applied to both medical school and dentistry school. The Friday before classes were about to start, Donna received a phone call from University of Toronto Dentistry.

"We have one spot left," they told her. "Classes start Monday. Do you want to take it?" Then they added, "Because of the last minute nature of this offer, if I hang up the phone, I will be calling the next person on the list to offer the spot."

Donna accepted the offer. A mad scramble to get Donna setup at University of Toronto began. It was a crazy weekend none of us will ever forget. Her parents had to mortgage their house to afford the tuition and dentistry tools. It was a big financial strain on them but they were willing to do it.

By the second semester, Donna discovered she didn't like working in people's mouths. But her parents had mortgaged their house to afford to send her! Donna felt trapped.

Not wanting to tell her parents she didn't want to be a dentist after all, she became depressed, trudging on in something she didn't want. Eventually, she became so depressed she was suicidal.

As her boyfriend at the time, even though I was an atheist, I noticed her good Catholic mother had made sure she had a Bible in her bookshelf. From my youth, I knew some comforting scriptures, so I started reading the Bible to Donna when she would hit low points in her depression.

The scriptures seemed to lift the depression. We kept reading the Bible until one day, we realized we believed, and so we gave our hearts to the Lord.

Shortly after, we were at my parent's house for dinner and we broke the good news. My mother went upstairs and brought down her Bible. Tucked in it was a tear-stained paper. On it was a prophecy my mother had received from the Lord. It read, "This day I have saved Doug from the jaws of the Lion. He will serve me all the days of his life..."

The prophecy went on. Then I noticed the date. It was dated for the exact same day Donna got that fateful call from dentistry school, which led to her depression and ultimately to our salvation!

I wasn't prophetic back then, but I knew God was saying to me, "Calculate the odds on that." The odds of getting struck by lightning was far greater than the odds of getting that prophecy on the same day as Donna got into dentistry.

Living in Two Worlds

I wish I could say I pursued God after that. The truth is, we always went to church on Sunday; I loved to worship on Sunday; by the third song I could feel the presence of God and I loved it, but then we would stop and listen to a message that almost always repeated some other message I had heard.

I used this time to catch up on my sleep.

God was not part of my everyday life nor my business. I wasn't having a personal relationship, even though I loved worship. I would almost never pray on my own, just at church or when others would pray.

I thought I loved God, but it wasn't enough to persuade me to change my life. However, even back then, I had a strong draw to evangelism and I would always get involved in any kind of outreach events. I even headed up a couple of major events using my marketing talents to bring 10% of our city's population into our "Family Fun Fair."

A Sign Brings Repentance

I continued with one foot in the world and one foot in the church for a number of years. As my wealth grew, so did my lavish spending. Though I would have denied it at the time, I pursued money. I felt if I could earn a certain amount of money, I would win the love and respect of people.

One night, my wife and I went out for dinner while my sister babysat our daughter of about 8-years-old whose eyes were not good. She couldn't even read the large text in children's story books. Not only were her eyes blurry, but she saw double. She had to have special corrective glasses to be able to read just about everything.

We were finishing dinner when we got a call from my daughter saying, "You have to come home right now." There was an urgency in her voice, and without any details given of what happened, we rushed home.

When I got in the door my daughter said, "Daddy, Jesus healed my eyes!" I didn't really believe it, so I decided to test her. I started with a story book. She could read it no problem.

Then I got a tube of toothpaste for her to read the tiny writing on the back. Finally, I found a pill bottle with impossibly small writing *I* could barely make out and medical terms my daughter couldn't be familiar with. She could read every word, every letter!

At first, I was in shock and excited over what had happened. But when I got alone, I said to God, "If you are going to be like that and heal my daughter, I am going to change my business."

There was a part of my business I knew wasn't quite right. I had justifications why it was okay. In my heart, I knew it wasn't okay. My response to a God so loving that He would heal my daughter was repentance. Not just to ask for forgiveness, but to change my ways.

Severe Anxiety and a Dangerous Irregular Heart Beat

Several years passed. I had made some changes in my business, though I still lived to make money. God was still mostly a Sunday event.

At the time, I had no idea what people were talking about when they said they "heard from God." I never heard a thing. I used to call myself the "deaf" Christian.

Looking back I'm not sure I was a Christian. If I was, it was only by the skin of my teeth. I seriously doubt I actually was saved. However, God was after me.

I was always a logical person, definitely not very emotional. My idea of helping someone with a mental illness was to tell them, "Get a grip. Think it through."

I considered it impossible I would ever have any mental illness.

Money had such a powerful grip on me that when my business took a turn in the wrong direction and I had to let people go, I began to experience anxiety. The anxiety grew until it was all-consuming. It was accompanied by an irregular heartbeat which sounded like a Harley Davidson Motorcycle.

The pattern was so erratic it terrified me, thus adding to my anxiety. Sometimes, the time between heartbeats would be so long I could feel myself wilting, almost lifting out of my body. From a medical perspective, when your heart is in such a rhythm, it can actually stop. You simply die.

The anxiety got so bad I had to sleep sitting up, because when I would lay down, my heart would instantly go into this horrible rhythm. Then, I was afraid to sleep at all. Even sitting up, I would often wake up at 4 a.m. because my heart was going nuts. It got so bad I couldn't drive to the corner store without feeling sick to my stomach.

Reaching My End

After about six months, I was so bound by this sickness I couldn't function as a normal person. I still had a lot of money so I called my travel agent and told her to book me a trip to Mexico. I figured all I needed was to lay on a beach and relax.

Once in Mexico, I tried laying on the beach. The sun, the wind, the waves crashing--it was all perfect. But my anxiety only grew worse. I tried drinking, even though it wasn't my thing. When I would get drunk, I had relief for about 20 minutes. It was only a very short term solution.

Finally, I reached my breaking point. One evening my heart was beating so erratically, I was literally lifting out of my body between beats — which were sometimes a few seconds apart! I called my mother who prayed for me. Then I decided to get up and walk around. I didn't want to just sit there and wait until my heart gave out.

I walked to a place in the resort where they were doing construction, but nobody was there because it was a Sunday. Then my moment of surrender came. I just gave up.

I dropped to my knees and said out loud to God, "Lord, I have wasted my life. I spent my life chasing money. I consider my life a waste. God, if you heal me, I will go anywhere you want and say anything you want. I won't care what people think because I know I won't live much longer like this. So, if you heal me, I will not count my life as my own because as of right now, I consider it over."

I felt something like a blanket of peace fall on me. When you have been in torment for months on end, nothing feels as good as peace. It was wonderful! The anxiety left me from that very moment. My heart got better and better every day and within two weeks my heart was completely healed. I have no idea whether or not I was a Christian before, but I can tell you at that moment I had finally, truly surrendered my life to Jesus.

An Unusual Message

A while after being healed, I attended a church meeting and heard the most unusual message. I had never ever heard a preacher preach about God like this. He wasn't even the senior pastor. It was the pastor's kid who was filling in while he was away.

He talked about how the priests couldn't even stand to minister when the Glory of the Lord came into the temple. Then someone at the meeting gave me a "Soaking CD" from an evangelist. I found myself weeping from the presence of the Lord, which I had never done before.

When I got home, I pulled up his website and watched video after video of miracles. I didn't know at that time what anointing or impartation was, but every time I would play a miracle video, this warm, sweet feeling would wash over me. I had never experienced such a wonderful thing before, but I knew I liked it. I literally played those videos for hours until I fell asleep. For the next few weeks I kept watching those videos. They propelled me to want to connect with God myself.

A Year of God Encounters

I purposed I would spend an hour a day seeking God. The first two weeks were like talking to a wall. My heart was hard from years of living with one foot in the church, and one in the world. But I had one thing going for me — I have always been a persistent person. Even though it was super dry and nothing was happening, I kept seeking.

One day while praying, I felt the tiniest little tingly feeling. Each day in prayer, that feeling began to grow. I could not manufacture it myself, but when I was seeking God with all my heart, it would intensify. I now know it was the Holy Spirit's rivers of living water flowing from within as Jesus explained in John 7:38, *"He that believeth in me, as the scripture hath said, out of his belly shall flow rivers of living water."*

All of a sudden prayer time wasn't boring *at all*. I knew I was really connecting with God Himself. I was so excited, now I loved to worship. Soon, that one hour a day would be four or five hours, and sometimes eight hours! I couldn't get enough of Him.

During this time, I went through a lot of training by the Holy Spirit. I devoured my Bible. It wasn't boring; it was now exciting. My favorite thing to ask God was, "What was it like? What was it like to be Moses, the Glory Cloud of Your Presence meeting him, talking with you like a man speaks to a man?" Wow. Even now I am drenched in the Lord just thinking about what that experience was like for Moses.

The Bible is chock-full of encounters just waiting. Jesus is the Word (John 1:1), and Jesus said He was the way to the Father (John 14:6). I had never realized that all the Word, the scriptures, were open doors to encounter God.

My prayer time very quickly turned into encounter time. Some things that happened during that year I cannot tell you because you probably wouldn't believe me. Miracles began to happen when I started to pray for the sick, because now I knew God and we were friends.

I don't have the space here to write all the amazing things I learned and encountered--that would take a book. I can say that 10 years later, I am just as passionate about the Lord's Presence! Propelled by love, we have an orphanage in Mwanza, Tanzania, and a widows feeding program in Ghana. I have preached crusades of 30,000 people, but I most love to do miracles on the streets, where I can minister one on one.

I am addicted to the shock and sometimes tears as people react to being healed. Often people with absolutely no knowledge of God will feel tingling, or heat, and are completely dumbfounded. I recently had a girl tell me she still had tingling in her hands 30 hours after being healed. Wow!

Getting people saved and following a God like this is easy. People often call me and text me after getting healed. They are already hungry for more of what just happened to them.

For too many years we have been avoiding the methodology Jesus himself instituted. For me, Luke 10:9 is my lifestyle. I only hope I can inspire others to do the same.

ABOUT THE CONTRIBUTOR

Doug Collins was a businessman that God radically changed through an extended season of prayer. He owned an online advertising company reaching 100 million people per week. When his business took a turn for the worse, he began to experience severe anxiety. His heart began to beat erratically like a Harley Davidson motorcycle engine. While in his worst state he went for a walk and promised the Lord, "If you heal me, I will go anywhere and say anything you want."

After his recovery, God set Doug on a new path. He sold his business and started praying for the sick.

One day while in prayer the manifest presence of Jesus came and personally anointed him for healing. People began to get healed of all manner of sicknesses and disease. On Doug's first trip to Africa God did something amazing. While Doug went out into the villages each morning, God healed every single person for three days in a row! Deaf ears heard, blind eyes saw and cancers dissolved instantly!

Recently through a visitation of Jesus, God has birthed a passion to spark revival in Canada outside the four walls of our churches. To prepare for the coming revival, Doug is incorporating praying for the sick on the streets of Canada (and the United States) and is seeing God do amazing miracles, including the blind seeing and the people in wheelchairs walking. All glory to Jesus!

CHAPTER 8

WHERE SHALL I HIDE?

Neavei Isaac

"Come now, and let us reason together, saith the LORD:
though your sins be as scarlet, they shall be as white as snow;
though they be red like crimson, they shall be as wool"
(Isaiah 1:18, KJV).

I want to tell you about the single most important event in my life. In doing so I will have to reveal some things of a personal nature; I guess almost everyone has things in their personal history which they would rather were otherwise. There is no profit in dwelling on things which have been cast into the sea of forgetfulness. They are recalled here only to provide some necessary background.

I was born in New Zealand. My mother rejected me for several days, claiming that I wasn't her child. Some days later she repented and took me home, where I was rejected by my dad. For the most part he ignored me, but that became more difficult as the months passed. Obviously, I don't remember much of that except these things were sometimes mentioned as I grew up.

I had a very difficult early childhood. By the time I was school age, my parents had become convinced I was evil and stupid. Whenever I got into trouble, which was often, they would tell me how evil and stupid I was.

Sometimes Dad would say that Mother should have given me away at birth. Throughout my upbringing I was treated differently than my brothers and sister. It was not until I was 48 years old that I discovered the reason for all this.

Before Dad died, he told my sister, who later told me, he believed I wasn't his son. He said my Mother had been raped and I was the result. The moment I heard that, many things that had puzzled me fell into place. Bits of overheard conversations and many bewildering comments from relatives all suddenly made perfect sense; words like "love child," "mamser," and "bastard" now had a context which made them understandable.

Once I understood the truth, I was able to have compassion for this man who had been presented with his wife's bastard child. I forgave him for all the bad things that happened between us, and was able to let go of a great deal of bitterness and resentment I had been carrying around with me all my life.

I want to honor my parents for doing the best they could in a very difficult situation. They were both God-fearing persons and although they were not taught to understand scripture, they did rely on Jesus and did their best to honor Him. I have no doubt we will all be together in eternity, and have the wonderful relationship we were unable to achieve on earth.

Meanwhile, by the time I was a teenager I was a real rebel. I constantly got into trouble of one sort or another. My parents were religious and regular church-goers. The family had to kneel in a circle each evening and chant long meaningless prayers. Unfortunately, the denomination of Christianity my parents belonged to was strong on dogma and doctrine, but weak on teaching understanding and wisdom. The particular church we attended was all empty form and little helpful function. Looking back, I see little evidence of the Holy Spirit or the love of Christ.

Surrounded by cant and hypocrisy, I rejected religion at age 13. I didn't know it then, but I had thrown out the Baby with the bathwater.

By then I was a liar and a thief. I stole a motorcycle and rode it all around the city. Eventually I was chased and finally stopped by a policeman. He said that if I hadn't been speeding, he wouldn't have noticed me; at an early age I became a "bikie," and got my first ticket. Before my fifteenth birthday I'd left school and started full-time work. Before my seventeenth birthday I had a motorbike and before my eighteenth I had a fast powerful bike and a V8 car.

Early in my teens I had decided not to take life seriously until I grew up. I was into V8s, motorbikes and girls. At the time I thought I couldn't get enough girls, but looking back I can see there were far too many and I treated them badly.

As for the cars and bikes, the road was a racetrack. Cops were just another hazard to be avoided. Speeding fines were just annoying taxes. Looking back, I am amazed that I wasn't killed or jailed many times. I can see the hand of God protecting me from my own stupidity. Only God knows why He protected me, but I suspect that it was His response to my mother's faith in Him, and her prayers for me.

At 21, I decided it was time to take life seriously. I began to look for some way to make a fortune. That turned out to be a much harder task than I had imagined.

I found that while I could get any number of jobs at the unskilled or semi-skilled level, it was not possible to find one that led to big money. I began to read more widely and began a search for wisdom. That too turned out to be a much harder task than I had expected.

After three fruitless years I decided that I should go to university. There, I thought, I was sure to find wisdom. Since I was looking for wisdom, it made sense to study philosophy. Since I had left school before my fifteenth birthday, I did not have a solid education and struggled with the academic requirements.

The social life was exciting. Most students spent more time partying than studying, and I was no exception. Four years later I took a bachelor's degree, majoring in philosophy. Though I had struggled with my studies, I had proven to myself that I wasn't as stupid as I had been brought up to believe. I had also discovered that wisdom was not to be found in the philosophy department, and I suspected that it was not to be found anywhere in the university.

So it was that at age twenty-eight I had an education, a house, a car, a wife and a baby, but I still had neither wisdom nor wealth. There were some good jobs offered to me but they were all long-term propositions. I wanted something with better prospects for "the good life" before I got too old to enjoy it.

One of my brothers, who was a foreman in a factory, had managed to save some money and was also looking for something better. We joined forces and bought a service station and motor repair business. We did very well, and soon built a level of affluence that neither of us had previously known.

One day the bank manager came calling to ask if we would like to borrow a large sum for a project. We certainly were doing well! Little did I know how soon I was to lose it all.

A beautiful young woman came in to have her car serviced. I just had to have her and pretty soon we were having an affair.

This was not the first time I had cheated on my wife. The "others" were just out for a good time, too, and my wife didn't seem to worry when I was out late. She spent a lot of time with her friends and seemed happy with that. There had never been any passion or romance in our marriage; we were really just companions.

Starved for love as a child, for many years I had been looking for love in the arms of women. When my baby daughter came along I had decided to stop all that, but now I was reverting to my former ways. I never found satisfaction.

Looking back, I can see what a rotten person I was. I was a liar, a cheat and very selfish. Knowing from my own admission what a rotten person I was, you may find it very difficult to believe what I am about to tell you. Over the years I've read and heard about several such accounts as this, but I wrote them all off as flights of fancy or delusions. I scoffed at anything that hinted of a knowing, caring God out there. Yet strangely, I was always ready to give credence to tales of E.S.P., or extrasensory perception.

I suspected that most religions had some truth in them, but not much. I was pretty much New Age in my thinking and outlook. I was such a habitual liar that my mind could no longer distinguish between truth and falsity.

If you can relate to what I am saying here, then you know how the mind can be swayed this way and that; it is only flesh after all. I can only advise that you put your usual mindset to one side and listen to your spirit — which knows the truth when it hears it.

One evening when I was with my lover, I had an over-powering desire to completely possess her. I was no longer satisfied with knowing her physically; I wanted my mind to enter her, my very awareness to be within her. I wanted to know her thoughts and feel her feelings. In order to do that, I forced my spirit to leave my body.

At this point, some of you may be ready to write me off as a fruit loop. Talk of out-of-body experiences can affect people that way. You need to understand that we all have two bodies; the physical one you are familiar with and a spiritual "body" that the soul cannot be separated from.

This spiritual "body" has no mind of its own any more than a physical body does. Mind is part of soul, along with emotion and volition. I can only tell you that I was familiar with out-of-body experiences, but that I had never before tried to enter another person. Well, I didn't succeed. I left my body, but instead of entering her I found myself surrounded by featureless greyness. I think at that moment, I died.

My lover later told me that she thought I had died of a heart attack. One moment I was with her, fully engaged in what we were doing, and the next moment I was a lifeless hulk. To all intents and purposes, I was lifeless for about forty minutes. She was skilled at first-aid procedures and attempted to find a pulse, or breath, several times without success. Of course, I knew nothing of that until she told me later.

I felt puzzled rather than afraid. This was not like anything I had known before. In vain I looked in every direction, but could see nothing at all. I continued to scan, but it was impossible to focus as there was nothing to focus on.

Just as I began to feel panic, I noticed a faint glimmer off to one side. When I looked I could see nothing, but when I didn't look in that direction I had the sense of a very faint light off to my right. Sometimes, when you look at the night sky you have the impression of stars which are so dim you are not quite sure they are there. It was like that, only there was just the one glimmer.

Suddenly, I wanted very strongly for that glimmer to be a light. I found that I could move toward it, and I did so simply by willing it. I had the impression of moving rapidly and eventually the glimmer became an undeniable light.

At the same moment that I knew there really was a light out there, I realized that I was surrounded not by greyness, but by impenetrable darkness. It is as if one cannot see darkness unless there is some light to measure it by.

As soon as I recognized the darkness as such, I became very afraid of what might be hidden in it. All I knew was to move toward the light, but even that was scary because the light also uncovered me. The light illuminated more and more of the space about me until the darkness had shrunk to a small area behind me. It felt as though the darkness was trying to pull me back, and I had to keep willing myself further into the light.

There came a moment when I was aware of a kind of portal, or doorway, ahead of me. I could see no door, just an opening. The light was coming from beyond that opening. At the same time that I saw the source of the light, I stopped moving forward.

I wanted to go through into the light as I felt that only then would I be safe. Try as I might I could not go forward, but I knew I only had to relax in order to go backward. I could still feel the pull of the darkness.

Looking more carefully at the opening I saw that it had parallel sides, but was rounded at the top having a narrow appearance. The figure of a man appeared in the doorway. I thought the doorway and its occupant were about 50 meters away from me until he stepped forth. My perceptions immediately changed.

I realized He was gigantic in comparison with me, and quite a long way from me. It seemed to me that I was no taller than the soles of His sandals. I was terrified. Amazingly, with each step He took toward me, He seemed to shrink. When He came near me He was just a little taller than me.

He stood there, about ten meters away, and gazed at me. There was nothing disdainful in the way He looked at me, but His gaze contained complete knowledge of me. He saw all of me. He knew everything there was to know about me.

Now I was even more terrified because His revealing gaze showed me what a filthy, rotten bit of muck I was. Every willful and wrong thing I had ever done was revealed for what it was. Every selfish and uncaring word or action, every lie, distortion of truth or rejection of God and His Word was there to see along with its effects in people's lives. As I saw myself revealed, I also saw that He was faultless and perfect in every way.

Then He spoke saying, "You know Who I Am."

"But you are not real," I replied. And He just looked at me with that knowing look.

A feeling of great hopelessness came over me as I began to realize that this could be Judgement Day for me. *What hope could there be for me?* I had been living a life of sin. I had denied Christ for more than half my life and had apparently died in the very act of adultery.

"What do you want?" He asked.

I knew very well that He knew exactly what I wanted, but He obviously wanted me to say so.

"I want to go in there where the light is coming from," I said, without any real hope that I would be allowed to enter.

"You can't go in there, and you know why," He said with finality.

At that, all remaining hope and strength drained out of me; I was in utter dread.

It was then, at the lowest moment of my entire existence, when there was not an ounce of pride or defiance left in me; the amazing grace of the Lord took me to the greatest moment of my life.

He led me to a low bench that I had not noticed before, and sat down with me upon it.

Drawing me close to His side, He said, "Neavei, I love you".

I knew it was true because He said it, but also because I could feel it. I cannot describe that love except to say it far transcends anything you can imagine. The most loving feelings you have ever experienced toward your own children pale in comparison. His love swept through me, touching every part of me. I could not comprehend what was happening.

For most of my life I had been denied love, and now the Creator Himself was infusing me with His untrammeled love. Here was I, this vile, mucky creature being loved by this perfect Lord of All Creation — Jesus. I felt I was being washed, touched and healed.

For a time I just bathed in glory. By and by, my wits returned, but just as I began to wonder about the apparent contradiction of being turned away from the door and yet being loved by Jesus, He spoke again.

"I am sending you back, for I have work for you to do," He said.

I could not reply, being completely overwhelmed with joy at this reprieve.

"There are many on earth who know *of* Me," He continued, "but they don't know My Word is true. Many have been raised in confusing circumstances and are deceived. They need to be told the Truth. You are to tell them: 'I Am. I love them. I am coming back soon.'"

The Lord explained to me that being familiar with the Biblical stories about Him is not enough. The people have to know the accounts of His life on earth, which are found in the Gospels of Matthew, Mark, Luke and John, are true. He further explained that although He has many servants, there is much to be done. He said there were many people who needed to hear the truth from me. He said He would empower my words to touch people who could not otherwise receive the truth.

When He told me how many people I must reach for Him, I was frightened.

"Lord, I can't reach that many people. I'm only Neavei."

Assuring me that I could indeed accomplish the task He was giving me, He again stressed that many souls depended on the work I was to do. He explained that He could accomplish His will without my help, but preferred to do things this way.

"I must start this work right away," I said.

"You will not begin this work for many years," said the Lord. Then He went on to tell me about many things I would do over the next twenty years.

I was aghast at what He told me. "I won't do those horrible things now that I see them for what they are," I protested. Realizing the futility of arguing with an all-knowing God, I was filled with shame at hearing these things I would do.

He then explained that I would do these things because I would not remember the truth. I would not be able to remember. "There is no light in you, only darkness," said Jesus.

Puzzled and fearful, I asked how I would ever be saved, and how I would become an instrument in the salvation of others? The Lord Jesus then explained to me that the day would come when I would call out to Him to save me from the mess I had made of my life. He said that from that moment He would hold me in His hand, and the light would begin to dawn in me. As the light in me grew, memory of these experiences would come to me. Even then, it seemed, I would tarry until the end of days when time was very short.

"How will I ever manage to reach so many people if I have so little time to do it?" I asked.

"Trust in Me, for My timing is perfect," He replied. "When the time comes, I will give you the means."

I awoke to find myself face down in the back of the car. I remember gasping for breath and then choking on the dust I had just breathed in. Pulling myself together, I stumbled out of the car only to be accosted by my lover.

She had thought me dead, and had been pacing up and down wondering how to get rid of my body without facing awkward questions. She was married, too, and was fearful of the consequences should her husband discover what she had been doing. Now she thought it had been a bad joke on my part that I had just been pretending to be dead.

It took me some time to calm her and assure her I had no knowledge of what had happened. Indeed, that was true. Even as I tried to explain I could remember only that I'd been out of my body and had some really great experiences up in the clouds.

Thinking that it was only natural for me to be a little confused after being in some kind of coma for more than half an hour, I said I would tell her everything in a day or two. But any vague memories I had awoken with were gone the next day.

I knew I had experienced something mystical, but beyond that I had no idea what it had been. Many times, I tried to recall what had happened that night but I couldn't. I could remember the occasion and what I had tried to do, but beyond that, nothing. Only the conviction that something wonderful and frightening had happened remained with me.

Through the passing of 20 years I did many things I am now very ashamed of. I have repented of those things and ask forgiveness from all those I hurt. I was degenerate.

In the year 1992, when my life was at an all-time low, I called out to God. It was a desperate cry for help but it came out in the form of a challenge.

"Hey there 'Big G'," I said, "I don't know if You are real but they say You are; I don't know if You can hear me but they say You can; I don't know if You care, but they say You do. I want to know the truth! If You are real and You are who they say You are, then I don't understand why the Creator of the whole cosmos would care about a nothing, hopeless, failure like me. I want to know the truth! If You are real, if You sent Your Son Jesus to live as a man and die on the cross to save us from our sins, then reveal Yourself so I may know the truth."

I did not notice any sudden change. I had not expected to. I thought the whole proposition was absurd and just another sign of the deluded state I was in. I put the matter out of my mind.

Weeks passed and I found myself sharing a house with a Christian. He had answered my advert for a flatmate. We had some common interests and enjoyed the same shows on TV so we got on quite well. He seemed an ordinary bloke in most ways but one night a week, and twice on Sunday, he did something weird — he went to church.

He always invited me but I never went. No way! I was not going to get mixed up in that kind of crap. About the same time, my children started to talk about the things they were learning at the religious education classes at their school.

One night my flatmate said, "I know you don't believe as I do, but I would like you to come along to church just for fellowship and to enjoy the good music."

I accepted his invitation, but was completely unprepared for what happened. To my amazement, there was a church full of people who were obviously enjoying themselves. That was a big enough shock, but soon I was listening to the preacher's message and something in me was responding. Afterward, my friend asked me if I had enjoyed it. I said I had in some ways, but I didn't want to go back again because it was too uncomfortable.

Months passed. I would occasionally go to an evening service with him, but always with the same result. During that time I was increasingly engaged with an internal debate. I did not know if I was talking to myself or if this was God I was talking to.

There were changes in my life; I began to care about things I had not cared about for a long time. Also about that time I visited my sister who had been a "born again" Christian for some years. She witnessed to me and shared with me some information that my dad had given her. These things had a powerful effect on me.

I wanted to believe in Jesus. He seemed to be the answer to so many problems. I wondered, *were all these just the delusions of an emotional cripple who couldn't make it without some sort of crutch?*

One by one the Lord dealt with the issues I raised. There came a time when I knew I had to make a decision about the direction my whole future would take. For the greater part of my life up to that time I'd believed there was no personal God. If there was a Creator, then He had done His work long ago and left the whole universe to fulfill its destiny in some autonomous way. Now I seemed to be discovering that there is a God who knows, cares and answers.

In my search for wisdom I had looked into the most popular religions, and some cults, and found them wanting. They were all dead, lifeless philosophies which created more troubles than they solved. I was being confronted with a sovereign God who took a personal interest in all who sought Him.

I prayed another prayer, "God, if You really are listening, and if You really do care, I want to know the truth no matter what it costs me." It was as if blinders suddenly were removed from my eyes. I saw evidence of God all around in plants, animals, mountains and especially in people. I saw things I had always been blind to. Previously, I had seen only the natural. Now, I saw something of spirit in all creation. It was almost as if I could see the blueprint for each thing, as well as the thing itself.

I felt an urgency to get the matter settled. One sleepless night I sat up with the Bible. I could not accept with my mind what I now know in my heart to be true.

Early in the morning, I prayed, "God, I have reservations about what is written in this Bible. There are either contradictions in these books or I lack the ability to understand what I am reading. Show me, in a way I can understand, the truth about just one of these apparent contradictions and I will take the rest on trust until such time as You may reveal more to me."

I instantly received an understanding of that particular puzzle. There and then I gave my heart to Jesus. In the years since, many puzzles have been sorted out for me.

Some weeks later I responded to an altar call at church, making my new faith a matter of public knowledge, and soon after I was baptized with water. Then I received the baptism of the Holy Spirit. I was saved, redeemed and made a part of the Body of Christ.

All that happened quickly, but then began the slow process of renewing my mind to conform to my status as a "child of God." I made slow progress in the things of God. I also joined the Full Gospel Business Men's Fellowship International and fellowshipped with men who knew and loved Jesus. And there came a time when sufficient light was in me for memory of that wonderful event from 20 years ago to come flooding back to my conscious mind.

It happens with anyone who has lived awhile, that a particular sight, or smell or happening will remind one of a time or place that has not been thought of for many years. When that happens, one is not confused; the memory of that event is clear and one knows it as memory. Such is the case with the memory I have of those events from long ago. I have recounted them here as accurately as I am able. This is a true account of real events.

The good Lord continues to improve me as the Holy Spirit deals with me, changes me and conforms me to Jesus. Praise God for the work He has done and continues to do in our lives. The fact that you are reading this account proves that Jesus has given me the means to carry out the commission He gave me so long ago. I pray that Jesus blesses all who read this testimony and calls them to a closer walk with Him.

Jesus lives! The Bible stories about Him are true. Jesus loves us and will save all who call on His mercy and receive Him into their hearts. These are "The Last of Days." Jesus is coming back soon.

ABOUT THE CONTRIBUTOR

If this has raised issues for you, please feel free to email Neavei at: gethelp@livingconnections.com. He will respond personally.

Neavei Isaac, author, has recently returned to live in New Zealand. He, and his wife, Lyn, are preparing to live in a large motor home as they travel and work throughout New Zealand. They expect this to provide more time that can be used for writing, and lots of opportunity to engage with the increasing numbers of "Grey Nomads" and "Freedom Campers," the majority of whom are not effectively reached with the Gospel.

An update and expansion of their website should be well underway before the end of 2016: www.livingconnections.com. It will grow to contain new articles that can help readers keep a clear view of the "Straight and Narrow Way" that leads to Jesus, with salvation and eternal life. The Isaac's pray their work will help people remain undeceived in this increasingly dangerous and immoral time.

PART II

But God commendeth his love toward us, in that,
while we were yet sinners, Christ died for us.

(Romans 5:8, KJV).

CHAPTER 9

THE ROUNDABOUT

The Story of Evangelist Roger Whipp, as written by Carolyn Curran-Fyckes

But as for me and my house, we will serve the Lord
(Joshua 24:15b, KJV).

Many of you will know what a roundabout is, but for those of you who don't, I shall explain. A roundabout, common here in the UK, is a traffic circle created in order to slow down traffic. There are several other routes to choose from leading off from the roundabout.

The path of life is much like a roundabout: some of us follow the wrong road and then wonder how we arrived at the end of that particular road; others recognize the way they are to proceed and arrive safely at their intended destination on time. However, many will be confused while on the roundabout. They may even drive around the circle several times before deciding upon the route to follow.

I was one of those drivers who kept going around the circle. My name is Roger Whipp.

For over 20 years, I worked first as an ambulance attendant and then as a police constable in London, England. My journey in life was, at times, both confusing and irritating. *Why was I plagued with stress? Why were others giving me the attitude and cutting me off on the road? Didn't they realize that I just wanted to be left alone to enjoy the trip and to make my own decisions when I was ready to?*

89

After 14 years of marriage to Maggie, we had both gone down different paths doing our own thing, and growing apart. Although Maggie was a Christian, she would be the first to admit she had wandered far off God's route when the dramatic incident that was to change both our lives happened.

The good news is that once invited into our lives, God never abandons us. He remains by our side whatever route or pathway we decide to take, ready to help us back on His route.

Although my parents never attended, as a child I was sent to church. I learned about Jesus and His sacrifice. I also knew what Jesus expected of a person. At the age of 13, as an act of independence, I decided not to attend church anymore. I wanted to have fun in life. I wasn't going to be bound by restrictive Christian rules. *Did God really exist anyway?* I didn't have time to think about such a heavy question. I put that unanswered question on the shelf, where it remained for many years.

With my future unfolding, I was frequently reminded of that haunting question. During both of my careers as an ambulance attendant and finally as a police constable, I witnessed first-hand much intense suffering and tragedy. *How would a loving God allow such sorrow? Why didn't He intervene?*

The answer to the question of whether a loving God existed or not was becoming clearer to me. I didn't need to trouble myself with such a philosophical question, though. Let someone else worry about solving it. I had to get on with my life.

On Easter weekend, April 19, 1984, my life came to an unexpected halt. Maggie had been on her way to visit her brother and had just taken her usual exit off of the roundabout. Without warning, another vehicle slammed violently into her car. The sound of metal ripping and crunching must have been terrifying. Blood poured from her mangled, glass-covered body. Ironically, the accident happened within a stone's throw of the City of London Cemetery.

The prognosis for Maggie was very grim. She was not expected to survive such a horrendous accident. Her parents and siblings, all

Christians, rushed to be at her bedside in the intensive care unit of the hospital. Perplexed, I observed that they all seemed to have an inner peace and strength to draw upon even though they were saddened and shocked to see their Maggie severely disfigured and unrecognizable. I didn't have the comfort of that unexplainable peace within me.

The doctor informed us that if Maggie, somehow, by some miracle, was restored to a modicum of health, she would probably exist in a vegetative state. I was asked to make a life choice decision. *Did I want the doctor to discontinue life support or not?* The doctor cautioned me to ponder this very serious question, and if possible, give an answer the following day.

The sensible response seemed obvious — yes. Maggie wouldn't want to be left in such an unfortunate state. She would be at peace, and I would find peace, probably, with that decision also. In the morning, having decided to give permission to turn off the life support, I slipped out onto the hospital grounds to have a smoke while awaiting the doctor's arrival.

Isn't it strange that it can take a tragedy to make us aware of how much someone means to us? My world had come to a road block with the devastating news about Maggie. Although, just a week previous we had agreed to divorce, the thought of losing Maggie was suddenly nauseating.

I quickly butted out the cigarette. There was no small enjoyment even in smoking. The cold realization of my love for my wife slapped me hard in the face. *How could my mind have deceived me into thinking that I no longer loved or needed her in my life?*

The mind is simultaneously awesome and scary because it is an incomprehensible puzzle. *Was there a Creator who had designed this mind? Was there a Creator who had tenderly painted each flower that graced the hospital grounds?* I was now determined to find the answers.

My plan was that I would make a bargain with God for Maggie's life. What did I have to lose if He wasn't real? I sent up a simple prayer in the hope that God was listening. I would agree to investigate the reality of Christianity if God would heal Maggie. At least, I reasoned, I had not committed myself to becoming a Christian.

Within an hour of saying this simple prayer (which even contained some strong expletives) God not only heard my prayer, but He also answered it. As the doctor turned off the life support, Maggie began to breathe again.

For nearly one month, Maggie lay unconscious. No visitors other than family were permitted to see her for the first couple of months. The family was fearful that visitors would be so overcome by the sight of her that they would be unable to control their emotions in front of her. Maggie didn't need that to happen.

According to doctors involved in her care, Maggie's recovery, if it occurred, would be excruciatingly slow and wracked with pain. The expectation was that she would require approximately two years of plastic surgery. Her right arm had been so extensively damaged that an orthopedic surgeon approached me and asked me in what position I wanted her arm to be set.

Puzzled, I questioned the surgeon as to why he would consult me regarding such a decision. After all, he was the one with expert medical knowledge, not I. The doctor explained to me that her arm, damaged beyond repair, would be totally useless regardless of what position it was set in; there was nothing to attach screws or pins to.

The ophthalmological surgeon delivered dismal news also. Maggie's optic nerve could not be repaired either, but he could make her injured eye appear normal by implanting a contact lens and moving her eye upwards, in order to line it up with her good eye. However, he could not eliminate her double vision. The damage was permanent.

All of the doctors working on Maggie were in for a huge surprise. Within 13 weeks, Maggie was discharged from the hospital. Plastic surgery to fix her horrendous facial injuries was never needed. Her face no longer showed evidence of this near-fatal accident.

Her useless arm became useful again without physiotherapy as the surgeon had said; there was no point to therapy in her case. The orthopedic surgeon was beyond convincing that her arm was healed. He was a man who relied completely on the facts of a case. Only the clear proof of repeated X-rays could sway his opinion. After studying the repeat X-rays intensely, the surgeon, with a bewildered expression etched across his forehead, turned slowly toward me and said, "I do not understand this. This is a miracle."

The expressionless ophthalmological surgeon was equally stunned with Maggie's incredible progress. After Maggie's eye bandages were removed, he was stunned to discover that she no longer had double vision. This amazing change was impossible. The surgeon's previous cool, aloof countenance melted with this exciting discovery. Completely out of character, he broke out into a huge, contagious smile.

At least ten churches were praying for Maggie's total healing by this time. God clearly had His hand on Maggie and His hand on others who would be placed strategically in her life.

The first car to come upon the scene was being driven by an off-duty ambulance attendant who managed to keep Maggie's airway open until a medical team arrived. One year after the accident, the same ambulance attendant contacted me to tell me that his cousin, who was a road sweeper, was dispatched to do cleanup work at the site.

Coincidentally, this cousin happened to have a camera with him on that particular occasion. He offered to provide graphic pictures of the scene. These photos would give people proof of the devastation done to Maggie's car. It *was* an accident. I also learned that of the 12 physicians who rotated being on call to attend such emergencies, the only Christian among them was on duty that terrible night.

More fascinating information regarding early intervention for Maggie was provided by Maggie's own mother. Maggie's mother had canceled an appointment with her dentist when she rushed to be at Maggie's side. When she finally did return for a visit to the dentist, she recounted the details of what had necessitated the cancellation.

She informed the dentist that Maggie had suffered 28 fractures to her jaw alone. Astonished, the dentist instantly remembered that her father, who was a maxillofacial surgeon, had been flown in from

Scotland to advise and assist with a woman who had 28 fractures to her jaw resulting from a motor vehicle accident. Yes, it was Maggie who had been at the center of all of that attention.

The coincidences didn't end there. Two young off-duty constables, who just happened to come across the accident on their way home, had worked with me. Paul, a Christian, who had shared supper more than once at our home didn't even recognize Maggie. He told me that he had spent all of that Sunday at church praying for the Lord's intervention in Maggie's health.

The doctor who cared for Maggie in the intensive care unit was a personal friend of one of the mates. The fireman who helped to free Maggie from the wreckage of her car was the brother of a former co-worker of mine. The night nurse was to become my cousin's future sister-in-law.

Many lives, not just mine, were being interwoven and affected by Maggie's miracles. Also; the name of the hospital was Whipps Cross, and my surname, not a common one, is Whipp.

However, no life would be more changed than mine. Even though God had proven Himself by the miracles He had undertaken for Maggie, I had not decided to commit my life to Him. That was not a part of the agreement. I didn't feel ready to make that change yet. I was holding up my end of the bargain by attending church services, wasn't I?

In conversation with the minister one day, I was surprised to learn that God would forgive any sin if He was asked to do so at any time. Pleased with this information, I posed an interesting question to him: wouldn't it be reasonable to delay any confession and commitment to God until I was 70 years old? Wisely, the minister said that he would like to conduct my funeral. Therefore he inquired what date he should mark down for the service. I was very taken aback.

One, Sunday, a guest speaker delivered the sermon. At the end of the sermon, the speaker gave the invitation for those who wanted to come forward for the prayer of salvation. In shock and against my own volition, I realized that my legs were taking me forward to the altar.

Finding myself now halfway up the aisle, I entertained the thought of returning to my seat, but I felt too embarrassed to do so. People in the congregation were smiling broadly at me and were whispering amongst themselves that it was about time for me to make this commitment. Not to lose face, I decided to continue forward. I would just repeat the prayer of salvation after the guest speaker, and then I would return quietly to my seat. That would be the best solution.

I didn't expect that God would use this opportunity to speak directly to my heart during the prayer. That powerful moment with God forever changed me and filled me with His peace and His love. Over time, through prayer and the studying of the Bible, I developed a close relationship with my awesome Creator.

God clearly showed me the way off the roundabout, miraculously healed Maggie's broken body and our broken marriage. I would never have even imagined that on this exciting new journey I would travel — with my beloved wife, Maggie, at my side — that I, a former atheist, would work for God as an evangelist.

But as for me and my house, we will serve the Lord (Joshua 24:15b, KJV).

ABOUT THE CONTRIBUTOR

Roger Whipp was born and raised in East London, United Kingdom, where he currently resides with his wife, Maggie. Professionally, he was first employed with London Ambulance Service for seven years, and then as a police officer in London with the Metropolitan Police for a following 14 years of service.

Since giving his life to the Lord in 1984 at the age of 37 and establishing an itinerant ministry in 1985, Roger has recounted his testimony from Albania, Northern Ireland, through and including 17 states in America, and much of the United Kingdom.

Roger has also obtained a certificate in Christian Studies from St. John's Theological College in Nottingham.

The main thrust of Roger's ministry is to encourage healing and deliverance through Christ and to provide an outreach to men. Roger is a recommended speaker for Christian Vision for Men, and currently heads up the men's ministry at his home church of St. Chad's, located in Chadwell Heath, Romford, UK. Roger may be contacted through writing at: Roger Whipp, 1 Clovelly Gardens, Romford, Essex, RM7 8NP. His Website is: www.evangelist-rogerwhipp.org, or he can be reached by cell phone at: + 4407952313544

CHAPTER 10

A SUPERNATURAL LIFE WITH JESUS

Krystyna Januszewski

Jesus answered and said unto him, "Verily, verily, I say unto thee, Except a man be born again, he cannot see the kingdom of God
(John 3:3, KJV).

Let me take this opportunity to introduce myself to you. My name is Krystyna Januszewski. I grew up in Poland when the country was under Communist rule. We were a seemingly normal, good Catholic family of four with high moral standards.

One thing I remember and regret was that I never had a good relationship with my mother. To me, she was an extremely negative person. I could never talk to my mother with an open heart. Although I loved her, I didn't understand her, and couldn't wait to finish my education in order to leave home and start my own life.

I came to understand something later on in my life that would have a profound effect on me. My mother went very religiously to church and followed all their traditions and rules. However, nobody taught her how to honor her husband, my father, nor how to reconcile differences with other family members. To this day, my mother's family is divided because of a lack of love between them. I believe that it is a generational curse.

In my imagination, I saw God as a hard, punishing God who would harm me if I did bad things (like being angry toward my mother) so I closed my heart to her. To me, life with God was a life of struggle and suffering — like Jesus suffering on the cross — the martyr's life!

So when I finally was able to leave my parental home, I was determined in my heart to be nothing like my mother. I went to college, graduated and became a responsible and independent person, the very opposite of my mother.

I worked in the hospitality industry where I met my husband, got married and had two boys. My husband was a good husband and father. We were a strong family unit, though I made my husband an idol as I was very much in love with him. He adored me and his adoration comforted my heart. My life was not going to be like that of my parents.

Eventually, my husband and I decided we needed to leave Communist Poland to pursue a better life. We immigrated to Germany where we became refugees. After three years in Germany, we finally made our way to Canada. In Canada, we struggled financially as my husband had to return to school in order to practice his profession. Things became even worse when my husband was diagnosed with terminal cancer.

I began to feel very empty inside. My life and dreams were over. I didn't know where to turn or what to do next. I would've liked to be dead. Instead, I read many books on psychology and psychiatry thinking that I would find the answer to my emptiness in them, but to no avail. I became more depressed and hopeless. I was desperate to the point I thought about taking my own life. I questioned the reason and purpose of life, if God even existed, and if He did to what religion He belonged.

I cried out to God for help. I was sinking in a deep, black hole. I called out, "God, if You are Muhammed, Buddha, Vishnu, Roman Catholic, Mormon, Jehovah's Witness,…please, reveal Yourself to me. Where are you?"

Suddenly, an unexpected thought came to my mind from a few years back. I had heard the words, "You must be 'born again'," while I was watching a television program. Since I was not familiar with the English language, I made myself a note and wrote those two words on a piece of paper. Then, I stashed it away in a book on our bookshelf to be found at a later date and understood more clearly.

I went to work in a factory to help make ends meet. We were in a very bad financial situation. It was in this dirty place that my prayers would be answered.

While working on the midnight shift, I met a man named Anthony Valdner. Seeing that I was down and depressed, he handed me Billy Graham's book, *How to be Born Again.* I looked at the cover and those two words, "born again," jumped into my heart. I remembered the note that I had made a few years prior and wondered how Anthony knew to give me the book. I thought it was just a coincidence.

At home, I had trouble finding the notes I had made a few years back. Can you believe where I found them? They were in a book, and the author of the book was also named Valdner.

He had the same surname as Anthony! *Was this a coincidence? An accident?* I didn't know that this was one of the ways the Holy Spirit draws us to Jesus! He works in mysterious ways, His wonders to perform.

I went to work the next day so excited to tell Anthony my news. He wasn't surprised, for he also knew the Holy Spirit. He told me that with God there were no "accidents" or "coincidences," and that everything happens for a purpose. He invited me to his church when we finished the afternoon shift at 11 p.m. They were having an all-night, Good Friday prayer meeting. I remember the date; it was March 31, 2002. I decided to go.

In that church, I saw and heard things I had never seen nor heard in my life. People spoke in strange tongues, others wept loudly and uncontrollably at the altar. I didn't understand what it meant to surrender my life and die to self. I thought I had to die physically, but Jesus had done that 2000 years ago. That's when Anthony opened the

Bible to the words, *"Jesus Christ [is] the same yesterday, and today, and for ever"* (Hebrews 13:8).

As I cried out to God on Good Friday, March 31, 2002, I gave my heart to Jesus Christ to be my Lord and Savior. I was a new creature in Christ. The guilt and shame I felt from my past melted away. I was "born again" and filled with the Holy Spirit.

I was so excited I didn't want to go to sleep. I just wanted to read my Bible the whole night; I felt so different. I read John 3:3, *"Jesus answered and said unto him, "Verily, verily, I say unto thee, Except a man be born again, he cannot see the kingdom of God."*

My husband was getting worse and worse. I so wanted him to come to know Jesus. I didn't understand that everyone doesn't have the same experience in being born again. Each individual's experience is the work of the Holy Spirit. The Bible book of John, chapter six, verse 44a, says, *"No man can come to me, except the Father which hath sent me draw him."*

My husband's initial reaction was to reject me. I was devastated and contacted the Pastor at Anthony's church. He explained to me that I was now in a war, a spiritual war for my husband's soul.

I was so hungry for more of God. Every moment of the day I wanted to read His Word. As I began to understand more and received revelations. Even though my husband's situation hadn't changed, I had changed. I was joyful and peaceful in the midst of the storm.

It was a very difficult but joyous time for me. I lost all my friends. My husband continued to reject me, yet I loved and cared for him unconditionally the same way that Jesus loves us--without conditions. Prayer warriors joined with me in prayer at the church for my husband's salvation: we were in a spiritual battle.

About a year after I gave my heart to Christ, about a month before my husband died, one Saturday morning I prayed and surrendered the one who was my idol, my physical husband, over to the One who had become my spiritual Husband, the Lord Jesus Christ Himself. The next day, Sunday, my husband was willing to come to church with me. God had answered my prayer because I had surrendered my will to His.

I watched as my husband made his way to the front in answer to the altar call from the Pastor. Now, I was really joyful. I praised the Lord all day long.

On Monday, my husband bought himself a Bible. He told me that on Sunday he felt as if someone was behind him, guiding him to the altar. I knew it was the drawing of the Holy Spirit. My husband asked if the Pastor could come to our house to teach him God's Word. The Pastor came as requested.

Moments before my husband died, in the presence of our Pastor, my husband testified of seeing a waterfall. The Pastor explained that water was symbolic of the Holy Spirit and His presence. At that very moment, my husband was transported to heaven. Glory to God in the highest.

I opened my Bible to 2 Corinthians 5:8, *"We are confident, I say, and willing rather to be absent from the body, and to be present with the Lord."* I heard the sound of a trumpet at that moment. When I hugged my husband, it was as if I was hugging his clothes; his spirit had gone home to be with Jesus.

I now have so much comfort and continue to praise the Lord for what he did for me. I have a peace that I never had before. I was so joyful and thankful because I knew that my husband was saved; that I would see him again because of the promise in John 3:15, *"That whosoever believeth in [Jesus] should not perish, but have eternal life."* I know that I will see my husband again. Praise God from whom all blessings flow.

At that point I had nothing: no house, no husband and my friends were all gone. But I had Jesus.

One day while I was reading my Bible, I read in Matthew 5:10, *"Blessed are they which are persecuted for righteousness' sake: for theirs is the kingdom of heaven,"* and I knew, I sensed in my heart, that I was not alone. Jesus' Holy Spirit was with me, guiding me and protecting me, and I had a joy and a peace that no one could take from me. I was free. I was in love with Christ. All my burdens just flowed away because now the Holy Spirit was living in me. I experienced just what the Word of God says in Matthew 11:28, *"Come unto me, all ye that labor and are heavy laden, and I will give you rest."*

Life moved on. One day I felt really sick and could hardly walk. I went into a restaurant and fell at the knees of a gentleman, asking him for some pills to ease my pain. He told me he would pray for me. I asked in whose name he would be praying and he told me he would be praying in the name of Jesus of Nazareth. After he finished praying, he gave me his telephone number.

What I didn't know was that this gentleman would later become my husband. He told me that when he saw me come into the restaurant the Holy Spirit told him, "This is your wife; take care of her. She is a widow." He had been seeking the Lord for a companion. Even though I was upset in my body, this divine appointment was a spiritual set up by the Holy Spirit.

After my husband had died I had many dreams, but there was one that hit me, one that I will never forget. Now I know it was more than just a dream; it was a vision, not a dream, for it is as real to me today as it was that night so many years ago.

I was flying over the Rocky Mountains. (At that time I had never heard of the Rocky Mountains.) It was so beautiful and I sensed my feet didn't touch the peak of the mountains.

I couldn't stop thinking about the vision I'd had, so I bought an airline ticket and flew to Calgary. I took a gondola to the top of the mountain in Banff and there it was: I saw exactly the same thing I had seen in my vision.

I asked the Holy Spirit to explain this, and that's when I sensed I should call the gentleman in the restaurant as he seemed to be a man of God. To my utter amazement, the man told me about my whole life. He explained to me how I am afraid of dying but that God was showing me I didn't have to be afraid. My freedom was in Christ and that's why I was flying: flying free above the troubles of this world.

This gentleman's voice penetrated my heart. As I was speaking to him, I looked through the window of the hotel room where I was staying and saw a silver cross shining through the window. That's when I understood in fullness how much of an idol my husband had been to me in my life. Now that I was free, only Jesus would be my husband.

1 John 5:21 says, *"Little children, keep yourselves from idols. Amen."* An idol is a false god. The real God is saying to keep ourselves from anything and everything that would occupy the place in our hearts due to God; keep ourselves from any sort of substitute for Him that would take first place in our lives.

God had other plans for me, not for bad but for good. Like it says in Jeremiah 29:11, *"For I know the thoughts that I think toward you, saith the Lord, thoughts of peace, and not of evil, to give you an expected end."* God knew that I wasn't going around looking for a husband, that I wanted to be a Godly woman who would be obedient to His Word. I didn't want to do anything that would jeopardize my relationship with the Holy Spirit. But then the Holy Spirit confirmed something else to me.

While I was in conversation with this gentleman, he asked me if I remembered the date I had accepted Christ. I told him it was Good Friday, March 31st. He told me that was his birthday! A coincidence? Not with God.

I began to realize there are no coincidences, no accidents with God, and that the steps of the righteous are ordered by the Lord (Psalm 37:23). What an awesome God we serve. I also began to recognize and understand that this gentleman was a man of God who was single, alone, and who desired a Godly woman by his side — and I was that woman!

I fell in love with James, but before I went any further I asked him what his thoughts were on Christian marriage, and whether Christians should live together without marriage. I knew that if he gave me a Godly, Biblical answer that he was the man I was to marry. This was the person God had put in my life to come alongside me, to take Christ's message to all those I would come in contact with as the power of the Holy Spirit leads me, in order to bring in the end-time harvest for Christ, and to tell people that Jesus loves them.

I continued to pray for my relationship with my mother and for her salvation. It was my husband who suggested I return to my homeland to see my mom. When I arrived back in Poland, my mother told me that she would like to change her heart. I asked if I could pray for her and she agreed.

When I began to pray the sinner's prayer, saying, "Lord Jesus, thank you for your Holy blood which was shed for our sins," both of us began to cry. My mom gave her life to Christ. Then she asked me not to leave. She told me she felt she was going to die, even though she was not sick. As I held her in my arms and prayed for the peace of Jesus to come and fill her, she peacefully passed into eternity.

During my mother's entire life she had been afraid of dying alone. But the Holy Spirit had directed me to her. I am the one whom she had not had a good relationship with, but because I had a relationship with the Holy Spirit and was obedient to His leading, the Holy Spirit sent me to her bedside to be with her as she passed from this life into eternal life with Christ. He is an on-time God.

What an awesome, wonderful, amazing God we serve. He is real. He is true and all He wants you to know is that Jesus loves you. If you will give your heart to Him, He will never leave you nor forsake you (Hebrews 13:5b).

When I lived under Communist rule we couldn't travel. My heart's desire was to travel and see the world. God's Word says in Psalm 37:4, *"Delight thyself also in the Lord: and he shall give thee the desires of thine heart."* Now that I live in spiritual freedom, I also have physical freedom to travel the world without any borders and closed doors. I am free to share the love of God with the power of the Holy Spirit.

Just in case you are wondering about my husband, James was born in the Gorbals of Glasgow, Scotland. He has accomplished many things in this life. He is a Messianic Jew ministering in the gifts of the Holy Spirit and is a prophet of the Lord. Together, we travel this world searching for God's lost sheep. We have seen the dead get up and walk in Jesus' name.

Acts 1:8 says, *"But ye shall receive power, after that the Holy Ghost is come upon you: and ye shall be witnesses unto me both in Jerusalem, and in all Judea, and in Samaria, and unto the uttermost part of the earth."*

"For there is no respect of persons with God" (Romans 2:11). What He has done for me, He can do for you. Open your heart to Him and He will give you your heart's desire.

ABOUT THE CONTRIBUTOR

Krystyna resides with her husband, Rev. James Thomas, in the lovely town of Ancaster, Ontario, Canada. Her joy and passion is working wholeheartedly for the Lord until He returns.

In recent years, she has traveled as an evangelist throughout the Caribbean, Mexico, Costa Rica, Panama, Columbia, Venezuela, Europe and Egypt. In her journey with the Lord her favorite time was when she visited Egypt and the Holy Spirit made it possible for her to climb Mount Sinai, the mountain of Moses.

Rev. Thomas and Krystyna are affiliated with The Tabernacle of the Congregation in Waterford, Ontario. James supports Krystyna in her work as an evangelist.

Krystyna has two sons, Peter and Lucas, and two grandchildren from Peter and Julie. Andreas is two years and six months old, and Samaia is almost six years old.

Before leaving Poland, Krystyna was working in a resort as a Clinical Dietitian. To this day, you can be guaranteed whenever you drop by the house for a visit there is always something good cooking on the stove. Krystyna's culinary expertise is a gift from God. What a great way to win souls for the Lord.

As an interesting note to this testimony, when Krystyna was brought up in Poland she was anti-Semitic. Now that she is born again, God gave her a husband who is a Messianic Jew.

CHAPTER 11

GOD IS NOT JUST ANOTHER FAIRY TALE!

Penny Oliver-Del Zotto

In my father's house are many mansions: if it were not so,
I would have told you. I go to prepare a place for you
(John 14:2, KJV).

Although I had been baptized Anglican, we certainly did not practice our own religion. My adoptive father was a raging alcoholic who was violent, profane, rude and completely out of control when he drank — which was *often*! I tried to stay out of his way, but I still endured many of my own terrifying moments.

One time, I remember sitting in the empty bathtub. I asked God, "…to just let him kill me, if this was how my life was always going to be."

My Dad never did quit drinking and things never did get better. In fact, they definitely got *worse* over the years. I figured God must either be asleep or dead. Due to my unanswered prayers, I suppose, I decided I was agnostic, not a full-out atheist. Deep inside I *wanted* to believe there really was a God, and that He actually *cared* about us.

At the young age of 15, I was put into a Pentecostal group home. Chapel was compulsory and most of the girls looked and sounded like heavenly angels! I also loved to hear preaching from the book of Revelation where the end times are described.

I most certainly enjoyed my long conversations with Pastor Paul as he patiently tried to explain to me why I "needed a personal relationship with Jesus Christ." I told him since I had so recently obtained my new-found "freedom" from the abusive situation I'd lived in, I had no intention of becoming "a Bible-thumping goody two-shoes." In fact, I planned on being bad. I didn't want to be a hypocrite and add that to the list of all of my other sins.

True to my own word, I "partied like a rock star" for the next few years and completely embraced the occult with all of its demonic practices. I knew there was an absolute, undeniable and very real power in it, but I didn't understand that I had tapped into the *wrong* source of power. Sadly, in retrospect, it would be another 18 years before I would hear the gospel message again.

I ended up pregnant at 19 and married at 20. I did agree to raise our children as Catholics, honoring their father's request. I, myself, never chose to convert, but I did sleep well during Sunday services!

We had a gorgeous house with a low mortgage so I could be a stay-at-home mom, a car in the driveway and perfect health. I truly believed it had all been acquired or accomplished without a bit of help from God.

However, in truth, what never *ever* went away was this deep ache in my heart and the pain that my childhood had inflicted upon my spirit being. I had never felt loved, safe, accepted or important. I believed if you just lived and died and that was all there was to it, what difference did any of it make? We could just choose to live however we pleased because life was brief and fleeting anyway. Then we would be gone and forgotten.

At some point I decided I wanted a part-time job. After my training seminar, we were asked to meet outside and pair up with other recruits. Because it was raining, I scooted over to a woman holding an umbrella whose name was Donna. I can see now that it was nothing short of "divine intervention." I noticed her personalized license plates which read, "PSA 40", and asked if it meant "past 40"?

She laughed and said, "No, it's a scripture," and then recited the entire passage. Before she was finished I jumped inside her car, but at the same time realized that I had now been paired up with a "Bible thumper"!

Awesome, I thought (because I had a mouth on me like a truck driver). Donna preferred, "Hallelujah," which she used all of the time (even though to this day she vehemently denies that she said it that often)! To me, even twice would have been too much. We were a match made in heaven.

We had a lot of doors slammed in our faces that day. I quite literally wanted to punch the really rude people, but Donna kept speaking blessings over them. I just didn't get it. *How was this terrible treatment not offending her?*

Donna certainly did have a peace that I simply could not comprehend. I doubt that I had ever had true peace in my life up to that point. Donna would tell me how much I needed God in my life, so I explained to her that I most certainly did not. Everything I had acquired was without any help or intervention from God and was entirely my own doing through hard work, perseverance, etc.

I told her about when I had really needed Him — back when I was young — He was nowhere to be found, it seemed. So, for what purpose or reason would I invite Him into my life now?? How very prideful and arrogant I was! Donna wasn't deterred. She began to expand on the stories of the Bible, and very excitedly explained most of the book of Revelation.

I do remember stopping her at some point to say, "You seriously don't *believe* those things, do you? They're just another set of fairy tales, not unlike all of the other childhood ones. You can't possibly believe that they are *true*? Come on now!"

I quickly found out that she believed every last one of them. She told me that the Bible was, "the God-breathed, God-inspired, God-ordained instruction book to those He created."

I stood corrected. I told her that I remembered *that* book from my stay at Bethel Girls Home. I asked her to tell me about the "end times" and what was going to happen. She obliged me because she was so excited about the world events that were lining up at that point in time.

All I remember thinking was, *if I, an "unlearned heathen," saw more of those prophecies were coming to fruition even since I had first read about them, then how much closer were we now to her "End of the Ages"?* I started to give some serious thought to what Donna was saying.

On the third day, Donna had asked me what I thought happened after we died.

"Worm food, blackness, nothingness...The End," I most self-assuredly answered. Of course, for her, that was the entirely wrong answer!

"What if I told you that there is a heaven and a hell?" she asked. "What if it's not the end and we are going to live forever in eternity?"

I wasn't sure whether I was right, or Donna was right. I began to think if *she* was right, then I'm in big trouble; but if *I* was right, then what would I have to lose by maybe embracing this Christianity — and this Jesus?

She said I could know for certain that I would spend eternity in heaven with God. It certainly was food for thought, and I began to doubt my own convictions. I completely understood I was potentially on the wrong side of this bet and it would cost me eternity in hell if I rejected this Jesus.

That night I went home and prayed out loud for the first time since I was a little girl. I wasn't sure about God yet and I did wonder if I was just talking to the air. *Would I simply feel stupid afterwards?* I asked Him: if He was real, and if He really wanted me to make this commitment to Him and believe on His Son Jesus, then I would have to wake up with such a burning desire to go ahead and get "saved."

I intuitively knew that this was a very serious commitment, and one that was not to be taken lightly. I didn't want this decision to be like so many of my other bad ones that I had made in drunken stupors, only to wake up the next morning and realize that I been a complete idiot the night before. It was kind of a weird prayer, I know, but it was what I needed to convince myself that God had actually heard me and that He was real.

The next morning, I *did* wake up with a burning desire to still commit my life to Christ and to start living a life that would be pleasing to Him. So I excitedly phoned Donna and she said we could meet at 1 o'clock. I honestly thought that I could possibly die and go straight to hell before then. I couldn't believe she was making me wait so long!

When we did finally get together, Donna kept telling me more, so I began yelling, "Stop the car! Stop the car! I want to give my life to Jesus!"

I was afraid something terrible might happen to her and I wouldn't know what to do then! As this would be a very special memory, she wanted it to be somewhere nice, like maybe under a tall tree. We drove around until she happily found a little parkette where we sat down at a concrete picnic table — but not before she tumbled down the hill and almost broke her ankle in a gopher hole! At long last, she led a repentance prayer and I repeated it all after her.

During the prayer I could quite literally see, as if in a "technicolor", the cross and the blood of Christ running down it, even pooling at the base of it. My hard heart was ripped wipe open as I finally and fully realized it was my sins that Christ had to die for. I was there for quite some time, weeping uncontrollably with the sheer magnitude of all I had done to put Christ on that cross.

I felt a huge, dark cloud lift off of me. I felt a thousand pounds lighter as I confessed it all to God. Afterwards, the grass really was greener, the sky really was bluer, and I felt so cleansed and finally free from such a heavy burden of guilt.

How could I have ever thought that I didn't need God, or that He didn't care about me? How had I lived all of these years without Him, and the hope and peace He offered me? How could I have shunned this exceedingly great deed that He had done for me, before I ever knew or loved Him?

I was in absolute awe of this salvation story. Oh, how much does fallen man, in our sin-sick state from birth, need this Jesus, this Prince of Peace (Isaiah 9:6)? How I needed His peace that passes all understanding (Philippians 4:7). I would never be the same!

It has been nearly 21 years since that glorious day and I am still in awe over why God would save a wretch like me. I will always and forever be grateful to Donna Martonfi for having the courage to tell a defiant, rebellious soul that I was dead in my trespasses and sins and destined for hell. I'm still learning how to be more like Christ and less like me!

I know now that He really does have a plan and a purpose for my life, plans to prosper me and not to harm me, to give me a hope and a future (Jeremiah 29:11). I know that I wasn't a mistake, but was *"fearfully and wonderfully made"* (Psalm 139:14b) and He cares for me! I also know that I *will* stand before Him one day (actually we all will whether we choose to believe that or not) and hopefully hear, *"Well done, thou good and faithful servant."*

Eternity is forever and this life is fleeting, but today, if you will "hearken" to my voice (Deuteronomy 28:2) and choose to believe in a God who is very real and very loving, you too can have your name written in the Lamb's Book of Life (Revelation 21:27).

ABOUT THE CONTRIBUTOR

Penny is a stay-at-home Mom of seven children ranging from nine to 32 years of age. She also has two grandchildren and a third one on the way! They are her first and foremost passion.

She attends the Outpost Ministry Church where she is the coordinator of "all things outreach," which she is equally as passionate about because she is "loving on people" and reaching lost souls.

She resides in Brantford, Ontario, which she considers her spiritual home as this is where she first committed her life to Christ nearly 22 years ago.

She can be contacted at: hisservantpen@yahoo.ca

CHAPTER 12

I CAN STAND THE RAIN

Rev. Dr. Bernie Miller

*That if thou shalt confess with thy mouth the Lord Jesus, and
shalt believe in thine heart that God hath raised him from the
dead, thou shalt be saved*
(Romans 10:9, KJV).

Every time I get a royalty check from Broadcast Music Incorporated, I think of how the song, *I Can't Stand the Rain*, played a pivotal role in launching my career into the music industry at CBS/Sony records.

I remember when I was working for the late James Brown at WEBB radio, a station he owned in Baltimore, Maryland. One morning, I decided to take the morning newspaper from our neighbor's apartment across the hall from our apartment. They had moved, but the papers kept coming. I decided to take it and sell it to the radio station on my way to school.

The news director, Ernie Boston, was so kind. You see, I knew how to sell newspapers because that was one of the first jobs I had at the age of nine years old. Now, at the age of 15, I had acquired a cigarette habit but I didn't have any extra money. In 1966, you could buy a couple of loose cigarettes for the cost of a newspaper. Ernie gladly bought the newspaper.

I was told years later by a Christian named Lewie Card, the CEO of Card/Monroe Corporation that if someone gave you money for something once, chances are they would do it a second time. I knew that instinctively at the age of 15. So, the next day I stopped by WEBB radio again.

This time Mr. Boston said, "We get the newspaper already. I just bought one from you yesterday to help you out."

Wow, what a letdown. Then, he asked me if I could read, and I said, "Yes."

Mr. Boston said, "Come back after school and I'll give you a script to read for a 30 second program called 'Accent on Youth.'"

That was the start of my broadcasting career. I went on the air March 1, 1967, at 6 p.m. with my own radio show.

In 1968, I met Smokey Robinson after his concert where I was the MC at the Baltimore Coliseum. I gave him some of my lyrics that I had written to get his opinion. After reading one, he asked me if I had any music for them.

I said, "No."

That's when he told me I needed to learn how to play an instrument or find someone with whom to collaborate.

In 1973, I bought a piano and taught myself how to play so I could write my own music to my lyrics. I worked in Memphis during that time for WLOK radio station. After my radio shift was over, I would hang around Hi Records' recording studio where Al Green and Ann Peebles recorded their music. Willie Mitchell allowed me access to the studio's keyboards.

One day while sitting at the baby grand piano, I started playing the chords to what would later become the chorus for *I Can't Stand the Rain*. As I was playing the chords, Ann Peebles' husband, Don Bryant, walked in and heard me playing my chords. He told me that he was working on something that would fit my chords.

A week later, I met him at his house to hear what he had come up with. It had rained all day. When he started playing the music, I asked for a pen and notepad. The first words out of my mouth were, "It sounds like rain against my window, bringing back sweet memories."

Then, he said, "Hey, windowpane, do you remember, how sweet it used to be." In less than 20 minutes, we wrote a song that would become my calling card for entry into the executive ranks of the music industry.

In 1987, Ray Anderson, the senior vice president of Epic/Sony Records called me and asked if I could edit a song by Sade because no one in their Artist & Repertoire Department could. He said, "Since you're a songwriter, I'm sure you can edit it to her satisfaction."

I edited the song that day and overnighted it to him. Two days later he called to tell me Sade loved my version. A month later Ray submitted my name to fill the vacancy in the A&R Department. When I got the call to interview, I remembered telling someone who worked for CBS Records in 1971, that I was going to work for them one day.

That day came in 1987. I was named Vice President of the Black Music Division of the A&R for Epic/Sony Records. I oversaw 52 artists, including but not limited to, Michael Jackson, Luther Vandross, Sade and Mtume, respectively.

I am an A type personality so I was driven by the goal of becoming Vice President of CBS. But a year after I reached my goal, I did a nosedive emotionally and didn't understand why.

One morning when I woke up in my New York apartment, I turned on the TV to catch the news. The night prior to that I was watching an X-rated movie channel. When I turned on the TV, it was on the 700 Club! Now, I know that those two channels never meet and to this day I'm still wondering, *How in the world did that happen?* I must have rolled over on the changer or something.

I honestly don't know, except, it was a "Godcident." That's a word I came up with when people attribute miracles of God to accidents.

As I was shaving, I heard someone on TV say, "There's somebody out there who is in the music business, but they are not happy. And, you know, the reason why you're not happy is because you don't have Christ in your life."

And I said to myself, "That's so general. They're just trying to get some money from me."

As I was going to turn off the channel, someone said, "If you're listening to me right now, stop for a minute and ask yourself: 'What does your life mean? What is it all about? Is it about you making a lot of money? Is it about you knowing all these famous people?'"

I stopped for a moment. They had my attention. That was me they were talking to.

They said, "I want you to repeat after me," and they led me through the plan of salvation. I got on my knees at that moment beside my bed, and I asked Christ to come into my life. From that moment on my whole life changed.

Every time I answered the phone I'd say, "God bless you." People at CBS made fun of me.

They'd say, "Did I sneeze?"

I'd say, "No. I'm just saying, 'God bless you.' Hope you have a great day."

So everyone always called me, "The God Bless You Guy."

A year later I found myself in the gutter emotionally. I had lost my job. I had to move out of my expensive apartment. I was in New York City without any income.

They were in breach of contract because they had gone past the period when they needed to renew my contract, so they paid me a sum of money and I left quietly. With the pay off, after taxes in New York City, I barely had enough money for soup.

Then entered the IRS. I'd made a ton of money after *Eruption* and Tina Turner recorded my song. I spent the money on riotous living and I hadn't paid taxes. The IRS took all the money I had in the bank and put a lien on all of my royalties. That forced me to totally trust God.

When CBS sold to Sony, they gave all the executives a bonus check but not all at once. They gave us a check every quarter. However, they said that if an employee left the company for any reason they would receive the balance. When I left the company, I had only received two checks. When I left I didn't think I would get another dime from them. But God!

One day I sat down and said, "God, you know I need money. I need rent. I need money for food, and I need money for some other things." I started searching the scriptures and found out that God provides. Psalm 84:11b says, *"...No good thing will He withhold from them that walk uprightly."* The next week I received my bonus check in the mail from Sony.

I wrote down all the scriptures that pertained to money and prayed them back to God. I then picked up the phone and called the IRS agent.

I said, "Look, would you have mercy? Would you release some of my funds? I am broke."

The IRS agent kind-of chuckled for a moment and asked me to hold the phone for a minute. When he returned he asked, "What money do you want me to release?"

"The quarterly royalties from BMI (Broadcast Music, Inc.) that are being held," I said.

I was shock at the agent's response. He said, "God bless you and Merry Christmas."

"Praise the Lord!" I shouted.

Years later the IRS worked with my attorney so that I could retire my tax debt.

When I had read the word "Father" in the Bible, I didn't believe I could trust Him until that day. At that moment, my trust bridge in God was established. I knew I could really trust Him. For years, I'd had "daddy issues." My father, the man who had impregnated my mom, also left her best friend with child around same time. Then he left town and moved to New York. I was born in January and my step brother, Gary, was born in February.

My "Godcidents" kept coming. One day I was asked to record a commercial for a friend. As I was waiting in his lobby, I was reading a music newspaper. In the want ads I read there was a job opening in Chattanooga at a Christian station.

I said to myself, *Christians don't pay any money. I'll probably be working half the time for free.* I recorded a simulated air-check to send along with my resume anyway. I also sent a very "to-the-point" letter. They probably should not have hired me. But the guy who read the letter was also very "to-the-point." He loved it.

"That's the kind of guy I want to hire," he said.

I went to the interview and he hired me. I arrived in Chattanooga to work but the job was not available at the time. The station was going through licensing difficulties with the FCC.

I got to Chattanooga by faith and trusting God. I was a greeter at Times Square Church in New York that David Wilkerson founded. The assistant pastor knew I was leaving. I told them about the station and that it probably wouldn't be on the air for another three months.

They said, "Well, you want us to give you some money?"

"I have to pray about it first," I said.

"If you need rent for three months that seems pretty easy," they said. "We'll give you that."

"I got to pray about it first," I said.

My rent was $470. So I prayed and asked, "Lord, how much money should I ask the church for?" Through much prayer God kept giving me a number: $700.

I said, "Wait a minute. Three times $470 is more than $700."

God said, "Trust me."

So I asked them for $700.

I got to Chattanooga having already paid the down payment and the first month's rent from some cash I had. Before the second month's rent was due I received a royalty check in the amount I needed to pay the next two month's rent.

In 1996, I founded a multi-ethnic congregational church called New Covenant Fellowship Church. My wife, Madelene, and I have a son named Zachary.

ABOUT THE CONTRIBUTOR

Dr. Bernie Miller lives in Chattanooga, Tennessee, with his wife, Madelene, to whom he's been married for 23 years. They have a son named Zachary. In 1996, Dr. Miller founded New Covenant Fellowship Church, "A Place for Every Race."

Dr. Miller has chaired numerous local and national boards such as the Chattanooga Housing Authority, Chattanooga Rotary Club's Information Committee, the Tennessee Advisory to the U.S. Civil Rights Commission, and the U. S. Census Bureau's Race and Ethnicity Board. He's a graduate of Covington Theological Seminary where he received a Doctorate in Divinity. Dr. Miller has received numerous awards in music and ministry. His complete bio and teaching resources can be obtained through his church's website: www.NCF.church.

CHAPTER 13

JOURNEY TO IDENTITY

Margaret Hampton

For whosoever shall call upon the name of the Lord shall be saved
(Romans 10:13, KJV).

"Daddy, Daddy, Daddy!" I twirled and danced before him, wanting to jump in his lap.

"Not now, Maggie." I was crushed.

Every little girl wants to be captivating to her Daddy. God made us that way. If that is lacking, affirmation will be sought elsewhere, sometimes in later obsessions, achievements and recognition, or relationships with men, but always from external sources losing sight of oneself. I was no exception.

My hard-working Daddy was emotionally unavailable. I knew he loved me, but he didn't know how to show it. Nine when his father died, he grew up surrounded by chattering women: grandmother, mother, maiden aunt, baby sister, sister's nurse and maid.

"Children are to be seen and not heard." On visits to my critical grandmother, I sat quietly on a piano bench at the far end of the living room in my Sunday best. Finally, at college graduation, for the first time I heard her say, "That's my granddaughter" — when I was graduating Summa Cum Laude with Honors, Gold Key, Mortar Board, Homecoming Court, fraternity Sweetheart, in the university's *Hall of Fame* and more.

By then, the "external identity" lessons had become well learned. Nothing was ever good enough. I vividly remember being crowned Military Ball Queen, handed the dozen roses and then enduring a panic attack as I began the runway walk wondering, *What can I do next?* I couldn't even enjoy the moment.

Soft, feminine and affectionate by nature, nurtured by preschool "loving sessions" with my Mama each morning, still I learned to be no-nonsense in the corporate world. There I rose fast and far after graduate school, always a direct connection with the CEO or CFO, the first or only woman in whatever I did, and often the first officer.

The label "Overachiever" defined me. I lived externally — through others' eyes — by titles, achievements and honors.

Personally, I wanted nothing more intensely than a warm, intimate, devoted marriage; to be by my husband's side, his "right wing" and helpmate "'til death do us part." I found my ideal husband — a powerfully built former athlete, young Wall Street attorney, natural in both Levis and formal settings and a great conversationalist. He affirmed my worth and identity as I entrained with him, lost myself in him and lost further sight of my own identity.

If life is a bed of roses, its beauty is atop many thorns. Proverbially, we built our house on sand instead of "The Rock." The foundation of our "house" turned to quicksand when my husband's partner stole a couple million dollars from us, and we inherited a couple million more business debts (which I had guaranteed).

All this time, I attended church and prayed to "God out there." I didn't know I could have a personal relationship with a loving Father God who knew and understood my every thought and need, saw my tears, heard my prayers and could carry me through life's storms. Instead, I was tossed by fierce trials as essentially everything imaginable happened — and the unimaginable. It was literally only by the Grace of God that my young son and I ultimately got out of the city alive as things got worse.

My father-in-law lived with us. He was my son's "nanny" and second father, and my best friend. He died suddenly of a stroke when my son turned nine. Then, my husband "handled" the avalanche of problems by having a fatal heart attack some months later, discovered by my son.

Stunned, we went from four to two in the house almost overnight. Mounting grief compounded by attacks from every direction, including daily harassment from over 60 unsecured credit accounts my husband had used for the business.

And it got worse.

In the first months following my husband's death, daily something happened I never had to handle before, even though I had handled almost everything for us. It started with a pipe bursting in the garage as my parents disappeared down the driveway on their six hour drive home a few days after my husband's funeral.

Large and small problems consistently occurred, such as the house filling with smoke so thick you could almost slice it with a knife (when I turned up the thermostat prior to awakening my son for school), or weird things like chipmunks shorting the computer in my car, or storms sending huge limbs catapulting through the roof of the pantry, guest cottage and pool house. Every day it was something new on top of abusive collection calls and ever deepening grief. Only "someone" who had been studying mankind for thousands of years could be so creative, suffocating and crushingly destructive without letting up.

Something profound struck me after a few months. For the first time ever I asked, *What have I done to deserve this?* Gazing out on the garden that bright spring morning, for the first time I saw a beautiful picture. Each day as things happened, someone always showed up to help! They couldn't make "it" go away, but they could help me get through it. And over half the time, it was someone I had never met before.

For the first time, I understood deep in my spirit the meaning of "grace," unmerited favor. There is no way even Mother Teresa could have been good enough for such an outpouring of love and support. It was so freeing to realize, to know, that I will never be alone to go through anything! As more "storms" struck, that sure *knowing* kept this strong person from crumbling.

Sometime later, my father, who never wrote letters outside of business and knew only a smidgeon of what was going on, sent a handwritten letter expressing admiration. It read, "I don't know anyone who would not have died or committed suicide." That was not an option.

Nor would I declare bankruptcy, because even those impersonal banks had relied on my word, my honor and my credit. I would somehow find a way to pay the millions off. Every penny went in that direction even when, with moist eyes, I counted pennies to see if I could buy milk for my son after making a series of bank payments with the thousands I just brought in.

At some point and in spite of a fierce mind-over-matter mentality, the extreme stress started causing my body literally to shut down from "circuit overload." One day, on my face, unable to summon strength even to lift my little finger, I vividly felt the life force ebbing from my body. Silently I cried out to my son, unable to speak, *I'm so sorry. I've tried so hard with everything in me, but it's not enough. I'm so sorry.*

Helpless, I was literally dying. Then I sensed a presence. I thought I saw, through blurred vision, feet and a robe. Then a hand stretched out toward me, yet did not touch me. Next I felt a sensation as though I could feel every cell in my body sequentially re-energizing, coming back to life. I did not die, but was alive to fight another day.

With such evidence and listening to well-intentioned New Agers, I just knew there had to be a way to experience deeper spirituality and connection, to be closer to God than my church, even with all its beautiful liturgy. So I started searching. Yes, I looked in some wrong places, too, including some potentially dangerous deceptions.

How the Lord saved me from myself in those is a whole other story. Although I didn't yet really know Him, He knew I was searching desperately with my whole heart for more of Him, not the counterfeit.

Then a friend told me about an intercessor who had prayed for him. I didn't really know what one was, but I definitely wanted prayer help.

So I called the intercessor. Without knowing or being influenced by my background, he "saw" intense images and messages. Then he emphasized one should always get confirmation from another intercessor, since all are fallible humans.

I was silent, leading him to ask, "Don't you know another intercessor?"

"No."

He recommended a woman who worked at the Vineyard Church. After prayer and sharing, she invited me to church. That first Sunday they announced the women's ministry for fall, all morning every Thursday. *I really need that,* I thought, *but I have to work.*

Then they announced the topic: Healing Our Brokenness. Oh, how I needed that! *But I have to work.* Next, they announced the location, the Hampton Room. (May I remind my Reader, my last name is Hampton.)

"O.K., God," I said. "It might have taken a two-by-four, but you have my attention. I will do this. If I'm about your business, I trust you to take care of mine."

Much happened that fall. I loved the Vineyard's services, with music I could lose myself in. It helped me "shed the layers of the onion skin," emptying myself of outside thoughts and fears.

Alone after one service as everyone exited the sanctuary, soft, recorded worship music kept playing, *"Jesus, Jesus..."* I found myself kneeling at the altar, baring my soul, crying out to Jesus with my whole heart and praying from memory the Episcopal wedding ceremony. That's when, with streaming tears, I surrendered all and accepted Jesus wholly into my heart. That's when I appropriated the free gift of salvation for myself, no longer the "churched unsaved" but now saved!

That's when I also knew that any future husband could only be one who knows and loves the Lord, for only then could he truly love and lead me within a covenant union — like a triangle with Jesus at the pinnacle serving as the glue to keep us together through thick and thin.

My marriage vows to Jesus mean I could only marry the one He sends to me to be His hands on the earth with me.

That has given me the courage to wait for the right husband, a couple of decades now celibate, without looking for affirmation and comfort from relationship with a man. The nightly torment ceased immediately once when I cried out to Jesus for help. The Lord took my pain away and I slept peacefully. I still do after two decades. Now the wait is easy. *"If the Son therefore shall make you free, ye shall be free indeed"* (John 8:36).

Women in our Vineyard "Brokenness" group had all been walking with the Lord for quite some time, but as a newcomer, I felt spiritually bankrupt, inadequate and alien. When someone is newly saved, the enemy (satan) wants to steal what has been sewn into her life. I was a weakened, hurting woman and perfect target. It was as though a demon perched on my shoulder whispering over and over, "You are a fraud. You don't belong."

During one Sunday worship I was on my knees, tearfully, at the back of the sanctuary. As the music played, I kept hearing that awful voice, "You are a fraud."

I cried out to God with silent screams, *Please, tell me I'm not a fraud. Tell me I belong!*

Then the bellowing voice of an intercessor pierced the near-silence with a word from the Lord, "You are Mine! I paid for you on the Cross. I will never let you go. You are Mine!"

I crumbled on the floor in tears. Those powerfully penetrating words were for me — and for everyone who embraces the Lord. I share this with new believers so they will not listen to the lies of the enemy and turn away in fear and shame, letting him steal their faith and joy. You, too, were bought with a price, with Jesus' precious Blood.

Finally, I know my identity — who I really am. I am a child of God. I am "captivating" to Abba Father (Daddy), the apple of His eye (Psalm 17:8). He removed my sins as far as the east is from the west (Psalm 103:12a). He says so. I am washed clean and sanctified by the Blood of Christ, a joint heir with Christ Jesus of the Kingdom of

Heaven (Romans 8:17). He sits at the right hand of the Father making intercession for me (which I will need as long as I'm here in my "flesh suit"). He lifts me up when I fall, saying, "Daughter, shake off the dust...," and helps me move on.

And do you know what else? I've paid off those millions now. In every tight circumstance, exactly what I needed was provided just in time. Yes, I liquidated the vast amount I had earned, invested and saved, plus all I worked for over another decade. But I knew throughout, *God hasn't carried me this far to let me go now.* He is faithful.

He carries my burdens and is my real security. I can rest in Him. *"For God hath not given us the spirit of fear; but of power, and of love, and of a sound mind"* (2 Timothy 1:7). I can go forth confidently because *"I can do all things through Christ which strengtheneth me"* (Philippians 4:13).

Call on Jesus, the Son of God. I *know* He is real. He is who He says He is, and will do what He says He will do. Invite Him into your heart. Let Him ease your pain, wash you clean and give you His peace which passes all understanding. Seize hold of the free gift of forgiveness and eternal salvation. Jesus has already paid the price for you.

ABOUT THE CONTRIBUTOR

Margaret Hampton is a business consultant and authority marketing strategist, as well as an editor, publisher and marketer for non-fiction books through her business, Authority Media Press. She is a syndicated journalist for *Newswire, Authority Presswire, Small Business Trendsetters* and other publications, and an *Amazon* Best-Selling Author in the business field.

Her newest book is different; it is comprised of personal, true stories from her life titled, *Not By Might Nor Power: A Book of Miracles and Rescues.*

For more information about her authority marketing, book publishing, Amazon Best Seller campaigns, public relations or other strategic business and marketing consultancy, leave a message for Margaret on 352-665-9878 or by email: mhampton.cai@gmail.com.

Acclaimed with numerous honors and recognitions throughout her career, Margaret Hampton is also listed in over 12 *Who's Who* publications including the *International Who's Who of Intellectuals* and had the honor of serving (formerly) as Trustee on the National Board of Trustees of the Leukemia Society of America. Yet, she has devoted her life to helping others whether in the workplace, for those with health issues, the elderly or hurting women.

A widow who has a heart for children, orphans and other widows, she fully embraces the mission of "The Global Friendship Run" and its related initiatives, led by world distance runner, international businessman and goodwill ambassador, Stan Cottrell.

But mostly, she loves the Lord — to Him she turns with every breath she breathes, and to Him she dedicates her whole life.

CHAPTER 14

HOOKED ON JESUS AND THE PROMISED JAIL BREAK

Katie Souza

Fear thou not; For I am with thee: be not dismayed; for I am thy God: I will strengthen thee; yea, I will help thee; yea, I will uphold thee with the right hand of my righteousness. Behold, all they that were incensed against thee shall be ashamed and confounded: they shall be as nothing; and they that strive with thee shall perish. Thou shalt seek them, and shalt not find them, even them that contended with thee: they that war against thee shall be as nothing, and as a thing of nought (Isaiah 41:10-12, KJV).

The sound of a prison door closing on the wrong side of me was familiar. I had been through the ritual more times than I could count. The pat-downs, shackles, sounds and smells were all the same. I felt less than human when being kept in a cage. And yet, here I was.

This time I was serving a federal sentence of over twelve years. It would start in one century and end in the next. Welcome to the new millennium, Kate.

The heavy, iron cell door slid into place with a metallic "clunk". The sobering sound affirmed I wouldn't see daylight for more than a decade. My future looked painfully bleak.

129

Lying back on my bed, I stared at the underside of the empty bunk above. I wasn't sure how I ended up without a "cellie." Hopefully, it would last.

The lights dimmed. Prisons are noisy, even late at night. I wished for a distraction, like a drink. Even better, a shot of dope.

I was a career criminal, living out the violence of drugs and drug deals, horrible relationships, fist-fights, stolen vehicles, gun fights and countless arrests. I was a collector, too; "assault with a deadly weapon" charges were a hazard of my trade. When I went to collect from people who owed me, they called the cops. Yes, criminals call cops on criminals, something I never understood.

For me, the only lesson I ever seemed to learn was how to avoid capture a little longer. So much for that.

I was caught by federal marshals in the act of cooking methamphetamines. I shared a kitchen with several inept cooks who left behind piles of chemical trash. Walking through their mess all day had burned holes through my boots and scorched my feet. I bet I could have outrun the cops if I'd had some traction left on my soles. Whatever.

The marshals took me to a hospital to treat my burns. After a quick stay, one of the officers came in and said, "Get up. You're going to jail."

He unhooked the handcuffs securing me to the bed while I pretended to be groggy. When he left the room I jumped up, quickly dressed and peeked through the curtain. His back was to me as he talked with a cute nurse.

This is it! I thought. *I'm out of here!*

I slipped quietly out of the cubical into a hallway and faced the exit. As I approached the big doors, they slid open automatically, welcoming me to the sweet smell of freedom! Glancing back, I saw the marshal was still talking to his nurse friend, unaware of my absence.

"Piece of cake," I said out loud.

My plan came together quickly. I would thumb a ride and explain my hospital stay as the result of a beating from a loser boyfriend. However, as I stepped forward to walk out on the street I suddenly froze.

A force I had never encountered held me there and then physically turned me around. It marched me back into the hospital, toward my captor.

The voices in my head, the ones that generated every debacle in my life, began screaming, *Stop! Turn Around! You can still escape. It's not too late!*

I fought hard. I wanted badly to obey those voices. But something stronger walked me back through those big doors, which again swung open without hesitation. The force propelled me along, retracing my steps which weren't even cold yet.

I approached the officer who was still engrossed in his conversation. The closer I got to him, the louder the voices screamed. Suddenly, I saw my hand involuntarily reach up to touch his shoulder. Now, I was fully committed. The officer turned to me and immediately went sheet-white, realizing I could have escaped.

Meanwhile, all I could think was, *What the hell have I done?* After a quick trial, I received 151 months in federal prison for my crimes.

Make no mistake, prison life sucks. I did myself no favors by fighting frequently with officers and inmates. This resulted in my being sent to the "hole," or lock down, repeatedly. Lock down was always freezing cold, filthy and lacked basic amenities like toilet paper or a bed. I frequently slept on a ten-inch wide metal bench and was lucky if I had a grimy plastic mattress to throw on the floor. I couldn't complain though. I did it to myself.

Then something happened.

Back in general population, I was bored and needed something to read. The only thing I could find was a Bible. I had never read a Bible, so I figured, *why not?* Soon, I found myself really getting into it. Some of the stories were vaguely familiar. I had heard about Noah and the flood and the one where the kid killed the giant. *Those stories came from the Bible? Who knew?*

When I got to the chapters where the Israelites were taken captive because of their disobedience, I was hooked. That was my life. I devoured each page. There was so much treasure and guidance in their story that I began teaching it to anyone who would listen. Girls professed Christ and I baptized them in the showers. I taught them Christian songs I learned from the radio. Our unit soon became known as the "God Pod."

After moving to a federal prison in California, I continued my mission. We soon had a large fellowship of women, all totally sold out to God. One night, God impressed upon me He would get me out of prison. I listened intently to His voice and felt the message was unmistakable. He said I would be released November 21st and gave me the number "57."

I instantly counted off fifty-seven days on my calendar. When I landed on November 21, I knew I had heard His voice.

I told everyone.

They laughed at me but, as the date drew closer, they became enthusiastic. Daily, it seemed, someone asked me how long before God would spring me. Even the non-believers rooted for me.

When my counselor heard I was claiming I would leave in November, she called me into her office. She listened to my story, looked at me like I was crazy and immediately sent me to the facility psychiatrist.

I patiently repeated the details to the doctor who wondered out loud if she should put me on suicide watch. Finally she decided to schedule an appointment for me on November 21, saying I would need to talk to her when my release didn't happen.

The day finally arrived. I was in a prayer meeting when the records office summoned me via intercom. Everyone in the meeting jumped for joy! They knew no one was called to records unless it was for something big. Sobbing, I crossed the yard as fast as I could and burst through the door.

"Why are you here?" the lady behind the desk asked.

"You paged me," I replied, out of breath.

After some discussion and obvious confusion, one of the staff said, "I'm sorry. That was a mistake. Go back to your unit."

To say I was crushed understates my emotions. I was deeply disappointed, not because I was still there nor because now *everyone* thought I was nutty, but I had not heard God's voice correctly. That mattered more to me than anything else.

Nevertheless, I pressed on, continuing to teach Bible studies. I even began writing a book about the captivities of ancient Israel and how they paralleled the modern day imprisonment journey.

Months later, without warning, my parents told me the court had agreed to hear my plea for appeal. I was flown back to the state where I was convicted to meet with my lawyer and the prosecuting attorney. The prosecutor made it clear he was not happy.

"If you pursue this," he threatened, "I'll bring additional charges against you based on the other chemicals at the lab. If you lose, you will end up serving 20 years, not 12."

As he spoke, I instantly heard the voice of the Lord say Isaiah 41:11a,*"Behold, all they that were incensed against thee shall be ashamed and confounded: they shall be as nothing."*

With this, I turned to my lawyer and said, "Let's go for it."

When the prosecution checked the locker for the evidence used to convict me it was gone. Having nothing tangible to prove my guilt, the judge ordered my sentence reduced by seven years. I thanked God continuously on the flight back to prison. But I was still troubled by the whole November 21st thing. *What did that mean?*

Two agonizing months passed before my new "out date" was calculated. When the case manager handed over my release papers, I saw the words, "Projected Release Date, November 23, 2003." I stared at the paper while the number 23 mocked me. *What did I miss?*

I ran to check my calendar. November 23rd was a Sunday. *Ah ha!* By law, when the release date is on a weekend, the prisoner must be freed on the previous Friday. In this case, November 21st!

A small group had gathered inside one of the cells as I checked the calendar. When I shouted out the date, they broke into celebration! News spread through the facility fast. Later, I realized that November 2003 was my 57th month in captivity.

God makes *no* mistakes!

ABOUT THE CONTRIBUTOR

Since her release in 2003, Katie Souza has devoted her life to pursuing God's healing revelations for His children. Her television show, *Healing Your Soul; Real Keys to the Miraculous,* is broadcast in multiple markets around the world.

Katie Souza's book, *The Captivity Series: The Key to Your Expected End,* is now in more than 2,500 prisons around the world. More than 300,000 copies are in circulation, almost all of which were given to inmates free of charge. The book is available in three languages with more translations in the works.

Katie Souza Ministries receives more than 7,000 letters annually from current inmates expressing their gratitude for this life-changing message. If you would like to help her make more books available, go to: katiesouza.com and donate.

CHAPTER 15

SHARING THE SIMPLE GOSPEL

Dr. Jerry L. Spencer

*For God so loved the world, that he gave his only begotten Son,
that whosoever believeth in him should not perish, but have
everlasting life.*
(John 3:16, KJV).

The year the Iron Curtain fell, my wife, Sue, and I traveled to Moscow. Our chief purpose was to distribute Bibles. Most Russians had never even seen a copy of this remarkable book.

One of the great joys of my life was watching Sue passing out Bibles on Red Square. The response was astounding! As the military guards received their copy of the Word of God they would kiss it, press it against their heart and with tears streaming down their cheeks they repeated over and over, "Spasibo! Spasibo! Spasibo!" They were saying, "Thank you! Thank you! Thank you!"

While in Moscow, I was invited by my host, Rick Amato, to accompany him on a private visit with Mikhail Gorbachev. I have vivid memories of removing my shoes, emptying my pockets, surrendering my passport and being escorted by soldiers with AK-47's.

Once inside his office I felt a sense of excitement. It seemed surreal to be in the presence of one of the most powerful men in the world. Following the formal introductions, the atmosphere became relaxed and cordial.

The President was warm and personable. We shared with him the gospel message and presented him with a beautiful copy of God's Word bound magnificently in ornamental brass. We also presented him with other pieces of beautifully printed Christian literature. Mr. Gorbachev was especially attracted to some children's books.

He smiled warmly and remarked, "My daughter and her children are dedicated Christians. I'll give these beautiful books to them."

As I sat in the presence of this loving grandfather the thought came to me, *in only a few ticks of the clock and flips of the calendar, this man will go the way of all flesh.* Soon the grandchildren will be his age and well on their way to that day appointed to all men. *"And as it is appointed unto men once to die, but after this the judgement:"* (Hebrews 9:27)

It occurred to me in that amazing moment that the daughter and grandchildren of this world leader were, surely, fervently praying that he would come into a personal relationship with Christ. I am certain it was the desire of their heart to spend eternity with him in the holy presence of the most powerful Person in the universe, at whose feet every knee would bow. This line from Scripture raced through my mind, *"a little child shall lead them."* (Isaiah 11:6)

It is a tragic mistake to underestimate the influence of children. It was a child who was responsible for my having first heard the simple Gospel message that changed my life.

As a child, my backyard was only a stone's throw from the Mississippi River levee in Osceola, Arkansas. Late one afternoon as I was out in my yard feeding my rabbits, my schoolmate from next door came over and invited me to go to church.

I had only been to church one time in my eleven years on this planet. As a small boy I rode to my grandmother's church in a wagon pulled by two giant red mules. It was a hot summer Sunday. Upon arriving at the church, I joined the other children running and playing before we went inside the little, white, church building.

I was thirsty, so when they served Communion, I reached out to get me one of those little cups of grape juice. To my utter surprise, my grandma slapped my hand and said, "That's just for Christians!" I remember thinking, *I don't know who these Christians are but they sure are stingy; they won't even give a thirsty little boy a drink of grape juice.*

I knew nothing at that time of the sacredness of the Lord's Supper. I certainly didn't understand that the juice represented the atoning Blood of Christ.

It was in 1950 that I accompanied my neighbor, James Allen Baker, to a revival service. The people were happy, friendly and very enthusiastic. The singing was joyous. The congregation was made up of people of all ages and from all walks of life. I saw some of my teachers and classmates from school. I even saw my Little League baseball coach and the star of the high school football team.

As the minister stood to preach I was mesmerized by his loving spirit. He was a compassionate man. I remember that tears ran down his face as he spoke of Jesus dying on the cross. As he shared God's love for sinners I was deeply moved. I still feel the thrill that ran through me as this loving preacher spoke of God's willingness to forgive me, come into my life and make me a new, "born again" person. I thought, *WOW, this is fantastic!*

As the minister came to the end of his wonderful message, he invited people to come forward and speak with the pastor concerning being saved. I wanted to go forward but somehow it seemed as if my feet were stuck in concrete. I just couldn't make myself move.

My neighbor, James, sensed my predicament and said to me, "Jerry, it's like the devil has a chain around you and he's trying to drag you down into hell. Go ahead and step out." I thought, *The devil is not going to get me!*

The next thing I knew I was standing before the pastor. Brother Russell Club was a very tall man. He got down on his knees, greeted me warmly and asked why I was coming. Then he opened the Bible, read the scriptures to me and explained what they meant. I embraced these simple profundities and, in childlike faith, made a willful choice against living my life in sin. Right then and there I invited the living Lord Jesus Christ into my heart.

In a miraculous, mysterious and invisible move, Jesus entered my life. He instantly translated me from the kingdom of darkness over into the kingdom of light. I look back on this experience of grace with joy, awe and deep gratitude.

My friend, the late, great Adrian Rogers, often said, "I have found that knowing Christ is simply glorious and gloriously simple." In both my undergraduate and graduate studies, I looked deeply into the secrets of God. I have spent my lifetime studying the Bible and seeking to incorporate into my life the precepts and principles of the Christian faith.

I find it absolutely amazing that the simple truths I embraced as a child remain the foundation of all else that I have learned. My years of study in college and seminary, as well as my lifetime of insatiable reading and research along with my life experiences, have confirmed over and over again the authenticity of my childhood conversion, the reliability of God's Word and the power of the Gospel.

What a blessing it has been to travel over much of the world sharing the *simple gospel*. After presenting Biblical truth for over six decades, I am more than happy to report that this good news is indeed the power of God unto salvation. I am extremely excited to finish my life's journey confronting people with the opportunity of passing from death to life through Christ.

One night on the Arabian Sea in South India, I saw dead bodies covered by the sands on the beach. I was told that it was a tradition to bury the body of the deceased under the sand and let the tide take them out to sea. My heart was stricken with a sharp sword of anguish to think that, century after century, the souls of men, women and children had been going out into eternity never having heard the gospel of Christ. In that moment, I reconfirmed the call to evangelism. I received that call at age 18 while working in a hay field on an experimental farm operated by the University of Arkansas.

That night, I preached to the 10,000-plus citizens of this remote fishing village. I preached the same simple message that I'd heard as a child. There were people present from two bordering states so as I shared the gospel, it was translated into both Malayalam and Tamil. More than 5,000 chose to receive Christ in simple, childlike faith.

On another occasion, as I addressed a most attentive crowd of over 25,000 gathered on a hillside outside the city of Soto in Southern Ethiopia, it was this same glorious gospel that I shared. As thousands came forward to receive Christ, I recognized it was in response to this same simple message. There is no limit to the reach of the *simple gospel.*

Through this simple message, I have seen holy men of India, witch doctors in South America, scientists in Russia, families in mud huts in Africa, men and women in prisons all over the world, those trapped in sin and those enslaved by addictions come to know God through Christ.

I recently baptized 14 former Muslims. We are seeing scores of them come to Christ. It is this same simple gospel by which they are becoming new creations.

I believe in the eternal verities taught in the Word of God. Surely the apex of wisdom is knowing Christ personally. Colossians 2:2b-3 says, "...and of Christ; *in whom are hid all the treasures of wisdom and knowledge."* Statistics tell us that knowledge doubles every twelve months. Regardless of our understanding inside our paradigm, there is no way that any of us can know everything. Wise is the man who recognizes his need to understand spiritual realities.

I once spoke at a conference at Baylor University. A very brilliant gentleman who spoke before me made this statement, "Having explored with great diligence a number of academic disciplines, I am convinced that you can go no deeper than the truths found in this simple passage, 'For God so loved the world that He gave His only begotten Son, that whosoever believeth in Him should not perish but have everlasting life,' John 3:16."

If you remain a non-Christian, let me humbly suggest that you courageously acknowledge you may not know all you need to know to be prepared for eternity. I find this quote by Robert Murray McCheyne very thought-provoking, "If you have not seen Christ, (experienced Christ personally) then you know nothing yet as you ought to know. What good will it do you in hell that you knew all the sciences in the world, all the events of history and all the busy politics of your little day?"

It was my privilege to open a joint session of Congress with prayer. After the session, I had the joy of drinking coffee with several of the Congressmen. One of the dignified gentlemen said to me, "Dr. Spencer, after years of being in denial, I have recently received the Lord Jesus Christ into my heart as my personal savior…my only regret is that I did not make this commitment years ago."

To all who read this testimony, I give this challenge: don't dare miss the destiny-altering power of the simple gospel.

ABOUT THE CONTRIBUTOR

Born in 1939, Jerry Spencer was raised on the Mississippi River in Osceola, Arkansas. A high school and college athlete, Jerry has always been enthusiastic about life. He did his undergraduate study at Union University and University of Tennessee. He studied at Southwestern Baptist Theological Seminary and has several honorary Doctorates including one from Liberty University.

He has been active in his Southern Baptist Convention denomination. He served as VP of the convention and was on their Executive Committee nine years. He was President of both the Conference of Evangelist and the Pastor Conference.

Dr. Spencer leads three mission organizations and conducts conferences and crusades continually. In addition to his other regular international work, he has ministered more than 60 times in India where he helped establish a hospital, college and seminary.

He has done extensive work in Ethiopia as well, including a school with over 1,000 students, a printing ministry, leadership training and evangelistic outreach. Along with his son, Van, he was led to start and nurture over 80 churches in Malawi.

Jerry Spencer Ministries may be contacted through their ministry website: www.jerryspencer.org or through writing to him at: Jerry Spencer Ministries, P.O. Box 6926, Dothan, AL 36302 USA.

CHAPTER 16

THE PRIZE

Bill Renje,
as written by Carolyn Curran-Fyckes

*Brethren, I count not myself to have apprehended: but this one
thing I do, forgetting those things which are behind, and
reaching forth unto those things which are before, I press
toward the mark for the high calling of God in Christ Jesus*
(Philippians 3:13-14, KJV).

The scene was surreal. Outside of my driver's side window, pointing directly at me, was a 9 mm handgun held by a plainclothes police officer. I heard his loud voice commanding me to stop. I decided in a nanosecond that I wasn't going to be arrested like the others who now lay face down and handcuffed on the grass in this drug raid. I would flee.

I hit the gas pedal and the car screeched forward. The sound of a blast filled the car. I screamed out in terror for God to not let me die.

I was only 17 years old, too young to die. I no longer had control over my life. The bullet had ripped open my body, severing my spinal cord and collapsing my right lung.

I hadn't always run with the wrong crowd. My childhood had been normal with a stable home environment and loving, nurturing parents who took me to baseball and football practices regularly. Sports were a central part of my formative years. In junior high school, my need to fit in with peers became more important to me than sports or even the values of decency which my parents had instilled in me.

Unfortunately, I was a follower, not a leader. I had discovered a very enticing lifestyle in partying and taking drugs with these new friends. As a freshman I only experimented with smoking weed recreationally. I had sworn that I would never take hard drugs, but by the time I was a senior in high school, I had progressed to using crack cocaine.

At first, I only indulged in cocaine on occasion. I saw no danger in this practice. After all, I was not experiencing any signs of addiction. I didn't realize that cocaine would subtly lure me in by requiring me to take larger and larger doses each time I used it in order to achieve the same high.

I had thought I was too smart to become a slave to this drug. I was wrong. In desperation, I began to sell drugs and to scalp concert tickets in order to stave off the unbearable pain of withdrawal.

Now my reality was a living nightmare. I was a quadriplegic.

One incident in the hospital will always stand out. I vividly remember being pushed, in my wheelchair, past a poster featuring a paraplegic rugby athlete. *How could I even dream of being like him?* The thought was devastating. At that time I wasn't even able to blow my own nose.

Pain-filled hours and days of rehab followed my stint in I.C.U. My life was over. There would be no more parties, drugs, girls or sports.

I was also heavily aware that I had let my family down. They didn't deserve such a son who only brought them heartbreak. I had to live with these deep, unrelenting regrets and feelings of failure.

While I was learning to accept my dismal future, I made a new friend in the hospital. This friend was a Christian. Despite all that had happened to him, he not only still believed in God but he still followed God faithfully. He planted a seed of hope for me.

A few years later an old friend, who was now out of prison, contacted me. This friend had changed his life and had become a Christian. He invited me to accompany him to church.

That day will be etched in my memory forever. In that very church, I accepted the altar call to repeat the Sinner's Prayer after the pastor. I realized without question that I needed to follow God's leading, not anyone else's leading. After saying that special prayer, I knew that I was a changed person. I was filled with peace, joy and hope for the future.

There was good reason for hope in my future. God already had unbelievable plans for my life. Over time, He opened up the way for me to fulfill my longtime interest in sports. I never would have dreamed that I would be on the U.S. National Paraplegic Football/Rugby Team. We won gold medals in Atlanta, Toronto and finally in Sydney in 2000.

I am now happily married to an amazing Christian woman and we have been blessed with three great children. The blessings from God continue. I am a university graduate and a successful businessman.

Through the power of God, I am able to minister to teens as a speaker for the Fellowship of Christian Athletes. I encourage teens to seek out what God's plans are for their lives and to be very careful about what values their circle of friends espouse. I also emphasize that the stigma of drug addiction must be removed in order to educate our children about the dangers the enemy places in their paths.

I want all of those who read this testimony, or who listen to me recounting it, to realize the invaluable lessons obtained by involvement in sports. I learned to work through pain, to have self-discipline in order to reach my potential, to be loyal to others and to myself, to not give up and to focus with determination on the goal ahead of me.

Sports definitely prepared me for my many struggles, but God took me through them. He was and is my coach. God will be your coach, too, if you let him. God will lead you, successfully, through this race of life to a much better life. There will be many stumbling blocks along the way but, if you trust in God, you will reach your greatest goal. The prize awaits you but you must press on.

"Brethren, I count not myself to have apprehended: but this one thing I do, forgetting those things which are behind, and reaching forth unto those things which are before, I press toward the mark for the prize of the high calling of God in Christ Jesus" (Philippians 3:13-14, KVJ).

ABOUT THE CONTRIBUTOR

Bill Renje is a respected Christian businessman, a married father of three and the author of *A Chosen Bullet*. Bill grew up in the suburbs of Chicago where he was shot in the neck and permanently paralyzed as a 17-year-old in 1989.

From there, he set out on a path of endurance and perseverance, ultimately earning a B.A. and an M.S. in Journalism from the University of Illinois. He was a three time member of Team USA's Wheelchair Rugby Team, winning Gold in the 1996 Atlanta Paralympics, the 1998 World Championships in Toronto, and the 2000 Sydney Paralympics.

Bill became an award-winning commercial real estate broker in the Tampa Bay area before being called into the ministry with the Fellowship of Christian Athletes. He shares his story and life experiences to influence coaches and young athletes with the Gospel.

Bill resides in the USA with his lovely wife of 15 years and their three children. Bill and Amy were touched by the gift of adoption when they adopted their oldest child, Nico, from Guatemala in 2006. They are active members of Eagles Landing First Baptist Church, where Bill serves as a deacon and youth leader.

To donate to Bill's ministry, please go to: my.fca.org/1743-renje-bill.aspx

PART III

For God so loved the world, that he gave his only begotten Son, that whosoever believeth in him should not perish, but have everlasting life

(John 3:16, KJV).

CHAPTER 17

FROM TRAGEDY TO TRIUMPH

Cherie Calbom

The Lord is my light and my salvation; whom shall I fear? The Lord is the strength of my life; of whom shall I be afraid?
(Psalm 27:1, KJV).

I knew about God even as a small child, but I had not known Him personally until I was thirteen. Loss of family members was familiar. My mother died of breast cancer when I was six. I lived with my maternal grandparents and my Dad in the years that followed.

My grandfather died suddenly of a heart attack when I was nine; it was a terrible tragedy that took him from us. Then, I was left with just my grandmother. The two of us were all alone in a large, three-story Midwestern home. *What if I lost her too?* She was a true friend of God who prayed fervently.

My incredible journey with God began with one decision in the attic of my grandmother's home and has never ended. My life has not always been easy, but my salvation testimony is one of finding hope in God every time I have prayed.

"Please, dear God, " I asked, "give me a family. Please take care of me."

He took me up on that request. Our extended family decided I should go to live with an aunt and uncle who led a church in Springfield, Oregon. It was there I found a new life of hope and community. Psalm 68:6 says, *"God setteth the solitary in families."* He truly did that for me. I suddenly had an earthly family along with a heavenly family.

One story I want to share with you before we go any further is how my life changed dramatically when I discovered the healing power of freshly made juices and whole foods. When I turned thirty, I had to quit my job. I had developed chronic fatigue syndrome that made me so sick I couldn't work. I felt as though I had a never-ending battle with feverish swollen glands and I was perennially lethargic.

I was also in constant pain. I ached as though I'd been bounced around in a washing machine.

I moved back to my father's home in Colorado to try and recover, and found an answer as to what I should do to facilitate healing. It was there I read about juicing and thought that it made sense. I bought my first juicer and designed a program I could follow.

I juiced and ate a nearly perfect diet of live and whole foods for three months with health ups and downs throughout. I had days where I felt encouraged that I was progressing; other days where I felt worse were discouraging. My good health seemed like an elusive dream at that point.

No one told me about detox reactions (which I was experiencing). I was obviously very toxic. My whole body was getting rid of toxins. There were days I felt very sick, but I also had hope that something good was happening to make me well again.

One morning I woke up early — early for me, which was around 8:00 a.m. — without the alarm sounding off. I felt like someone had given me a new body in the night. I had such an increase in energy that I actually wanted to go jogging. *What had happened?*

This new sensation seemed like it just appeared with the morning sun. Actually, my body had been healing for some time, and had not manifested this new state of well-being until that very day. I felt completely renewed.

With my juicer in tow and a new lifestyle fully embraced, I returned to Southern California a couple of weeks later to finish writing my first book. For nearly a year I felt terrific, with great health and more energy and stamina that I'd ever remembered.

Then, shockingly, I took a giant step back.

The Event That Took My Breath Away

July 4th was a beautiful day like so many others in Southern California. I shared the holiday with friends that evening at a backyard barbecue, then returned to a house that I was sitting for vacationing friends. I crawled into bed around midnight.

I woke up shivering some time later. *Why is it so cold?* I wondered as I re-checked the clock. It was 3:00 a.m.

That's when I noticed the door to the backyard was open, and then I noticed him. A shirtless young man in shorts crouched in the shadows at the corner of the bedroom. I blinked twice, trying to deny what I was seeing.

Instead of running away, he leaped off the floor and ran toward me. Pulling a pipe from his shorts, he began attacking me, beating me repeatedly over the head and yelling that he wanted me dead. We fought. I should say I tried to defend myself and grab the pipe; it finally flew out of his hands. That's when he choked me to unconsciousness.

I felt life leaving my body in those last few seconds. From accounts of other people's experiences at the end of life, I knew I was dying. This was it; the end of my life.

I experienced a sensation of popping out of my body and floating upward. Everything was peaceful and still. I sensed I was traveling, at what seemed like the speed of light, in black space. I saw what looked like little lights twinkling in the distance.

All of a sudden I was back in my body, outside the house, clinging to a part of the fence that surrounded the backyard. I don't know how I got there. I attempted to scream for help, but each time I screamed I'd pass out, landing on the cement. I'd then have to pull myself up and scream for help again.

Finally a neighbor heard me and sent her husband to help. Within a short time I was en route to the hospital.

Lying on a cold gurney at 4:30 a.m., chilled to the bone and in and out of consciousness, I tried to assess my injuries, which was virtually impossible. The next thing I knew, I was off to surgery.

Later, I learned I had suffered serious injuries to my right hand, multiple wounds to my head and neck, and part of my scalp was torn from my head. I also had numerous cracked teeth, which resulted in several root canals and crowns.

My right hand sustained the most severe injuries: two knuckles crushed and fragments of bone that had to be held together by three metal pins. Six months later, I still couldn't use it. The cast I wore, with bands holding up the ring finger (which had been torn from my hand though remained attached by a small piece of skin), had various odd-shaped molded parts and looked like a something out of a science-fiction movie.

I felt and looked worse than hopeless. I had a gash on my left cheek, a useless right hand, and barely enough energy to get dressed in the morning. My eyes were red and swollen.

To top that off, I was an emotional wreck. I couldn't sleep at night—not even a minute. I would lie in bed all night and stare at the ceiling or the bedroom door. I had five lights on all night. I'd try to read but my eyes would sting. I could sleep for only a little while during the day.

The worst part was the pain in my soul that nearly took my breath away. The emotional pain of the attack joined up with the pain and trauma of my past to create an emotional tsunami.

My past had been riddled with loss, trauma and anxiety. My brother had died when I was two. My mother died of breast cancer when I was six. (My cousin said I had fainted at my mother's funeral.) My dear grandpa John died when I was nine. I couldn't remember much except death. The memories seemed blocked. The impact of this all was huge upon my life.

As you can probably imagine, a lot of anger was wrapped up in my soul. It took every ounce of my will, deep spiritual work, faith and trust in God, alternative medical help, extra vitamins and minerals, vegetable juicing, emotional release, and healing through numerous detox programs to heal physically, mentally and emotionally. I met a holistic medical doctor who had healed his own slow mending broken bones with mineral IVs. He gave me similar IVs.

Juicing, cleansing, nutritional supplements, a perfect diet, prayer and physical therapy contributed to my healing.

It was truly a miracle that my hand healed when my hand surgeon had said, after months of therapy, there was nothing he could do for me. My hand wasn't healing. He said my hand was in such bad shape he couldn't even put in plastic knuckles. The day I heard that bad report I returned home very discouraged. I began to pray.

I told God that if a handicapped hand could bring glory to Him, I would accept it. But if healing me could bring more glory to Him, I would much prefer that. I really wanted to know where I stood with Him on this matter.

The next morning at 5 a.m., I heard the sweet voice of an angel saying, "Cherie, look at your hand." My cast was off and I was moving my fingers as though they were normal. The angel then said my hand would go back to its injured state, but I would get better and better until I was completely healed. That's exactly what happened.

What my hand surgeon said was impossible became real — a fully restored, fully functional hand. He had told me that it wasn't even possible to put in plastic knuckles due to the poor condition of my right hand, but my knuckles did indeed re-form. A day came when he told me I was completely healed.

Admitting he didn't believe in miracles, he said, "You're the closest thing I've seen to a miracle!"

It was a miracle! I had a useful hand again and was able to return to writing my first book.

My inner wounds were what seemed severest; in the end, nevertheless, they mended too. I experienced healing from the painful trauma of the attack and the wounds from the past through prayer, laying on of hands and emotional healing work.

I called them the "kitchen angels" — the ladies who prayed for me around their kitchen table week after week until my soul was healed. I cried endless buckets of tears that were pent up in my soul; it all needed release. Forgiveness and letting go came in stages for me. I had to be honest about what I really felt, the pain and toxic emotions confined inside, and then let them go.

Finally, I felt free. A time came when I could celebrate the Fourth of July without fear or inner pain.

When I look back to that first day in the hospital, after many hours of surgery, I cannot believe that I made it through to the place where I am now — my hand was resting in a sling hanging above my head wrapped in so many bandages it resembled George Foreman's boxing glove; my face was black and blue; my eyes were red — no whites — they were completely red.

As I lay there with tears streaming down my face, I asked God if He could bring something good out of this situation. I needed something to hang on to.

My prayer was answered. Eventually I found that my purpose was to teach people how to be healthy, and to love people *to life*. Through my writing and nutritional information, I could help them find their way back to health and healing. If I could recover from all that had happened, anyone could. No matter what anyone faced, there was hope.

I have a juice recipe called, "You Are Loved Cocktail." I named it that because I want you to know that you are loved. I send you my love through these pages. There is hope for you, no matter what challenges you face. There's a purpose for your life, just as there was for mine.

God can take all the broken places of your life and weave them together into your purpose and destiny. I want you to be strong and well. I want you to complete your purpose. You can be greatly served by a positive and optimistic attitude. Have faith in the Lord. I encourage you to give your life to him. He has never failed me nor forsaken me during all of my difficult moments and losses.

If you give your life to Him, He will lead you to your own restoration, to your purpose and His plan for your life. I pray you live abundantly happy, whole, and truly blessed, fulfilling your God-given dreams and purpose in your life in Christ Jesus!

> "For I know the thoughts that I think toward you, saith the
> LORD, thoughts of peace, and not of evil, to give you an
> expected end"
> (Jeremiah 29:11, KJV).

ABOUT THE CONTRIBUTOR

Known as The Juice Lady, TV chef and celebrity nutritionist, Cherie Calbom has helped in pioneering the fresh juice movement around the world. She is the author of 31 books including bestsellers, *The Juice Lady's Turbo Diet*, *The Juice Lady's Inflammation Diet*, *The Juice Lady's Big Book of Juices and Green Smoothies*, *Juicing, Fasting, and Detoxing for Life*, *Sugar Knockout*, and *Juicing for Life*.

She earned a Master of Science degree in whole foods nutrition from Bastyr University. Through writing, speaking and teaching, she has devoted her life to helping people learn how to care for their bodies so that they can complete their destiny.

Years ago, she had a vision where she saw God's soldiers lying across the battlefield with their armor askew. Written across their bodies were labels such as heart disease, diabetes, obesity, cancer, migraines, chronic fatigue and much more. She saw the demonic forces especially attacking these people because they were down and unable to fight spiritual battles effectively. They were completely sidelined from their destiny because their focus was on their sick bodies.

Cherie teaches people how to make the healthiest choices with juicing and whole foods, and how to detox and clear toxins from the body. She has helped hundreds of thousands of people all over the world heal from a wide variety of ailments and diseases, gain energy, lose weight and get focused in her programs for vibrant health.

Cherie has worked as a nutritionist with George Foreman and Richard Simmons, and appeared for 13 years on QVC with the George Foreman Grill. She has appeared in numerous shows on *It's Supernatural* with Sid Roth; *Jewish Voice* with Jonathan Bernis; *Daystar* with Marcus Lamb; and a number of shows on TBN with Matt and Laurie Crouch. She speaks at conferences and conventions, conducts health cruises, and hosts a variety of on-line courses.

Cherie and her husband conduct health and wellness juice retreats throughout the year and have seen hundreds of lives changed and people healed at these retreats. She has been featured in scores of magazines including a cover story for *Charisma*, *Woman's World*, *First for Women*, and has appeared in scores of print publications including the Los Angeles Times and The Miami Herald. Visit her at: www.juiceladycherie.com

CHAPTER 18

LIFTED UP BY AN ANGEL

John Elliott

But they that wait upon the Lord shall renew their strength;
they shall mount up with wings as eagles; they shall run, and
not be weary; and they shall walk, and not faint
(Isaiah 40:31, KJV).

When I was five years old we lived in Brussels, Belgium. Dad's work with Pan American World Airways took us to many parts of the world, but for the first six years of my life, my little existence was right there in Belgium.

Our house way back then was a three-story, brick-fronted place on a cobblestone street having the name of "Valle de LaCambe", number 24 to be precise. Entrance into and out of that dead-end street was through an enormous stone archway.

From the windows of our house, I used to look towards the end of the street, through that archway, to the ever busy four-lane roadway that lay just beyond. Trolley cars on tracks used to speed to and fro on that road, and the automobile traffic was endless.

Under the shadows of the archway was a sweet shop. Not sweet as in, "Oh, how lovely," but a tiny, glass-fronted store run by an elderly couple who sold vast varieties of candies from all over the world. I used to walk to the little sweet shop on my own several times each week, each time being sent home by one (or both) of the elderly couple who must have wondered how on earth I'd managed to leave my house without being seen by my parents.

It was a gray and gloomy morning. Dad was at work at the airport and Mom must have been upstairs doing something. That busy roadway beckoned me. I walked out the front door and made my way toward the archway. Not stopping at the sweet shop this time, however, I stood on the curbing of that four-lane road wondering what lay beyond.

Without a rational thought in my head I started to run across the road. Over the tracks I went, happy as a lark, not paying attention to anything. I almost made it to the other side — almost — but failed to see the trolley speeding down the second set of tracks from the opposite direction.

I ran right into the side of one of the fast-moving trolley carriages. The force of the bone-jarring impact threw me backward several feet, right back onto the first set of tracks I had just crossed, right into the path of yet another speeding trolley.

I remember seeing the growing red stain on the front of my shirt and the stream of blood as it gushed from my nose. It felt as if my face had been shattered. I also remember looking up to my left and seeing the oncoming trolley driver, his face frozen in fear. He knew what was about to happen. The impact was less than two seconds away.

Just then a strong pair of arms lifted me up from the tracks and held me tight, right between the two speeding trolleys, right between the two sets of tracks. The voice was clear and distinct, sounding as if it emanated from the inside of a hollow tunnel, yet somehow soothing and calm.

"Be still," it said. "Be still."

Somewhere on the road behind me a car slammed on its brakes and came to a screeching halt. I thought I heard someone shouting something in French in the distance. Once the trolleys had passed, those arms carried me back to the sidewalk and put me down right at the door to the little sweet shop.

I looked up to see the man who had saved me, but no one was there.

No one was anywhere for at least a full block all the way around. A few pedestrians could be seen walking about, around a hundred feet or so away. One of them was pointing at me and whispering to her companion. Another female pedestrian started to run in my direction, her arms outstretched, her mouth wide open in a silent scream; the look of shock and utter befuddlement was clearly written on her countenance, but she stopped short and stared trying to fathom what she had just witnessed.

I was stunned, unable to believe my eyes, unable to speak, dumbfounded. There was no blood at all, not even on my shirt. I touched my face, my nose, felt inside my mouth with my hand. Everything felt normal, no pain or discomfort of any kind.

I reached up for the black iron handle on the door to the sweet shop, the same one I had walked through so many times before. The little bell tinkled as I walked inside. The elderly shop owner was behind the counter. He held his hands in front of his mouth; his eyes were as wide as saucers.

"*Comme?*" he asked, "How?"

Seeing how I was brought to the front of his shop and deposited at his door by those strong invisible arms, he, too, was stunned and utterly confused. He quickly walked around from behind the counter and took my hand. He then allowed me to fill a paper bag with as many sweets as I could carry, and walked me back to my parent's house at the end of the street.

I saw him looking up and down the cobblestone road in all directions, looking, I suppose, for an answer, something that could explain what he just witnessed. He had tears in his eyes, tears that streamed down his face. His lips and lower jaw quivered uncontrollably.

It was the first time I ever remember seeing a man openly crying.

He and my mother spoke for several minutes. They embraced, and he whispered something to her. When he leaned down and hugged me closely, my ear pressed to his chest and I could hear his heart beating rapidly.

I watched him walk slowly back to his shop under the shadows of the archway. To this day I don't know what he said to my mother, but from that moment on my movements were severely restricted. I was never again allowed to venture out onto that four-lane roadway with those two trolley tracks.

"How?" the sweet shop owner had asked. The answer is so very obvious. Those strong arms comforted me, the arms of an unseen angel. Somehow, someway, I was restored, with not the slightest hint of an injury.

I didn't know it at that time, but over the coming years, on so very many occasions, that same angel would be right by my side saving my life countless more times, and very probably so many more times I'm not even aware of. I heard that unmistakable voice again and again over the years, telling me to, "Be still."

When I listened, when I paid attention, I was somehow restored — every time. I don't know why. I have no idea what our Lord has in mind for me. But I do know that an angel walks beside me every day of my life, the very same kind of angel who watches over all of us.

The Bible tells us that angels are ministering spirits sent to look after human beings who are the heirs of salvation (Hebrews 1:14), given the promise of life after death because of what Christ did for us on that horrible cross — that's us folks! Jesus indicated that little children have angels assigned to them, because He said their angels always behold the face of God (Matthew 18:10). I truly do believe that; I believe every word of it.

You have an angel watching over every single minute, every second, of your life as well. Did you know that? Don't you now just want to go dance in the streets? But please make sure the trolley trains have passed before you do!

That was the start of my journey, one that eventually took me to nearly every continent on the globe where I would live and work. As an adult I became a member of the government's Special Operations Group and was involved in a great many assignments, some of them resulting in the capture or death of a number of high profile criminals or terrorists.

But that work impacted my life in so many unfortunate and negative ways. My wife and I, the mother of our children, divorced after 27 years of marriage. Then I was involved in a number of relationships, but they, too, all failed.

Before that happened, when I was 20 years of age, I'd surrendered my life to Christ. But it didn't stop the pain and feelings of guilt because of the work I did. No.

In some odd ways, my love for our Lord was constantly being challenged. It wouldn't be until many years later, years when I was faced with one struggle after another, that I would rededicate my life to Christ.

I finally put my former life behind me, sold off much of what I had accumulated over the years, and moved to be close to my daughters and the grandchildren. I learned some harsh lessons along the way and realized that the life we choose for ourselves may not be what God had in mind for us at all.

We are all incredibly unique, one-of-a-kind creations that came into being for a reason. As I look back on my less-than-illustrious life, I now realize full well that God had something else in mind for me all along.

I also realize that whatever we choose to do *can* be used for His kingdom, for His honor and glory. It took me an awfully long time to get to this point but I truly believe that God is not finished with me — not at all. That rededication I made to Christ came after four decades of constant work and struggle, much of it a complete waste of time and effort.

Finally surrendering my life over to God and allowing Him to guide and direct me, to control my words and actions, was nothing short of an amazing unburdening of immense proportions. When all else fails, when we at last allow the Lord to have preeminence in our lives, we have a fresh start, a renewal of strength, and an amazing determination to do whatever we can for His kingdom.

Be still, and know that I am God
(Psalms 46:10a).

ABOUT THE CONTRIBUTOR

John Elliott is a forty-four year veteran of Israel's Mossad and the CIA's Special Operations Group. For nine of those years he was assigned to Interpol in Lyon, France, as well as to a number of law enforcement agencies in the United States, and to the Royal Canadian Mounted Police in Ottawa, Canada.

He holds a Bachelor of Science degree in business, an MBA, and a Doctorate of Law degree. Growing up in the Middle East, Europe and the United Kingdom, he is fluent in English, Gaelic, Hebrew and Hungarian, and can easily converse in both French and Italian.

As a trained investigator, his keen instincts have taken him to places such as Yugoslavia in order to recover 300 pounds of gold bars stolen by the late Serbian strongman Slobodan Milosevic. It also took him to the Vatican in order to uncover the church's incredibly vast treasure troves of stolen Jewish Old World art; their interwoven connections to the Mafia; their collusion with the Nazis during World War II; their hidden ranks of pedophiles, and so much more. Those same investigative instincts led him to a luncheon meeting with Sergei Khrushchev, the son of Nikita Khrushchev, a meeting that will inevitably result in history books being rewritten.

The author of twenty-five published works, he is an active member of the International Association of Bomb Technicians and Investigators, and also a consultant to the Mines Advisory Group. A public and motivational speaker, he conducts crime avoidance and safety seminars nationwide, and is an advocate for America's military veterans.

He is an on-air contributor for the BBC in London, England, and in Belfast, Northern Ireland, as well as a commentator for Radio Zabok in Croatia. Segments of his extraordinary life have appeared on various television outlets including CBN's *700 Club* and the BBC's *Sunday Morning Live* shows, as well as the Family Channel. Hollywood is producing a full-length motion picture based on his upcoming autobiography entitled, *Zephyr-The Life of a Counter-Terrorist.*

More importantly, he freely admits, he is a single father to two incredible daughters and grandfather to six wonderful children, three girls and three boys. As a Christian, he tells people if they have a pulse they have a purpose, and encourages them to believe in Christ and allow God to guide and direct their lives.

CHAPTER 19

SAVED IN THE BELLY OF A WHALE

GiGi Erneta

And said, I cried by reason of mine affliction unto the Lord, and he heard me; out of the belly of hell cried I, and thou heardest my voice
(Jonah 2:2, KJV).

Life is a journey; an awesome experiment put divinely together by the One who loves us. As far as the east is from the west, that's how much He loves us. That is a *lot* of love, which I never thought I deserved.

It's truly amazing how we grow up believing so many things the adults around us say. Hence, be careful what you hear. Protect your ear gates. Thank God there was some truth poured into mine so that *those* seeds would grow.

The only problem was I heard a lot of ugly things growing up, too, so it's hard to see the flowers through the weeds. Enough about planting, especially since I'm a city girl. Well, sort of. Let me start from the middle. After all, starting at the beginning would be too cliché.

I was in the middle of chaos as a result of my own poor choices. When I was in my 20's I left for Hollywood...

My story is a little different than most in that I started performing professionally when I was 8, chosen as a child to perform in the Nutcracker with soloists and prima ballerinas in the Houston Ballet. My parents had moved me from New York to Texas. (Keep in mind the culture shock as a child, not to mention I was a little on the dark side as a kid. I inherited some awesome tan skin from my mom. Both my parents are from South America and so no one ever knew quite where to categorize me — a blessing in my career later on.) I had been in Union commercials and a few other things while I was in the South, and had a nice reel to take around landing me an agent right away. I ended up getting work pretty quickly, too, and kept modeling which also paid rather nicely.

…When I got to Hollywood my marriage was on the rocks, but it was palatable because my purpose was coming together. I was able to bury the problems of my marriage into my work.

There were times in my marriage where I would beg my husband to go to church with me. I would end up alone in the back, a distant observer.

I struggled with the rules that were created by man in the church. In fact, when I was a teenager and confirmation came up, my gut was not okay with standing before God and making a commitment to doctrine I did not believe in. I took anything that had to do with God very seriously so I felt it better to run from Him, at times, than face the music. The closest I could get was Sunday mornings and that wasn't cutting it. I continued to reach out through prayer and even went as far as journaling, hoping maybe the connection would come. It didn't.

My marriage ended badly. My now ex-husband did some rather irreparable things that left me with scars, mentally and physically, and had it not been the Lord's hand and angels around me I would not be here to tell you just how *awesome* God is all of the time.

We had been in counseling when it really unraveled. Looking at the error of your ways can really make you upset. Putting up the mirror is scary when there's a monster looking back at you.

After the divorce, my greatest fear haunted me: failure. My ex took everything and made it really clear he hated me. He even told me that he hoped I would get trapped working in an office somewhere for the rest of my life. He envied that I had found my purpose and he had yet to find his.

It was so unnerving to him that he would get crazy angry. It manifested in strange ways. Unfortunately, when you are yoked with someone who has poor boundaries, it is contagious. I found myself broken, with poor boundaries, seeking to understand the mess I was in.

I went into very poor relationships, one after the other. Maybe to prove I wasn't all messed up. Maybe to see if I could really find love, or maybe to hide. At one point I decided that any relationship with any depth was for fools.

The blessing in all this train wreck was, I was actively hunting God. I'd go to a variety of different churches from New Age to Christian to Catholic to non-denominational to meditating to mountaintops...all to try to connect with God. Nothing worked.

As for my career, I was starting to get bigger offers in films, most of them in not-so-good movies. In fact, I recall getting an offer to be a Series Regular on a cable television network show. The caveat was in the details; there was a lot of nudity. Even then, and I'm not proclaiming I was always innocent, I had the sense to know that being naked every week on TV would not be a career booster. Remember, this was all before social media, thank God.

Like I said, I did make poor choices, including very dark, gory movies, and yes, late night television, as well as hanging out with some not-so-great people. I went to some really wild parties, dabbled in things I shouldn't have and took way too many risks with my life and my career. There were times I was terrified and didn't know how it was all going to work out.

A few years passed as I continued living "la vida loca," or "the crazy life," and still no signs of direct contact with "the Man Upstairs." Even in the midst of all of it, I would crawl out on various Sundays for my possible encounter with God.

In the middle of my search, God sent me earthly angels to wake me up. I ran into a casting director, Judy, who pointedly asked me if Jesus was my Lord and Savior. I honestly did not know. I told her that because I had no idea. Asking me about Jesus felt just a little too disheartening and overwhelming. God wasn't even speaking to me. How could I say Jesus even knew who I was? I left her place slightly annoyed. She had no clue as to where I was and what was going on, but I know the Lord used her that day to break through a barrier.

At this point in my career I was exploring different options in territories and started looking into other markets for employment. My immediate family had started migrating back to Texas from California and other places and I thought, *why not?* I started secretly commuting between states which proved to be lucrative.

In Hollywood there's an unwritten rule that if you are out of the Los Angeles area, your career is over. The mindset is like this: there's only an east coast and west coast, the rest is "flyover" country. Needless to say, I started my commuting in secrecy.

In the middle of my traveling back and forth I met a nice gentlemen who at one point told me to get my stuff right with God. He got under my skin with that comment but many years later I ended up marrying him. You'll have to read about that testimony in my book later because it could fill quite a few pages.

Then the Lord sent me another messenger, Sonia. I get introduced to her; she prays for me and even over me, and takes the Bible and practically knocks me over the head with it. Okay, maybe that's dramatic but it kind of felt that way. After a couple of encounters and prayers with Sonia, my relationship with my boyfriend disintegrated, literally. *Why would anyone seeking to find God move in with an atheist anyway?*

One day he says, "I don't even know why, but you have to leave, like, right now."

He had no explanation and no idea why. I actually remember him saying that.

Emotionally spent, confused and literally no idea where I was going to go, my friend Kimber came to the rescue. She blew up an air mattress in her house for me. I cried like a baby. Not because of all the stuff I'd been through but because she was so incredibly kind to me. Receiving that kindness at that very moment seemed foreign to me. Heartbroken to the core, I stood in the doorway and wept.

Later on that evening I lashed out at God. I couldn't sleep and I was angry and hurt. *How could a God so great be so elusive and allow me to be now homeless, without direction and so broken?*

I had this Bible that made no sense to me. I shook it up to God. I told Him it was ridiculous…and how I was told to read John…the book which speaks of love? Ha! It made zero sense to me. Many extraordinary words came out of my mouth that night as I cursed at God for all these things that ailed me.

In the midst of my crying, curled up and trying to sleep, my room made an obnoxious noise. Of course, I was mad at that, too. It wouldn't stop. *Great…. add sleep deprived to the list. Thanks God, now what?* It was so annoying.

I couldn't wait until my friend was awake to share with her this insane sound that came from her room. It sounded like I had been hiding in the stomach of a rather large mammal.

The moment she got up I grabbed her and made her stay with me to hear it. I'm sure she probably thought I had really gone off the deep end.

"Hi, I'm on the inside of a whale. Won't you join me?"

Confirmation came shortly. She heard it; it sounded like the inside of a whale. It is still a mystery, many plumbers later, but at the time it *was* my hiding place.

I couldn't wait to tell Sonia, so I called her to tell her about the whale noise. She laughed at me, told me to read Jonah and hung up. *Hmmm, guess that was my answer from God after I yelled at him.* I read Jonah and I cried and I knew every single word was for me as it pierced my hardened heart. The sorrow that left me that day was gone forever. That emptiness I carried around with me was gone. Every single word made perfect sense.

I laid my head down before God and apologized for everything, especially the anger. He had called me directly, no more busy signals. He was there with me and I was raw and ready to listen. Hollywood was my Nineveh and I would have to start my journey in order to return to deal with it.

God was merciful to me as I had a few very rough weeks from that point. My car was hit by an uninsured motorist. My hand received a dog bite and doctors told me I would have to have surgery in order to re-wire my hand. I knew I had to leave it for now and trust Him to get me through. He allowed me my first healing miracle as I watched my skin close up where the wound was on my hand, defying what doctors had spoken to me. I knew God was with me.

As I was being pushed out of Los Angeles in a most supernatural way, I had been called to the third meeting with a network to host a TV show. It was not yet time as my gifts and talents were ready but my soul was not. Thank you, God, for being the King of second chances.

I've left Nineveh until I am called to return. In the meantime, I have been blessed abundantly and continue acting in movies and television shows. I have learned to let God handle the steering wheel in life. I have learned to appreciate being the passenger as I go on this magnificent journey, the rest of the way, with My Lord and Savior, Jesus Christ.

ABOUT THE CONTRIBUTOR

GiGi Erneta was born in New York to Argentinean parents and is most notably known for her role as Captain Judith Rainier in the feature film, *Flag of My Father*. She's had several recurring roles on several TV shows including *Veronica Mars*, the CW show *Desire* and Spanish soap operas. She's also had roles on *Queen of the South*, *American Crime*, *Dallas*, *Friday Night Lights*, *Strong Medicine* and many others.

Her professional career began at 8 years old and her training started in the Royal Academy of Dance program. GiGi studied at Playhouse West under the direction of Robert Carnegie and the Second City Los Angeles, which gave her opportunities to share the stage with Martin Short, Fred Willard and Catherine O'Hara. Over the years she's had the opportunity to write, produce and direct, and looks forward to spending more time in faith-based and family friendly projects.

She's also the Host of the radio show, *Standing Freedom*, and is a Fox News Latino contributor.

You can find out more about the radio show, public speaking engagements and writings at: www.gigierneta.com and at the internet movie database.

CHAPTER 20

KIDNAPPED BY THE DARKNESS, ADOPTED BY THE LIGHT

The Story of Nico Hill, as written by Holly Anderson

But God commendeth his love toward us, in that, while we were yet sinners, Christ died for us
(Romans 5:8, KJV).

The only reason I am alive today is because God has a mission for me. I ran from Him and His calling on my life for many years. I turned to everything imaginable — promiscuity, porn, alcohol, drugs, fame, fortune and witchcraft. I ingested so many poisons: like Drano, paint thinner and all the other chemicals that were put in my drug of choice (which was smoking meth) that it's only by the grace of God I'm still breathing.

Do I have collateral damage? Yes. A person doesn't disrespect their body and cloud their brain with a drug that's known to destroy certain receptors, combined with all the blows I took to the head while traveling the world underground cage fighting. But the head blows were all too familiar to me. They began as a child.

I was born in California. Not in glamorous Beverly Hills or Hollywood, but in a blue collar town called Covina. My parents had a violent relationship full of drama, accusations and no peace, which offered little stability to me and my younger brother.

My father was a salesman but became a 1% biker. My mother took in as many foster children as possible, at one time harboring several in our home. I remember one day as a young boy walking home from school seeing an ambulance take away one of the teen female fosters because she had tried to commit suicide in our home.

For whatever reason, and to this day I don't know why, my father had it in for me. He would beat me so bad my mother wouldn't send me to school on many occasions because of the bruises, broken noses, and swollen cheeks and eyes from the many punches he rained down on me — as if I was a grown man — yet I was just a little child.

I remember once around 8 years old after one of their many fights (this being one of their violent more ones) my mother exploded into my room as I lay curled up in a ball hoping to disappear, hoping they would think I was asleep.

"See what your father has done!" Blood on her face, she continued screaming at me, "Did you hear?"

She often would do this, sharing adult problems on young ears that were unprepared to process such things. I looked up at her and spouted out a poem that poured out of my mouth:

"Winners and Losers, preachers and boozers, if you ask me it's all the same. And no one gives you nothing; you must try and try again. Even though it's often to the bitter end. And there is a moral to the story: You mean after all this, can't you feel the glory? Is there a silver lining around that cloud, Or do we go through life with our heads bowed? The dreams we have, they stay inside, the people with the power keeping our hands tied."

There was a moment of dead silence and she stormed out of the room, but not before interrogating me on how and where I got that.

The truth is I got it from within. I had never had the peace or guidance to read and learn much.

God was trying to reach out to me, even then.

My parents divorced but each repeated their tumultuous relationships with new people. One of those people sexually abused me when I was 11 years old, stealing my virginity. My father was living with a woman and one of the many drunken nights he did not come home, leaving my brother and me in her care, she molested me. It was another blow to me and another reason to never trust anyone.

My father would drive to porn stores with me as an adolescent child being exposed to things even adults shouldn't see. I wish my head could forget what my eyes have seen.

I began to excel in martial arts and boxing. I also had a natural athletic ability in football, getting scholarships to college even though I barely made it through high school. Considering I went to many different high schools, it's no wonder.

I married twice in my life, neither marriage lasting over a year. I was becoming a selfish, perverted man. I was becoming my father, but even worse; I was becoming a disciple for the devil.

From fighting in Russia, Brazil and various locations in the United States, then acting in almost 35 films (some of those being shot out of the country) to then being given my own TV series on Spike TV, I often think, *had I been grounded in the Bible, my life would have turned out differently.* But I was obsessed with power, custom cars, Harleys, custom made suits, the thousands of women I went through, the money — all the things someone like myself thought would bring a person peace.

I remember in my 30's during my Spike days, my father coming to visit me at a wild party in my "flavor of the month" mansion I was living in.

He proudly told me, "Son, you have finally arrived."

My mother was not around at that time because she had committed suicide. She had gone from pharmaceutical addictions to smoking crack all while working at a suicide prevention hotline. She took her own life but, of course, since the world revolved around me, I blamed myself for that as well, giving myself even more excuses to go get high.

Get high I did, blaming everyone and everything for my problems — jobs that fell through, my show being cancelled, being ripped off on business ventures, failed relationships, movies that did not make it to theatrical release, ones that did. It didn't matter. I was a strong, tough, handsome guy that people feared, hence my name, "Nico, the Dragon."

I was a professional victim and a professional manipulator.

I used my looks and clout to get what I wanted, but nothing made me happy until I found meth, or it found me. Really, it didn't make me happy. It destroyed my life, taking everything I owned. It drained my bank account. All but one of my championship belts was stolen along with any nice jewelry I had. The custom clothes, cars and looks I had? All gone.

Worst of all, my soul was gone. I went into the dark perversion that meth takes people to. I overdosed many times. I smoked it, drank it and snorted it. It was my wife and my life.

When I realized it was devised to destroy and take my life, it was too late. I had gone too far.

Not only was I addicted to meth, but also to any other chemical that was in arm's length. I had been an alcoholic for most of my life but this was a whole other level of obliteration. I screamed at God to kill me. I begged the devil to take me, for I had become one of his minions.

I could no longer form sentences without stuttering so badly people would glare. My hands shook so badly I could no longer hold a pen and write. I had moved to a condemned building and the garbage I found on the street or in dumpsters filled my floors knee-deep. My room was enveloped with chains, pornographic and occult drawings and blood smeared walls, all done by me.

I had planned to die in that room so it was only fitting I decorated it with reflections of my heart. The only thing I still cared about was my cat, Squeaky, whom I had received in the beginning of my decade-or-more-long addiction.

The most annoying thing during my addiction were the words. Words would be downloaded into my spirit — words I had nothing in common with, nor did I wish to hear. Some of them were redemption, grace, love, forgiveness and Jesus.

They were relentless, to the point where I thought if I could just write them on a scratch paper they would leave me alone; that is, while I could still hold a pen. I had black plastic trash bags full of these words that I would sit on the floor and piece together like a puzzle. But I had no picture on a box cover to show me what I was making.

When I had finished placing these words together what lay before me was a miracle. Many miracles to be exact. I had spoken word poetry that was all about God and His love for us and about things that would happen in the future. Throughout every single poem, the presence of God was weaved through the words like a beautiful, intricate tapestry.

How could I accept my true destiny when all I had wanted most of my life was to get high and die? God showed me how much He cared for me when no one else did, with the evidence of His existence through these Holy Spirit-inspired poems. He chose me — a broken down, used-up addict — to tear out from the abyss and restore me, to move me among the least, the last and the lost, to reach the unreachable.

God uses the foolish of this world to confound the wise. No one was more foolish than I was. I blame no one now for my past problems. I know there are people out there who came up worse than I did and made good choices in their lives. I had let the devil rule me, but no more.

The Bible is my guidebook for life now. God strategically placed His people around me to strengthen my faith and gain Biblical knowledge after I made a prayer for help on that last, suicidal, demonic, drug-fueled night.

I am convinced God was trying to reach me, giving me supernatural gifts in spoken word from a young child. Had I listened, I would have been leading many to Christ way before I actually did.

Just as the shepherd had to chase down that one wayward sheep and break his legs to bring him back to the flock (Matthew 18:12), and with my many demonic spirits I had invited in through the years of selfish living, God had to break my legs and place me over his shoulders to bring me back home. Boy, was I ready.

They say the devil will build you up to tear you down and God will tear you down to build you up. I believe I am a walking example of that. God will use for his glory what the devil planned for our bad.

When I was almost dead in that room, after smashing my head and body through glass, mirrors and walls, I made a simple prayer asking God to save me and I would become his soldier. He did, and I have. Until my last breath on this earth, I will never stop being His soldier.

ABOUT THE CONTRIBUTOR

Nico Hill formed God's Soldier Ministries and with his ministry partner Holly Anderson, they have worked tirelessly to spread the gospel. They are strictly Bible based and Holy Spirit led.

By God's grace, Nico goes into high security detention camps, men's high security prisons with the "Chosen Generation," men's homes, and middle and high schools with "Fellowship of Christian Athletes", leading as many souls to Christ as possible. He has spoken at Seventh Day Adventist Churches, Victory Outreach Church, Church of God in Christ, Baptist churches, and from Christian events in stadiums and parks to skid row.

He has spoken across the country leading many to Christ. To order the book on his life and make a donation to help this ministry continue their work for God's kingdom, go to:godssoldierministries.org.

CHAPTER 21

WINNING AT THE RACE OF LIFE

Sammy Maloof

*Verily, verily, I say unto you, He that believeth on me, the
works that I do shall he do also; and greater works than these
shall he do; because I go unto my Father*
(John 14:12, KJV).

My name is Sammy Maloof. I am a Hollywood stuntman. I build
race cars and I race.

Most of all, I am a Christian.

I can tell you this: about 29 years ago, when God reached into the
cesspool of this world He pulled me out of it. He had nothing better to
do than roll up His sleeves, reach down and pull me out of the mess
that I was in.

The great thing about God was that He never told me to quit racing;
He told me to quit illegally street racing. He never told me to quit
fighting; He told me to quit fist fighting. He never told me to quit arm
wrestling; He told me to quit arm wrestling for money.

That's how I made my living. I was a bare knuckle bar fighter. I
illegally street raced and I arm wrestled all over, and I can tell you this:
I was making two to five grand per week in illegal street racing.

I arm wrestled the World Champion, Dennis Jewels, four times in a
row. I beat him and he gave me his equipment.

He said, "I want to take you around the world to arm wrestle."

But God had a bigger plan for me, but I didn't know it at the time.

I can tell you this much, people are always asking, "What's your testimony?" Then they give their one testimony. It's been 29 years and I've got hundreds of testimonies! The proof that God exists far outweighs the proof that He doesn't. The evidence of God being real and real today far outweighs the evidence of Him not being real.

God showed me a long time ago in Jeremiah 1, where He says, "I knew you before I put you in the womb of your mother." He didn't say, "I knew of you." He said, "I knew you."

The gentleman that led me to the Lord was Ken Cooper. He was the morning DJ from KZLA radio station in Los Angeles. He wouldn't let me run around and tell everyone that I got saved. He came around every day at 10:30 a.m. after work and he mentored me a little bit...and he mentored me and he mentored me.

The first church that I went to was Church On The Way with Jack Hayford in Van Nuys, California. I went there for a few years. It is a powerful church with a great foundation but I knew I had to have a relationship on my own — one on one with my Heavenly Father.

I put two chairs in my back room, one chair was for God and one chair was for me. I lived alone. I had my own home and I told God every morning I would be there at 6 a.m. to meet with Him.

I was up at 5 o'clock, cleaned up and ready to go. I walked in that back bedroom with the two chairs. One was for Jesus and one was for Sammy.

I walked in there to meet with the Creator of the universe. It would be something maybe to meet with the President of The United States, but I was meeting with the Creator of the universe who created him. So when I went in there and I sat down for the first time.

There was an empty chair looking at me and my mind started screaming right away. *There's no one there. You've got race cars to build. You've got this going on and you've got that going on...* I excused myself from the room.

I asked, "Lord, will you excuse me for a minute?"

I walked into the other bedroom where I had a full length body-building mirror and I spoke to myself.

I said, "Sammy Maloof, you're going to go back in there and you are going to sit down and you are going to worship the Creator of the universe or I am going to make you sit in that room until next Wednesday!"

I spoke to my flesh. I made my flesh obey me because my mentor taught me in the beginning that we are three parts. We are a spirit, we have a soul and we live in a body, and our body doesn't have its own nature. We teach it what to do. I taught it to train. I taught it to build race cars. I taught it to drive. I taught my physical body.

Now at that point in time, I went back into that room. I told God I could give him five minutes. That five minutes led to 10 minutes. Ten minutes led to 20 minutes, and that 20 minutes led to 40 minutes, and 40 minutes led to an hour.

Right at the two year mark I was in that room for two hours straight and that's when I heard my Heavenly Father speak to me. You see, each time I told Him I could only give Him five minutes, it was like that week I gave him five minutes and then it moved up to 10 minutes and then it moved up to 20 minutes, but then it got to the two hour mark.

For two years I met with my Heavenly Father in that room every morning at 6 a.m. until I heard His voice. When He talked to me that day, it marked me. Ever since then, in the last 29 years as a Christian, everything I've believe and prayed for when it comes to me, myself and I, it happens.

It always comes to pass. Even when it looks like nothing is happening. In the last 29 years, I've got testimonies that will rip the roof off of most believers' houses and unbelievers would say the roof probably isn't bolted down!

I have been translated through vehicles twice. That means, myself and an LAPD cop were going down the Santa Monica freeway in a '66 Ford pickup when traffic on both sides of us came to a complete stop. My lane was still going.

All of a sudden they locked the binders up in my lane and everyone stopped. I hit the brake and the brake pedal broke and fell on the floor! I yelled at the top of my lungs, "Jesus!" and we were translated. She and I went directly through the car in front of us, through the car next to us and stopped in an open spot.

Another time I laid hands on a lady that had thirteen lumps of breast cancer. In front of my eyes that breast cancer melted and went away.

I was using a chop saw that spins at approximately 3,000 RPM. I was building a roll cage for a racecar when the material slipped out from underneath the blade and my thumb went under the blade. The motor was still running. Right when the blade touched my thumb, the motor continued to run, but the blade didn't. It stopped instantly with my thumb underneath it.

God reminded me that no weapon formed against me will prosper and no evil will befall me (Isaiah 54:17). The enemy can rise one way but he will flee seven (Deuteronomy 28:7).

You've got to understand who God is. To know who God is, you've got to make the distinction by knowing who He isn't. He isn't sickness, disease, lack or poverty. He doesn't have those things in Heaven so He can't give those things to you. God is never your problem. He is always the solutions to your problem.

Look, people sit there and say they have faith and they have belief. Really listen to them and you'll know where their faith is. See, your faith will never rise above the level of your confessions. I learned this as a young Christian. Our words have a big position to play in our life. Our words are containers and they carry power. I learned the three ways that you fail, or have victory is your thoughts, your words and who you associate with.

Now at this point in time in my life as a Christian, as a person who has his heart's desires according to Psalm 37:4, I get to operate in the gifts and talents that God gave me before He sent me to this earth. Now I make my living at it the right way, because God says the blessings of the Lord will make one rich and add no sorrow with it (Proverbs

10:22). He says a workman is worthy of their wages. So why don't you use your talents and get rewarded for it?

Now I get to go all over the United States. The churches, schools, colleges, prisons, juvenile halls, corporations, etc., bring me in so I can speak, train and mentor people on how to win at the race of life.

I can tell you this much, walking with God is the biggest rush of my life. I would highly encourage anyone who's making a decision about whether there is a God, or there isn't a God, to get a hold of me. Give me 30 minutes with you and I promise you that you will know there's a Heavenly Father and He's alive, and He's the same yesterday, today, and forever according to Hebrews 13:8.

God said that He created the heavens and the earth and it was seven thousand years ago. It wasn't 100 million years ago. It was seven thousand years ago, and God is still alive.

Sisters and brothers, I wish you all the best. If you ever need to get a hold of me, you can get a hold of me via Winning at the Race of Life. I love you.

ABOUT THE CONTRIBUTOR

Sammy Maloof is a Hollywood stuntman, automotive safety and technical advisor and stunt coordinator appearing in numerous TV shows, commercials, music videos and major motion pictures such as *Mission Impossible, Ghost, Protocol, The Fast & The Furious, Spiderman 2, Rush Hour, Three Kings, Burn Notice* and *Gone in 60 Seconds* (just to name a few).

He is also a race car driver, owner of a thriving race car shop in southern California, motivational speaker, mentor, author and husband and father to three girls. Sammy's passion is telling everyone everywhere he goes about the great things God has done (and is still doing) in his life. Sammy receives numerous invitations to share his supernatural testimonies and life-changing principles all over the world.

Sammy started a nonprofit organization, Winning at the Race of Life, several years ago as a way to give back to those in need. Sammy has a unique way of encouraging others to overcome obstacles in their own life. He and his team bring along his 1967 Camaro, powered by a 415 cubic inch Chevrolet engine, and they put on spectacular "Hollywood Experience" stunt shows all over the country. They give children and young at heart adults the opportunity to ride next to him in a real stunt car! These events are life-changing, especially for teens who are at a critical time in their life and in need of answers and direction. Sammy is also in development of his own reality TV show.

If you would like to book Sammy Maloof

Please call: (626) 292-2258

Or email: sammy@sammymaloof.com

Or visit: www.SammyMaloof.com

And Like his Facebook page:

http://Facebook.com/WinningattheRaceofLife

CHAPTER 22

MY 400 POUND TESTIMONY

Tom Rice

*Let the redeemed of the Lord say so, whom he hath redeemed
from the hand of the enemy*
(Psalm 107:2, KJV).

The Bible says, "Has the Lord redeemed you?" Then say so! You have to tell someone!

In Mark 5, Jesus delivered a man who spent his life night and day in the tombs crying out and cutting himself with stones. This man was so violent that the Bible says he would be bound with chains and shackles and no man could tame him. After Jesus cast out a legion of demons from the man (about 2,000 demons) the man sat down, clothed himself and was in his right mind. Then, when Jesus got into the boat to leave the man *begged* Jesus to go with him.

But Jesus told him, *"Go home to thy friends, and tell them how great things the Lord has done for thee, and hath had compassion on thee"* (Mark 5:19b). So the man left and began to tell everyone in Decapolis all that Jesus had done for him and all men marveled.

Decapolis means 10 cities! The man gave his testimony in 10 different cities and the Bible says that all men marveled! So when Jesus said, (my paraphrase), "Go home to your friends and tell them what great things the Lord has done for you," I take that seriously.

I want to share my testimony with you and what great things the Lord has done for me. I want to share with you what I call my "400 pound" Testimony.

Here's the story of how I got that way. My dad was raised in a foster family. He eventually became a marine and a big city cop. I always felt I had something to prove to him. Growing up I was around many parties, alcohol, arguing and playing cards. I remember waking up in the morning and stepping over bodies on the floor.

It started by me sipping my dad's beer at parties. By the time I was eight, I was drinking five to six beers a day, sneaking scotch and blacking out. I was a shy kid and had a speech impediment, so the alcohol took the shyness out of me.

By the time I was in 5th grade, I had to leave school and go to a BOCES (Boards of Cooperative Educational Services) program. In the 7th grade, I was already in a gang, having keg parties, and smoking and growing pot. In the 8th and 9th grades, I started snorting speed which only kept me up to drink more.

My mom would wake me up in the morning with my shirts ripped and my wrists bloody and I wouldn't remember how it happened. In the 10th grade, I started robbing houses to get money for drugs and alcohol. I even robbed the judge's house.

In the 11th grade I was charged with a felony and went to prison. I saw hell. I saw people getting raped. At one point my feet were set on fire. I sliced my wrists and tried to kill myself while I was in prison and then was transferred to a psych ward. I continued to drink and do drugs, even in prison. There was no escape from the addiction, not even in prison. After I got out of prison, I drank more. I could drink 50 beers a day and a quart of scotch.

One night in 1985, after celebrating the end of my five year probation, I was speeding and drunk driving and wrapped my car around a tree. I spent three days in a coma, lost 80% of my teeth and my mouth was wired shut. The doctors said I flatlined. I got out of the hospital and started drinking again. In 1986, I ran a red light at 85 mph, my car hit on the driver's side and I went through the windshield.

Through all of this, I got married, worked and had a daughter. I went through a series of injuries at work. By 2006, my weight had reached 400 pounds. I could barely walk. I used a cane and my legs were covered with open sores from my weight.

I was hitting depression; I was suicidal. I ended up having weight loss surgery and lost 175 pounds in 5 months. I continued drinking because I was still looking for a solution. It was really dangerous because I had no stomach after the surgery. It was the size of an egg. I would drink and black out while standing up.

I went into liver failure. My eyes and skin were yellow. The doctors told me I was going to die.

I believe God called me that day. My wife found me on my knees in a church crying out to God for help in a drunken stupor. Other than the picture my wife took, I don't remember it.

In 2008, I had my last car accident. I drove my car into a telephone pole, crushing another car. I thought I'd killed someone.

I went through the windshield again but the driver of the car was okay, and I was transferred to the police ambulance where God began to work miracles in my life. Instead of getting arrested, they took me home. I became so violent that night it took five guys to hold me down on the bed until I passed out. I should have been in prison.

My wife finally gave me an ultimatum, and I ended up going to AA (Alcoholics Anonymous) meetings. I met two different people who told me about the Vineyard Church, a one woman named Cheryl, and another named Marilyn, who was a receptionist at my doctor's office.

In 2010, I was invited to a Christian retreat that changed my life. The pastor prayed over me and he said, "The chains were broken." When I left the prayer meeting that night, there was fog over the lake where I was walking. I took the "chains" and visualized throwing them into the lake, then I crossed the bridge that was over the lake. I walked into my new life.

It was what I was looking for all those years. I came home and could not stop talking about Jesus!

Since then, the Lord has led me to different places to minister. I was in the prison ministry for three and a half years, ran the 12 step program for the Veterans Hospital and in adult day cares as well as individual groups in Nassau, Suffolk and Queens. The Lord has led me to become a lay minister in the Methodist Church and also to lead their prayer meetings.

The Lord has allowed me to become an interfaith minister at the hospital where my hands have been used by God to heal, including a man I prayed for while he was having a heart attack being completely healed. People on their death beds have become healthy enough to leave in a couple of days instead of being moved to hospice. Even tumors go.

What the enemy intended for destruction God used for good (Genesis 50:20). So now you know why, when Jesus said, "Go home to your friends and tell them what great things the Lord has done for you," I take it seriously.

ABOUT THE CONTRIBUTOR

Tom Rice currently resides in Long Island, New York, with his wife Liz, daughter Alicia, and their Beagle Terrier named Scout which they adopted on Columbus Day. Tom is disabled, and to keep himself occupied he has started to visit patients in the hospital--having been a patient himself.

This led to his prison ministry, prayers meetings, as well as Tom volunteering to lay hands on congregants for healing prayer during church services, and his involvement with Twelve Step Programs. You can contact Tom and his wife, Liz, at: kcmo1993@aol.com

CHAPTER 23

HIDDEN ANGELS, TOUGH GIRLS CRY TOO

Holly Anderson

*For whosoever will save his life shall lose it:
and whosoever will lose his life for my sake shall find it*
(Matthew 16:25, KJV).

Alone.

Words are so powerful. God created the universe with words. Sadly, the word "alone" sums up my childhood.

I was born to a mother that never wanted me. She was very cold most of the time. I never had the touching, caring or laughing I notice now between most mothers and daughters. As a matter of fact, she would seem to enjoy digging her nails in my young arms while violently shaking me, spewing curse words in my face at close range and demanding to know why couldn't I be more like my sister. Many times I would cry, sitting on the floor alone, tears running down my face with no one to comfort me.

She would send me to school sick. Once a teacher looked at me and stated, "I can't believe your mother sent you to school like this."

I ended up in the hospital for a long time from throwing up so much blood. I needed many transfusions to save my life. My father only came to visit me once. My mother and her own mother (who used to beat me) would come once a day.

Before the hospital incident, when I was around five, I had gotten a skin infection called "impetigo" all over my body. I was painted purple from the medication. It was an extremely hot, humid, August summer day. My mother and her mom made me stay in the car while they went shopping. They said they were embarrassed to be seen with me.

I remember getting so hot in the back seat I just stepped out of the car to get some air and stood by the car door. As luck would have it, they were walking towards me. My grandmother got in the backseat with me and beat me with her open hand and arm, slamming it into my body. I was screaming and crying for help and my own mother ignored me; a scenario I would repeat many times in my future to come.

My mother used to lay on the couch watching soap operas, or lay on the floor stretching and doing splits and backbends. She had been a child contortionist traveling with the carnival. She made it very clear, the grandstand acts did not associate with the rest of the carnival. She'd met my father as they were paired doing a dance called "the Adagio."

He came with his own luggage. His parents were immigrants from Greece. While his mother was pregnant with him, his father beat her and kicked her down stairs, which could have killed my father before he was born.

His mother also read tarot cards, tea leaves and held séances. I never really knew her because my mother kept me from her, and she died when I was just a child.

My father had been married before my mother and had a child that died young. He beat one of his many stepfathers so badly the guy almost died. He was a boxer in the Marine Corp.

His brother (my uncle) was an alcoholic and beat his wife. Their young daughter used to jump on his back to try and get him off her mom; she grew up and had a son, my cousin, Kelley, who was shot at close range with a shotgun at a drug house in Florida and died immediately.

My mother's sister's son became a crack addict after a life of alcoholism.

When I was seven to 10 years old, my father's alcoholic girlfriend tried to run over me with her car.

The only bright spot of love in my life, other than my neighbor's dog (since any dog I had would be driven and dumped in the country as I was forced to sit in the back seat crying, watching him chase the car as my parents drove off) was my older sister. She seemed to have a very different upbringing than me. But as soon as she hit 18, she left home leaving a 5-year-old me to be alone. Naturally.

She had no idea what I went through and she had her own life to live, but she was the one that got me my first bra, my first car and took me to the beach. She tried to make me feel like I was beautiful and a "somebody", but she had to work and live her own life. Don't ask me why I never resented her, but I never did. I always looked up to her like she was some kind of angelic being placed on this earth.

I learned in an AA (Alcoholics Anonymous) meeting once that one child can be singled out and abused when the siblings are not. Research shows this is more common than people realize in homes of abuse. In some strange way that made me feel so much better.

My mother used to discount my thoughts and feelings by telling me every time I said something I thought to be true, "Oh, Holly, you just dreamed that."

She also used to tell me to never have children; they ruin your life. Also, she said, when a baby is born, you don't love it; you have to grow to love it. She was pro-abortion and there's not a doubt in my mind if she could've gotten an abortion with me she would have. But abortions were not that easily available before being made legal in 1973.

Fast forward to teen years of drinking and drugging. It made my pain go away, but created new pain and new drama. I had no idea how to have friends because I had no idea how to be a friend. I just hung out and pretended to be cool. But I was a mess.

My father was never home. My mother was only physically home, but emotionally unavailable for the most part. I was kicked out of school once or twice and as soon as I graduated I went to work. I had no mom or dad to guide me to better myself.

My father told me we came from monkeys. He never beat me. He only put his hands around my throat to choke me once and my mother screamed.

My mother kept a dusty Bible on the coffee table for show. We never had prayer times or had deep family discussions about faith and God. Or anything for that matter.

One night after work I came home and everything I owned was thrown in black trash bags and stacked in the living room. No warning, dead silence. Alone, I stood. They threw me out. Not any discussion. Just three, shiny black trash bags piled up there — which also was a symbol of what my worth was to my parents at that time.

I was still a teen. I grabbed the trash bags filled with my clothes and few other things and got an apartment.

An older abusive boyfriend moved in with me. He used to sit outside and time me coming home from work. If I was even a minute late he would beat me. He kicked holes in my walls. He threatened to rape and kill my sister. He threatened to place me in a dumpster, pour lighter fluid in it and set it on fire.

I was down to 90 pounds with black eyes and bruises, until I had enough. I tried to leave; he tried to kill me. He beat and choked me until I blacked out. I was on my hands and knees in the middle of the street and he was kicking me in the face. I had my hands over my face and they were swollen and black and blue for weeks after.

At that time I was trying to move back into my parent's small, modest home. I'd asked a lady from work to follow me to my parents. I called my mother that night from work and told her, "If I don't make it home, call the police."

Unknown to me while I was setting that up, he was waiting for me at my car. He forced his way in my car and that's how it all started. I was forced to drive to his house and the lady that followed me saw him beating me in the street. She made a quick turn and screamed for me to jump in her car. Somehow I managed to break away.

At that time he had a guy with him. One of the times I broke free and ran to my abusive boyfriend's friend for help. He turned his back on me as I was bleeding and fighting for my life.

The strange thing is, three months later, this abusive boyfriend killed his next girlfriend. The guy that turned his back on me that night was her brother.

My mother made that night about her. She always did. She would often have what we referred to as "the vapors," where she would fall back, have to breathe in a brown paper bag and shake. So when we got to the ER, they thought she and I had been in a car wreck and treated *us*.

She would not get me therapy. My general doctor who was treating the physical wounds told her if she did not get me help I would repeat this. She told me when we were alone she would never do that because, "what would the neighbors think."

Once I healed from the physical wounds, I figured *that's just life*. I found my way into one of the most notorious motorcycle clubs in the world. I worked for them; I dated the VP; I felt protected.

The narcotics unit kicked in my door and held guns on me. Nothing phased me by then. I was tough and hard, and not even 21! But I was protected at that time, by a God I did not know. The Hell's Angels were always good to me. I know now God was covering me while I was with them. I smile now when I see the last part of their name is Angels. I certainly have had many Angels protecting me.

Many things happened in my life after that because I still was not searching for the only true thing that would have filled the emptiness inside. I went on to New York City and acted, doing theatre, independents and modeling. I dated a lot of wealthy men and took extravagant trips with expensive gifts. We went to the most popular, exclusive restaurants and clubs, and hung out on yachts with the mafia and their attorneys, but I still wasn't happy.

I got married and we moved to Los Angeles. I booked a VH1 commercial within the first year or two. I was also hired by Playboy but even though I was not strong yet in my walk with God, I refused to do nudity. So I worked at the studios doing stand-in work, fully clothed. They gave me my own dressing room and treated me great, but I felt like a fish out of water there.

I also discovered my husband was having an affair with the one person in Los Angeles that called me her sister, her best friend. I had even hired her to be his assistant.

I was devastated. I tried to kill myself. I ended up in the hospital for seven days and went into therapy for a year which helped me tremendously. My therapist told me she was having to re-parent me because I had never been parented. She also told me my mother was mentally ill.

It lightened my load to hear those words come from her lips. I had blamed myself all those years and I also didn't know how out of the ordinary my upbringing had been. I assumed everyone was raised like me.

God will use for our good what the devil means for our bad. I may not have gotten therapy if I had not tried to do something that would be a painful, forever regret.

During that time and slightly before, by accident, I had seen Joyce Meyers speak on TV. She captured my attention because her upbringing had been not so great either. I started listening and before I knew it, I was soaking up every word about God like a sponge. I learned about this loving God that was always with me. I was never alone.

I would have given anything to have come from a loving family where I could have experienced true love and shared about Christ. I see pictures of my guy friends taking their daughters places or spending time with them and I think, *how blessed those girls are*. I never had a real dad or a real mom. They did the best they could with what they came from. I know for a fact if I had a father who talked to me and made me feel loved, my life would have been completely different.

But that was not my journey. You cannot give something that you don't have.

I have accepted Jesus as my Savior and God has changed me and filled me with His love. I now have something to give. I have love! I rescue unwanted dogs off death row and have found homes for too many to count. My own dogs I love so much. I give them the affection and caring I never received from my earthly parents, but God has placed that ability in me now.

God chose me and has been using me for the last several years to build God's Soldier Ministries with David "Nico" Hill. By God's grace, our ministry has reached thousands of unsaved by going into detention camps, prisons, schools, streets and churches. God is no respecter of persons.

As long as I place God first where He has always belonged, and give him all my trust and all my faith, then I am a happy woman. With God all things are possible. He will change us from the inside out.

I had no idea when I asked Him into my heart that slowly, piece by piece, He would start rebuilding and remolding me. I love Him so much. With Him in my future, I know I will never be alone again, and I happily look forward to the great surprises He has in store for me.

ABOUT THE CONTRIBUTOR

In addition to her tireless work on God's Soldier Ministries, Holly continues to act in Los Angeles in commercials, music videos and series. She has created an Urban Faith-Based Super Hero TV series that she not only co-wrote, but cast, called, *Duality*. She is in the process of getting funding to begin shooting the episodes.

She loves to box and hike in the mountains. She is a grateful and blessed member of Faithful Central Bible Church in Englewood.

To see what Holly is doing on *Duality* and other projects, go to: officialhollyanderson.com.

To see ministry updates visit: godssoldierministries.org

TESTIMONY OF MY SUPERNATURAL SALVATION: "FROM LIFE IN THE MUD TO LIFE IN THE BLOOD"

Bob Griffin

*Whosoever therefore shall confess me before men, him will
I confess also before my Father which is in heaven*
(Matthew 10:32, KJV).

I remember standing in the cool mist as the fog rolled in, late in September of 1989. The LSD was mixing with the reefer and the beer.

It was at that moment that I heard Him say, "You are dying." And I laughed.

"I know I am," I said, "and my whole life has been hell. Just let me go there now. It doesn't matter."

Suddenly, like a television show in the heavens, I saw them — my parents. Their backs were to me and my father was consoling my mother. My mother was sobbing, her knees weak.

I asked, "What's that?"

"It's the rest of their lives."

"What happened?" I asked.

"It's your funeral," He said. "And it's the rest of their lives."

I suddenly was filled with emotion as, maybe for the first time in years, I thought of someone other than myself.

After all, that's what the 1960s, '70s and '80s taught us: a mindless, soulish elevation in a lifeless form. Following after "love" through sex, drugs and rock 'n' roll, the trinity of deception led to another kind of Mount Rushmore — the rush of death with Janis Joplin, Jimmy Hendrix and John Belushi — all engraved in stone cold death and preserved in time for all to see, overdosed and overexposed, as history repeats itself.

I could hear the music pounding and the rain began to pick up, yet, frozen in time, no one moved. The icy rain penetrated our clothes. Then my friend handed me a huge trash bag with holes for my head and arms. Where he got it, I'll never know!

The steam began to rise from within the edges of the bag while the icy rain dripped onto and into my shoes. I was crying and no one could see it — the tears of pain. The love lost mixed as a giant cocktail from within, seeping over the edges of time; tears sown into the field.

Neil Young was banging out a legacy of 25 years like a scroll of pain, a generation clinging to his testament of life.

Then I heard myself saying, "Jesus, come back. Come back into my life, I'll try this again. Anything. Just tell me and I'll do it."

I heard a voice. He was standing in the shadows, saying, "Turn around. Wake up, America. There is a generation following in your footsteps. Turn around and tell them 'This is not the way.' Wake up, America! Tell them this is not the way!"

I shivered from the cold and turned to Craig and said, "Let's go, dude!" I wondered if he had heard the voice. I realized I was getting warmer and warmer. *What was all of this really about?* I didn't really want to die! I just didn't like the life I was living...drugs, sex, addictions, divorce.

My mind began searching the wasted years — the S.W.A.T. team surrounding my house after weeks of free-basing cocaine; my family in a failed intervention; the gun suddenly firing in my hand. There were bullets flying, the sirens, the lights, guns drawn and tear gas being loaded.

I had been high for months with kilos sifting through my fingers and all of it up in smoke. At times, the coke-pipe was so hot it seared my identity as I crawled around on the floor smoking anything that resembled a rock. My own fingerprints melted off by the heat, the cocaine anesthetized my body, my kidneys nearly destroyed, my frame reduced to a mere 130 pounds, maybe less. I have but a few, clear memories of that night.

I still regret the bullets that chased my brother off the front porch and the one that went through the collar of my former wife's coat as he raised her arms to receive the coat to flee into the cold, dark night from my anger and rage. That night, I proclaimed that cocaine was my god! Then the room was empty except for the smell of crack mixed with the gun smoke.

I quickly grabbed the Quaaludes, 10 to 12 of them; I didn't know anymore. I just started chewing them with no water. They formed a thick paste in my mouth; dry, no saliva. Dehydrated from weeks of free-basing, I stood in the kitchen cooking up the crack and baking dishes full of free-base with chemicals all around as I stared at the wall, chasing the dragon when the pipe got too hot.

The rest of the coke flushed as the police cars came flying up the street, lights off, like stealth bombers targeting my home. The demons were screaming with glee to receive my soon dead body. I ran out the back door only to see the police cars on the next block swiftly descending from every direction. I could hear the helicopters and see the news crews arriving.

I had long lost the gun — *in the bushes? On the lawn?* I couldn't remember. I only remembered my own family turning on me. Tears were flowing.

I would become crazed when I possessed less than an ounce of coke. No longer would I share. A demoniac, I'd become.

I was crouched in the corner next to the fence. I could smell the fear on her; the police officer who was crouched just inches from me with only the rotted slats of a wooden fence between us. With her gun drawn on my front door, my mind began searching out the future.

Soon they would fire the tear gas. The house would go up in smoke. All would be ruined. If they only knew I was here crouched next to this officer they would fire at me, and my life would truly fade as the dry ground thirsted after my blood, a wasted pile of flesh!

I had to run to get them away from the house, to follow me instead. I ran and as I jumped over the fence, there they were. The police, rising up while I was in mid-air, grabbing, pulling, slamming my face into the ground.

Handcuffed and into the squad car, they berated me with questions, "Where's the gun? Where's the drugs? Who sold it?"

In arrogance, I mocked them. Suddenly, a fist into my face, my nose shattered as I felt myself slipping into darkness. The Quaaludes quietly doing their job, killing me softly.

I heard their voices. The doctor was saying, "We're losing him! He's going!"

The police officer to my right was saying, "He's the scum of the earth. Let him go!"

Suddenly, I was rising up out of my body. It was then I saw her, a nurse at the foot of the bed, reaching to cover my feet. But wait, she was praying something in a foreign language. I was rising farther up and away when I remembered thinking, *What is she saying?*

From somewhere in the shadows I heard a voice say, "Just say, 'Jesus!'"

I said, "Jesus!"

Instantly, I was sucked back into my body, and that was the last I remembered.

Three days passed when she stood before me calling my name. I tried to rise up not knowing where I was nor how I got there, part of me not wanting to wake up.

I glared through the bars as she began to say, "You've really done it this time," she said. "Have you seen your face? Have you even eaten?"

I found I had been in that cell for three days without awaking for even food or water!

I said, "I don't even know who you are."

"I am your attorney," she answered, "and I must tell you right now that the DEA and FBI are out there. The OSBI, the Sheriff, the OKC Police — the line is endless. There is only one solution I see for you. I can put you in a drug rehab for thirty days and they can't speak to you or even touch you."

I said, "Sign me up."

After 30 days I was back on the streets. My wife was gone, my brother moved out of state, my house was destroyed and all that was in it. The locks were broken and everything was gone and destroyed. The furniture was broken, cabinets emptied, and all that was left was the bills and the pain — my life!

Life in rehab was a blur — detoxing, isolated, insulated and the feds appearing regularly. On the 27th day my wife appeared and handed me "the papers." Divorce. I was released on the 29th day.

I struggled to rebuild my life, but I was hounded by the feds and tossed out by every person I had ever met. There was no city where I had ever dealt that anyone, anywhere, would open their door to me.

My own friends would simply say, "Sorry!"

The newspapers and television reports carried the story as fast as the underworld!

I bought an old car for four hundred dollars and just drove out of town. I headed north, with no money for gas, and I cleaned the restrooms of a filling station for six bucks which carried me to the next city. I finally arrived in the parking lot of an old friend's apartment building just as my motor exploded. The car sat there for a month. I found odd jobs for a year or so.

It was hard to read the signs for vacancy through the tears. I bought another car that carried me west toward Denver, where I would attempt to find a new life. Halfway there, that motor threw a rod. I walked until I found a hotel that would comfort me for the night, but I could find no comfort.

Soon every hotel began looking the same — roach-infested, dirty carpet, peeling paint, noisy exhaust fans and fuzzy cable. The broken knobs and handles on everything from the television to the toilet testified of someone else's pain, with fist-sized holes in splintered doors, musty curtains and the stench of smoke and mildew on stained mattresses.

I pulled out a Gideon's Bible from the drawer of another orange-doored hotel. I cried and sighed until daybreak. Not much money left after the hotel. The garage rigged the engine. I must have looked as pitiful as all the others who had gone before me on dusty trails heading west, in hope of nailing down the dream of a simpler life.

I hobbled into Denver a broken man. I cried until I could cry no more. I found myself sitting in a huge Baptist church. For weeks on end I would go, until one day I decided to be water baptized. I didn't know anyone in there and no one knew me.

A sweet gray-haired lady in perhaps her late '60s or early '70s spoke out while I was seated, ready to go into the water. "Sonny, how is it that you came to be here?"

I replied, "The Holy Spirit told me to come."

She looked startled and turned to the Pastor, "Isn't that cute, Pastor? He thinks he heard the Holy Spirit!"

Long hair or not, I knew I had. This wasn't my idea! It was just time for my life to change. I felt empty, like a bottle of Southern Comfort rolling around on the floorboard of another broken-down truck — gathering dust, empty and hopeless, writhing around in pain, with the lingering smell of yesterday's answers. They only delayed the judgments and kept me a prisoner.

I couldn't do a thing. Every corner, every turn, there He was.

Looking back to the Red Rocks Concert, I remember asking for, "Just one more bag of pot." I'd bought a quarter pound of buds and smoked it for months until the last day of the last joint.

That's when I heard Him clearest. I was listening to old love songs on the radio and flipping through the channels of the television when all of a sudden I was staring at what could only be described as a wild-eyed televangelist speaking in tongues. I didn't even say it out loud; I simply thought it in my heart. *Who does this clown think he is? And what on earth is that language?*

He suddenly looked up and said, "You — smoking that joint right there!"

Well, I dropped the joint on the floor.

He said, "You just dropped the joint on the floor!" My mouth hung open and I fell to my knees as he said, "Whoever receives a prophet in the name of a prophet receives a prophet's reward!" He went on to say, "Jesus has never left you! You keep leaving Him but He's right there with you even now, following you wherever you go."

I was crying so hard when I read the words, "Pre-recorded Program," and then I lost it. I was thinking, *He's the God of the future and He went out there on this program just for me! Who is this one who would drop this message in time?* Time was being penetrated with a message from the future being deposited in a "Kairos" moment, meaning "a certain season", for someone to discover, recorded for someone to awaken to and discover Him.

The essence of His voice drew me. *But what did He look like?* I searched for this voice everywhere — hoping, desiring — but nothing came.

Time was closing in on me with rent due again. It had been months since I made a payment to anyone. My gas and power were due to be shut off any day. The sheriff's department was serving me judgments for payments due and lawsuits against me. I stepped outside and wanted to scream, but who would hear me? It was quiet. The light in my garden apartment was too bright. I wanted to hide in darkness.

People were calling for drug deals. In an attempt to drown out their voices, I told Pat, a friend of mine, that I was going to chill for a while and that I wasn't going to deal for a while.

He laughed, and then with chilling words he said, "You didn't just get born again, did you?"

Startled, I said, "Ah,...no. I,...ah, just want to chill for a while."

He blurted out, "You're born again, aren't you?"

Like Peter denying Him around a fire in the night, I, too, had denied Jesus publicly. I couldn't sleep for three days.

No matter what I did, whether putting blankets over the windows to block out the light, towels under the doors, or covers and pillows over my head, still the light was there and I could not sleep. Restless, I kicked the covers, paced the floor, returned to bed, covered all the windows and soon cursed the day I was born. Pain was all I could feel: empty, hopeless, lonely pain.

On the third day, I flew out of bed with dark circles and pain under my eyes, hair matted, and three days of stubble. I talked to myself. *Where was He now; where was that voice of hope now? Why so quiet now?*

Then it happened. I heard that voice, standing in the shadows, "If you confess me before men, I will confess you before the Father. But if you deny me before men, I'll deny you before the Father."

Still angry and somewhat alarmed, I said, "When did I deny you before men?"

He replied, "When Pat asked you if you were born again! I gave you many opportunities to speak for Me!"

I said, "I'll go call him now!" And I did. When Pat answered the phone, I blurted out, "Pat, I asked Jesus to come into my heart and I lied to you."

Pat simply said, "I know."

I asked him how he knew.

"I heard it," He said. "I tried that Jesus stuff before. You'll come back. You'll be calling me soon."

I don't know if it was the fresh memory of the painful corner I had been driven into or the sinful temptation in Pat's voice, but I vowed right then that this time it was forever. I would follow Jesus and never again go back to dope.

***

You can now see that I went from, "Life in the mud to life in the Blood!"

In the midst of all this, when I had just turned 31 years old, He was teaching me deep spiritual truth about Israel, the church and the last days when I suddenly asked Him, "Why are You teaching me all of this?"

He replied, "Because you're Jewish."

"No, I'm not." I said. "My Father was German and my mother was Dutch."

He replied, "Your grandfather is Jewish. His name was changed twice. Call home and ask your mother."

I continued to argue with Him for the next three weeks.

He continually challenged me to, "Call and ask your mother."

Which I finally did late one Friday night. I picked up the phone and as my mother answered the phone I calmly said, "Mom, what's my heritage?"

"Of course, you're Jewish," she said abruptly.

In shock I said, "Mom, I'm 31 years old; when did you think you might tell me this?"

"Well, you never asked."

"I never had any reason to ask."

"Well, why are you asking me now, then?"

"Well, someone told me I was Jewish and that Grandpa changed his name...twice."

"Who have you been talking to?" she asked, anger in her voice.

I gulped as I said, "Jesus."

After a quiet moment of dead air, she replied, "Well, it would have to be Him, because no one else knows."

She went on to say that both of my great-grandparents had migrated from Belarus, one from Minsk and one from Pinsk. With no papers to hand over they only spoke their name, which was Perez, but was misspelled as Pearce.

Then, when my grandfather was only 8 years old, he was teased in school and he himself asked for his name to be changed from Isidore to John. Thus two name changes: one at Ellis Island, and the second some years later, a detail only Yeshua would know! A sign to my own mother!

My own name would later be changed "twice" as well.

ABOUT THE CONTRIBUTOR

Bob Griffin has been strategically Spirit-led now for over 25 years to "go into all the nations!" The Lord has been leading him to preach, prophesy and lay hands on the sick to "revive" the hearts of countless people in over 25 nations.

He accurately both prophesied and dreamed the events of 9/11 — prophesying five and a half years prior to the events of 9/11. As guests on the popular, *It's Supernatural,* program with Sid Roth, Bob, and his lovely wife, Jayne, were privileged to share on the show in 2002 of the events leading up to that tragic day that changed the way we live today.

Bob's own television program, *Stepping into the Future*, has been aired through multiple global networks, reaching the multitudes in every culture and with the advent of the Internet and YouTube channels, even further. The Lord led Bob and Jayne to produce over 500 radio programs which fed entire regions both in America and abroad. With the prayer lines always full, the revelatory, spiritual gifts flowed directly from Heaven for 6 years.

As an Apostolic Revivalist and Reformer, Bob carries the Heart of a Father for these generations following. As an author, Bob has published many books including: *Dreams and Visions; Supernatural Dreams and Visions; Standing in The Shadows Of 9/11 — The Vision*; and *Prophesying the Heart of God.*

Bob's heart for "True World-Wide Revival" led him into the Middle East to Turkey, Iraq and the regions of Kurdistan to pray with governmental leaders in Mosul (Nineveh), Irbil and Duhok. The ministry is now being positioned by The Lord to begin new outreaches in Jerusalem, Israel.

"House of Liberty for All Nations" is a world-wide, non-denominational Apostolic Revivalist movement dedicated to seeing True Revival in the hearts of God's people. "Jesus: To know Him and to make Him Known." Bob has ministered house2house and temple2temple for over 20 years in 27 nations, and has logged over 8600 preaching dates as he traverses the earth following Jesus wherever He leads.

For more information on this ministry or to contact us to minister in your church, please go to:
www.bobgriffinworld.com, or YouTube channel/bobgriffinworld, or bobgriffin2thenations@ yahoo.com.

Bob and his wife, Jayne, have 5 beautiful children, from their oldest at 22 to their youngest at 12, who are also spread out over America — each actively searching out their destinies from Florida to Tennessee to Arizona. The Lord's hand has been upon each of them. They are Jasmine, Jordan, Joel, Rachael and Benjamin. Each of them are uniquely and wonderfully blessed and equipped of The Lord!

PART IV

For by grace are ye saved through faith;
and that not of yourselves: it is the gift of God:
Not of works, lest any man should boast
(Ephesians 2:8-9, KJV).

CHAPTER 25

FINDING ULTIMATE REALITY

Mike Shreve

Come unto me, all ye that labor and are heavy laden, and I will give you rest. Take my yoke upon you, and learn of me; for I am meek and lowly in heart: and ye shall find rest unto your souls. For my yoke is easy, and my burden is light.
(Matthew 11:28-30)

A near-death experience in my freshman year of college proved to be a blessing in disguise because it compelled me to reevaluate my life. After years of being somewhat insensitive, I turned my gaze once again toward religion, more importantly, toward *spirituality*.

I had been raised a Roman Catholic but at that pivotal point, I decided I could no longer embrace ideas just because they were part of my cultural or family belief system. So, I wiped the slate clean to start from an unbiased beginning point and explored every new philosophy or religious belief system that crossed my path.

Even though I recognized I was studying the supposed revelations given to others, my goal was to experience God for myself. I had faith that something, somewhere, would prove to be my connecting link with Ultimate Reality.

In the fall of 1969, I met a guru from India named Yogi Bhajan. He claimed he came to North America to help the "flower child" generation find their way spiritually. He taught us about "yoga," a word meaning "yoked with God." With his full beard, long black hair and intense dark eyes he was very persuasive. However, it was much more than the mystique surrounding this tall, turban-clad Sikh that attracted followers or the stimulus of a new approach to spirituality through Kundalini Yoga; it was the promise that we could personally experience higher spiritual realms for ourselves.

I became increasingly consumed by the disciplines he taught until I finally left Florida State University in Tallahassee, Florida, to help start an "ashram," meaning a "yoga commune," in Daytona Beach. Every day involved hours of meditation and Mantra Yoga (the chanting of certain Hindu words and phrases designed to supposedly carry a person to higher levels of awareness). We also devoted ourselves to the study of Hatha Yoga — "asanas," meaning "physical exercises," and "pranayama," meaning "breathing exercises," both of which advocates said were aimed at opening "chakras," or "spiritual energy centers in the body." Our daily routine also included the study of various writings considered sacred like the *Bhagavad-Gita* and the ancient Hindu writings called, *The Vedas*.

Peculiar things began happening to me: a deep sense of peace, occasional out-of-body excursions into the "astral realm," and vivid spiritual dreams. A kind of spiritual adrenaline surged through me daily, in essence, the prospect that I was wrenching myself free from what my teachers called "*maya*," or the "illusion" of this present world. I followed hard after God until every waking moment was pulsating with the heartbeat of a holy quest.

Not long afterward I moved to Tampa, Florida, to open a yoga ashram there. Four universities in the area opened their doors allowing me to use their facilities for extracurricular classes. Several hundred students began attending.

One night during meditation I was absorbed into a brilliant white light. Though now I have a different interpretation of what really happened during the phenomenon, at the time I felt I had passed into the highest state of meditation. More assured than ever that I was truly on my path, I intensified my efforts.

Then something unexpected happened! A divine appointment interrupted my predictable pattern of life. I wasn't even seeking for new direction — but God knew my heart, so He intervened by orchestrating certain events that brought about…

A Dramatic Change

Several key happenings took place within a few weeks. First, the Tampa Tribune newspaper published a half-page interview with me. I was thankful for the exposure, certain this free publicity would increase the attendance in my classes.

Little did I know it would also alert a local Christian prayer group to begin praying for me. They cut the article out of the paper, pinned it to their prayer board and assigned someone to be praying for me every hour of every day until my conversion took place.

Several weeks later, I received a letter from a college friend describing an abrupt change that had taken place in his life. Though he had also been devoted to yoga, Larry shared how he walked into a church and heard an audible voice say, "Jesus is the only way!" At the same time, the Holy Spirit fell on him and he claimed he was "born again" (John 3:3).

At first, I assumed this was another way of describing what Hindus call "Samadhi," or New Agers call "Christ Consciousness." But Larry insisted it was completely different.

The Far Eastern view claims a latent "spark of divinity" exists *within* all human beings that must be "awakened" to achieve God-consciousness. However, the Biblical view explains because of our fallen state God is separate from us, and that spiritual rebirth comes only when we are washed clean from our sins by the blood of Jesus. Then the Spirit of God enters into our hearts *from without*. At that point, we are brought into true oneness with God.

Larry's words were emphatic, "Mike, you have to go through the cross. Jesus is the way to eternal life."

I wrote my college friend back explaining that I was happy he'd taken the path of Christianity but that my beliefs embraced all religions. Strangely, though, I couldn't get Larry's words off my mind.

After several weeks, I decided I needed to deal with this issue. Dismissing Christianity without fully exploring its claims would be inconsistent with my claim of being open-minded. I also concluded, *If Jesus really was who He claimed to be, and if I don't test His teachings, I might miss the very thing I've been passionately pursuing.* So one morning, instead of following my usual yoga routine, I decided to...

Dedicate One Day to the Lord Jesus Christ!

As usual, I got up about 3:15 a.m. Normally, in the ashram, by 3:30 we would be doing Hatha Yoga. Then from 4:30 a.m. to 6:30 a.m. we would sit motionless doing various kinds of meditation.

That morning, though, I decided to break from the ordinary. Retreating into a room by myself, I dedicated the entire day to this "One" Larry claimed was the only "...mediator between God and men..." (1 Timothy 2:5b).

Quite a few times I confessed, "Lord Jesus, I commit this day to You. I believe, if You're real and if You're the Savior of the world, You will show me today."

Then I began reading the Bible, spending most of my time immersed in the Gospel of John and the book of The Revelation. I was especially stirred by the latter with its powerful, prophetic visions, especially those verses foretelling that final conflict between the forces of good and evil at a battleground in Israel called Armageddon.

As I read, I kept praying. Even though I was fully expecting some kind of powerful, supernatural visitation initially, like a vision or an audible voice, it didn't happen that way. For about eight hours that day I continued seeking the Lord Jesus. Then, right when I was about to give up, I arrived at my...

Moment of Destiny!

Kent Sullivan was a senior at the University of South Florida, however, his educational pursuits had not brought him lasting answers. A few months prior, he was an avid follower of the teachings of Yogananda, a well-known Indian guru who authored *The*

Autobiography of a Yogi. Kent was respected in the yoga community but though we had never met, I heard that he had abruptly switched from to Christianity. Unknown to me, he was part of the very prayer group that was praying for me.

That divinely appointed day, Kent decided to wash his dirty clothes.

He got about halfway through the door of the laundromat when he felt impressed by the Holy Spirit, "Don't go in there. I have something else for you to do. Get back in your van and drive where I lead you."

Kent had no idea that about two miles away, the yoga teacher who had been the object of his prayers for several weeks was hitchhiking, trying to catch a ride to the University of South Florida.

Even though I had spent the majority of the day focusing on the claims of Christianity, I left the ashram that afternoon to conduct one of my classes still praying that if Jesus was "the Way," He would reveal Himself. As Kent approached me in his van, he felt compelled by God to pull over and pick me up.

As I opened the door, my heart started racing, because taped to the ceiling of Kent's van was a large picture of Jesus. I knew this was no mere *coincidence*; it was a *God-incidence.*

A few moments later, Kent asked, "Have you ever experienced Jesus coming into your heart?"

Surprising him with my eagerness, I responded, "No, but when can I? I've been praying about the experience all day long."

He said, "You can come to our prayer meeting tonight."

"I don't want to wait for a prayer meeting," I replied. "I've been praying all day. If this is a valid approach to God, I want to experience Jesus right now."

Thrilled over my high level of interest, Kent pulled out of the traffic into the first parking lot he could find. Carefully, he took me step-by-step through Scripture, explaining the true, Biblical path to

God. Then, right when I was on the verge of embracing the Christian approach, my own intellect became....

A Very Challenging Stumbling Block!

If I was going to be sincere during this time of prayer, I decided I had to first deal with some Biblical doctrines that troubled me. One by one, I brought them up.

Each time Kent would reassure me with the words, "Don't worry about that. Just try Jesus!"

Then I pinpointed certain Far Eastern beliefs I felt I could never give up, like reincarnation.

Kent kept emphasizing, "Don't be concerned about those things; just try Jesus!"

Kent understood my apprehension, but he also knew that if we got involved in some deep discussion over doctrinal issues, I might turn my heart away from the experience of Jesus altogether. So he kept emphasizing the essential thing: that if I truly experienced Jesus coming into my heart, many of my questions would automatically be answered.

That logic persuaded me. I was so hungry to know God, temporarily setting my intellect aside wasn't too much to ask. Just repeating a single petition seemed *far too simple*—but again, I was willing to try.

We bowed our heads together and I prayed, "Lord Jesus, come into my heart. Wash me in Your blood. Forgive me of my sins. By faith, I receive Your gift of eternal life. Fill me with Your presence and Your love. I acknowledge that You died for the sins of the world and that You arose from the dead. I accept You now as Lord of my life."

I felt a warm sensation in the deepest part of my heart. It wasn't an overpowering supernatural sensation, but I knew something dramatic had transpired, different than anything I'd ever experienced before.

The Bible calls this wonderful experience "the washing of regeneration and the renewing of the Holy Spirit" (Titus 3:5b). Though

I still had many questions, the inner *knowing* that I had finally been restored to a right relationship with God filled me up. I was confident that if I died, I would spend eternity in heaven.

For several days following, I announced to my students that I'd finally encountered Ultimate Reality. I admitted that I had been wrong in my previous world view, that I never encountered the true Spirit of God until I went through Jesus, and that consequently, all of my yoga classes would be discontinued.

Though such a sudden change was shocking to my students, many of them trusted my insights and became followers of Jesus as well. As Plato once said, "God is truth and light his shadow." Because the God of heaven was finally overshadowing me with His personal and gracious influence, the light of truth began shining more and more with every passing day.

ABOUT THE CONTRIBUTOR

Mike Shreve has traveled as a teacher of God's Word with a healing and prophetic emphasis, ministering around the world since 1970. He has written fourteen books including *In Search of the True Light* (a comparison of over 20 religions), *65 Promises from God for Your Child*, and *Who Am I? Dynamic Declarations of Who You Are in Christ*.

He and his wife, Elizabeth, pastor The Sanctuary in Cleveland, Tennessee, and have two children, Zion Seth and Destiny Hope. www.shreveministries.org / www.thetruelight.net

CHAPTER 26

A MIRACLE IN THE DARKNESS

Patty Mason

Then they cry unto the Lord in their trouble, and he saveth them out of their distresses. He sent his word, and healed them, and delivered them from their destructions
(Psalm 107:19-20, KJV).

I remember the day I began to fall into the pit of depression.

I was standing on stage in Dallas, Texas, before an audience of thousands being recognized for one of the highest levels of achievement in the company. Yet, as I stood on that stage surrounded by joyful celebration I found myself thinking: *Is this all there is?*

Abruptly, everything I had poured myself into that year became worthless. As I stood on that stage listening to the loud music and thunderous applause, I began to think to myself: *Is this what I shipped my children off to a babysitter for? Is this what I did the changing of the guard with my husband for?* In the middle of what should have been a magnificent moment, my soul began to plummet from that momentary high to a miserable point of confusion.

In the days that followed the conference, I began to turn my back on everything and everyone I thought would bring me happiness. I found fault and became critical of everything my husband and children did or didn't do. The career I once loved became pointless.

I wandered through each day like a blind beggar, not knowing what I was begging for. I couldn't get over the overwhelming feelings of sadness and worthlessness. Each day became increasingly harder, every minute increasingly darker.

It was ironic; I was 35 years old and had everything this world deems valid. I had a husband who loved me, three beautiful, healthy children, a nice home and a successful career. I had achieved everything I set out to accomplish since I was 18 years old. Yet, I was miserable. I had everything I dreamed of, yet none of it brought me the happiness and fulfillment I craved.

I made every effort I could think of to find answers, to get better, to stop feeling the way I did; but nothing helped. It was difficult for me to come to the conclusion I couldn't help myself or free myself from the emotional turmoil. I had to look beyond myself in order to find relief. I had to tell people something was wrong and I needed help.

At first, I was afraid of what others would think. I wasn't sure how they would react when I told them about the depression. *Would they judge me, criticize me and condemn my feelings? Would they stop loving me, or stop being my friend?*

Up until this point, no one, not even my husband, knew about the pain I was going through. So, when I finally found the courage to start talking about the depression, to my surprise, no one judged, criticized or condemned. Instead, they simply didn't believe me.

I felt cheated and betrayed by the people I loved. I began to push them away. I never felt lonelier. Even my sweet husband didn't get it. Almost every night I tried to tell him that something was wrong.

Every time he would respond by saying, "Oh, you'll get over it."

My husband loved me, I knew that, but he didn't understand what I was going through.

After I exhausted all efforts to find help through family and friends, I turned to the medical profession for relief. With phonebook in hand, I began to call one doctor's office after another on the mission that if I could get some pills, I'd be fine. I had a get-fixed-quick mentality. I knew I needed help, but I figured a simple prescription would do the trick.

I went down the list, calling doctor after doctor, only to hear responses like: "I'm sorry, we don't take your insurance," or, "I'm sorry, we don't handle that kind of depression."

In less than an hour, I had made my way through the entire list of professional doctors I thought could help me. Finally, when I dialed the last number on the list, a kind woman answered the phone and listened patiently to my heartfelt plea.

She told me at the end of our conversation, "I'm sorry, but we can't help you."

As I hung up the phone a thought swiftly dawned on me, *No one can help me — I'm utterly alone. This is never going to end.* It was at that moment the darkness went deeper and thoughts of suicide entered my mind.

Hopelessness turned into utter desperation when I realized I was completely alone in my struggle. I had to do something to end the suffering, so I convinced myself that everyone would be better off without me.

I knew committing suicide was wrong and my actions would hurt my family tremendously. The darkness was so thick and heavy. I didn't see another answer. Death seemed to be the only way out of the darkness.

In the days that followed, I found myself doing something I never did. I prayed.

I didn't know God. I grew up being told about a God who lived in heaven. To me, God was nothing more than showing up for church on Sunday, and sitting through an hour or two filled with nothing more than a meaningless structured agenda. We sang a few songs to no one in particular. We listened to someone we didn't know talk. We put money in a basket, offered up shallow, superficial prayers, received a blessing from the host and then left only to return the following Sunday to do it all over again.

As a child my exposure to God and church was punitive. When my parents took me to church, I remember the priest standing up front calling all of us sinners. I didn't understand the allegation, so his accusations only made me mad. Church intimated me. In my eyes, it was a place of burdensome rules and mechanical rituals. When I became old enough to make my own decisions, I stopped going.

Praying to some God I didn't know felt foreign, but I didn't know what else to do.

I was desperate to end the pain, but I didn't pray for God's help, mercy or healing. Nor did I call on Him to find answers. Rather, I asked him to take my life.

Every morning I prayed for the insanity to end. Every night I prayed to never wake up.

The most crucial point came on December 12, 1996. On this day I knew I couldn't go on one more day. When I awoke that morning, I felt angry. I lay in bed, staring at the ceiling as if I were looking toward heaven and thought, *Why won't you let me die?*

I got up reluctantly and stepped into the shower. Hot tears of frustration poured from my eyes. Naked, drenched and ashamed, I felt like I had been ground into the ashes from which I came. There was nothing left. I had reached the end of myself.

"I have nowhere else to go but to You," I said to God. "You have to do something. No one can help me; only You can help me! Please, help me."

This was a completely different cry for relief and freedom. I didn't ask Him to end my life. I asked Him for much more; I asked for a miracle. I knew as I cried out this was a desperate make-it-or-break-it moment. If God didn't do something that day, I feared I would.

My plea was not an ultimatum. I wasn't bargaining with God. I had hit rock bottom. I had nowhere else to go.

Suddenly, through the sobs, I heard what sounded like a faint voice, "Go to MOPS." (MOPS stands for Mothers of Preschoolers.)

At first, I moaned. I didn't want to be around people. I didn't want to pretend everything was fine. As my emotions tried to persuade me to stay home, I heard it again, "Go to MOPS."

Once I arrived at the meeting, I put on the mask that communicated to those around me I was doing well. I was really struggling, but the last thing I wanted to do was let the ladies know about the emotional turmoil. I certainly didn't want them to know about my suicidal tendencies.

Toward the latter part of our MOPS gathering, the speaker came forward and stood behind the podium. She shared about what it's like to have a lack of joy and no real purpose in life. She didn't specifically talk about depression, but what she was saying fell right in line with what I was feeling. The real crux of her message was about finding joy and purpose in life, and that the only way to find pure joy was through Jesus.

As she stepped from the platform, I watched her make her way to the back of the room. Without thinking, I got up and quickly made my way to the back. She looked at me and smiled warmly. Honestly, I don't remember how the conversation started, but before I knew it, I was dumping my life at her feet.

Without warning an emotional dam broke, and I found myself rambling and sobbing uncontrollably. She didn't say a word as I continued to ramble. I couldn't control what was happening. I couldn't stop crying and I couldn't stop talking — not even when I realized that every woman in the room had turned around to stare at us.

But at that point, I didn't care who knew or what anyone thought. I needed help. This woman seemed to have the answer.

She listened quietly for several minutes. Then, without a word, she reached out and touched me on my left arm. When she did, the hysterics stopped. The crying and run-on sentences instantly stopped. There was no more nausea in the pit of my stomach. The dark cloud that had been my constant companion was gone. The heaviness lifted — everything — all of the darkness that had consumed my life was completely gone.

My spirit and soul felt light, like they had taken on wings and could fly around the room. For the first time in my life, I felt free.

I was stunned and completely amazed. I stood there and stared at her, frozen by the event that had just taken place. At that moment, I had no idea if she knew or understood what had happened. She still hadn't said a word. Yet, there was something about her I hadn't noticed before. As I looked into her eyes, I could see great love and tender compassion.

As I turned and walked away, my mind filled with thoughts. I struggled to comprehend the experience.

I knew this woman didn't possess the power to heal me. Yet, as I remembered the prayer I prayed that morning, a sense of peace washed over me. There was no other explanation. It was a miracle. Even though I didn't fully understand what had happened, I was convinced the power I felt rush through me was God answering my desperate plea for help.

Prior to the depression, I didn't know Jesus as my personal Savior, but since that day He has changed my heart, my old attitudes and my life in ways I never dreamed possible. He took all my striving, all my efforts to find happiness and self-worth and offered me something of greater value. I was living in despair, but when Jesus touched me everything changed. In the blink of an eye, I went from having no hope to having hope and a future.

The full version of this story is found in *Finally Free: Breaking the Bonds of Depression without Drugs*. Now available on <u>Amazon.com</u>, at <u>www.libertyinchristministries.com</u> or wherever books are sold.

ABOUT THE CONTRIBUTOR

A Nashville, Tennessee, resident and the founder of Liberty in Christ Ministries, Patty Mason is a wife and mother who found hope and healing when Jesus reached into her well of depression and set her free. Since 1997, she has been sharing her story of God's redeeming grace on numerous television and radio programs such as CBN's *700*

Club. Her story has also been published in several articles, blogs and books such as *Unshackled and Free* and *LifeWay Magazine*.

As an author, speaker and Bible teacher, Patty has reached audiences in 170 countries through Sisters on Assignment, Christian TV, Salem Communication's Light Source, and as the host of Joyful Living Radio.

Her books include *Transformed by Desire: A Journey of Awakening to Life and Love; Finally Free: Breaking the Bonds of Depression Without Drugs; Experiencing Joy: Strategies for Living a Joy Filled Life,* and her newest book, *The Power of Hope.*

For more information about Patty Mason, her books or ministry visit: www.libertyinchristministries.com

CHAPTER 27

MR. INSPIRATION

Bob "Mr. Inspiration" Wieland, as written by Katelyn Rose Gondell

*Greater love hath no man than this, that a man lay down his life
for his friends*
(John 15:13, KJV).

In 1966, the number one television show in America was Batman, and I lived in a complex which my buddies and I referred to as "The Bat-cave." Let's just say, myself and the other twelve men that lived there were a little "rough around the edges." I lived in the attic where there were literally bats flying around my ceiling.

One day there was a knock on our door. It was some folks from an organization called Campus Crusade for Christ, founded by Dr. Bill Bright. The team came by our apartment in La Crosse, Wisconsin, to ask if they could share some good news with us. We had no idea what it was about but we were willing to hear what they had to say. With the help of some little booklets, they began to talk with us about an opportunity for salvation.

This was all new to me; I'd spent most of my life focused on sports and we weren't exactly a church-going family. I didn't really give much time to thinking about any spiritual laws before then. But basically, in so many words, they expressed that you cannot save yourself. They drew two circles; one with Jesus Christ and Bob Wieland inside together, and the other with Jesus Christ inside the circle and Bob Wieland outside.

The question was, "Which would best describe you?"

So I said, "I guess I'd be outside the circle."

And they said, "Well, here's how you can get inside the circle: by realizing you're a sinner and that you cannot save yourself, and by confessing this simple sinner's prayer."

That night, on November 28, 1966, I opened up the door to my heart and invited Jesus Christ to come into my life as my personal Lord and Savior. Then, I lived happily ever after.

Oh, wait a second, I almost forgot. There were a couple of challenges along the way: the first was deciding what professional baseball team I was going to sign with and then I had one other draft offer — that was the United States Army.

So when I ended up getting blown up and remaining unconscious for about a week, the very first thing I recalled was that evening at "The Bat-cave" when I invited Christ into my life. In essence, I recalled Jesus saying, *I will never leave you nor forsake you* (Hebrews 13:5). That was very prevalent in my heart, in my mind and in my spirit during that time as I floated in and out of consciousness.

During this season, I wrote an interesting letter to my parents:

"June 14, 1969

Dear Mom and Dad,

I'm in the hospital. Everything is going to be O.K. The people here are taking good care of me. It won't be that much of an adjustment, maybe I can help you out in real estate.

Love, Bob.

P.S. I think I lost my legs."

Now, wouldn't you think someone would know if they had lost their legs? But as I floated in and out of consciousness, these were the only words I had to offer them.

See, not only was I blown up, I was zipped up in a body bag and carried to the chopper. I was pronounced DOA, Dead On Arrival, when they brought me into the hospital, and it was only by the grace of God that my life was spared. I should've been dead in less than a minute, but God is still in the miracle-making business today. I don't know how it all worked out, but that's why they call it a miracle.

The doctors told me that because of the seriousness of my injuries, I should plan on being in the hospital for a year and a half to two years or more. Much to everyone's surprise, I forgot to listen and basically left the hospital within six weeks' time.

I told the doctors, somewhat jokingly, that someday I would break the world record in the bench press. This didn't make any sense to them, so they sent me to the psychiatrist. We talked for 20 to 30 minutes before I got him straightened out.

"What are you smiling about," he asked me, "are you trying to cover up what happened?"

He just couldn't understand where my peace came from. I told him that he could find me on ward 4CD if he ever needed any help. Eight years later, I did break the world record, *against able-bodied athletes*, and four times since.

You see, another scripture which relates to my life is in the book of Luke, the first chapter, verse 37, which of course says, *"For with God nothing shall be impossible."* I believe that 100%, and that's why God has allowed me to do the things I've done. I always knew, beyond a shadow of a doubt, that I would finish whatever I started, because that's what God says.

In 1981, the Lord placed it on my heart to walk across America on my arms. I didn't want to tell anyone initially because people would think I was nuts, but I really felt compelled to do it. Besides telling one or two people, I kept it to myself.

I began training up and down the mountains of Southern California. I would run up Santa Anita Boulevard on my arms, which is a pretty steep hill, and then I'd go train at the beach. I'd train from 'Gladstone's 4 Fish' to the farthest hill in Santa Monica and back. People didn't have a clue as to what I was doing, until I took off. That's when all of the national coverage began.

I started my journey across the United States of America on September 8, 1982. Since my story had gotten so much exposure, hundreds and hundreds of people came out to meet me, shake my hand, pray, get an autograph, etc. There would be times where, in two or three hours, I'd only go one step because I was ministering to the people.

My prayer every day would be, *"Lord, send people into my life that need to know more about you."*

Every day something was happening, I guarantee it. Rain, snow, sleet or shine, I was out there walking. I started with a whole team of folks; that lasted about a year. Afterward, I went on by myself for a good five and a half months.

In Las Cruces, New Mexico, a man who saw the story on television came to join the journey. His name was Marshall. He was a Christian, and his heart was very moved by what he'd seen. Marshall resigned from his job to go with me the rest of the way and when I look back on it, he really was sent by God to help.

When I had some quiet time to myself I would pray — throughout the day, before we started every morning and basically every night. It was at this point in time, in Joplin, Missouri, that the Lord impressed it upon my heart to switch directions. In the natural this did not make any sense.

We were heading east to Washington, D.C., we'd been out there for two and a half years, and *now* I felt led to change directions and head north towards Canada? Marshall initially got a little upset about it, but he came back and continued to support me.

We headed north and for 15 days nothing happened.

My mind was screaming at this point, *Was this, in fact, what I was supposed to do? How come nothing was happening?* I knew eventually I'd find out what the purpose of all of this was, and 15 days later I did.

Up until that moment in my life I'd been trying to piece together what had really happened that day in Vietnam. Since I had been unconscious for almost seven days, I couldn't recall a lot. I'd gathered information from medical records and by talking to the actual doctors and nurses at the Twelfth Evacuation Hospital in Cu Chi, Vietnam, I found out as much I could.

Eighteen years later, as I'm walking across America, I would receive some of the missing pieces I'd been looking for. Fifteen days after we changed direction, a man drove up next to me on the side of the road.

"Hey, are you that veteran walking across America?"

"Yep, that's me."

"Well, God speed to you, man."

We chatted for a few minutes. It turned out we both served in Vietnam the same year: 1969. In fact, we'd both served under the 25th infantry division, but there in Miller, Missouri, population 748, our paths happened to cross. After some small talk, he was on his way.

Fifteen or 20 minutes later, he came back with his scrapbook. I thought it was an interesting scenario for him to leave and come back. I'd been out there for two years and four months — 10 minutes wasn't going to goof up the project — so right there on the side of the road we decided to take a minute to look over some pictures.

When he opened up the scrapbook, I recognized the very first picture. "Ralph!" I said.

What are the odds that a picture of the North Vietnamese soldier we had captured was in this man's scrapbook?

That's when he asked me the question.

"Wait a second," he said, "is there any remote possibility that you were a combat medic in a place called the Hobo Woods?"

"Yes, I was," I replied.

"Herc," he said, "you're still alive! I'm the guy that carried you to the helicopter."

Then it dawned on me; this was Dennis Cooper, my very dear friend.

There's so much more to the story. On June 14, 1969, when I was injured, word came back from the Twelfth Evacuation Hospital to the field. The men, including Dennis, got word that "Herc" (short for Hercules) had died.

In the minds of the remaining men of the 1st Platoon, Alpha Company, 2nd of the 14th Battalion, 25th Infantry Division, this was their confirmation that I was killed. In Dennis Cooper's mind, I couldn't have been "Herc," because he'd gotten word that I had died.

I didn't recognize him at first either; when we had fought together, he was about six foot one and maybe 155 pounds. Now, he was still six foot one, but about 295 pounds. But it was him, Dennis Cooper, and that meeting brought a lot of closure to the whole story for me.

From a technical standpoint I might never have gotten my legs blown off if I had run in the opposite direction for safety, but then there's that commercial with the Marines that asks the question, "Which way would you run?"

That's a very heavy question, and it's not a really popular concept. A lot of people aren't interested in answering that, but to me it's a very important statement. Nobody forced me to go up there; it was my choice. It was a big risk, but when you're tight like that with your fellow soldiers, it's automatic. You do what you have to do.

I hear a lot of people say they want to help veterans out, but what it really comes down to is this: just be sincere. Any veteran that is seriously injured needs more help than what meets the eye. To really think about the severity of the situation, let's put it this way — we have as many challenges as the next person, multiplied by 100. In this great country, we have so much to rejoice about and we must continue to love and respect our soldiers, because it's the right thing to do.

Three years, eight months and six days after leaving Knott's Berry Farm in California, approximately 4,900,016 steps later, I ended the walk across America with some of my fellow soldiers at wall 22 west, line 47. There lies the name of our fallen soldier, Jerome Lubeno, whose life I had tried to save.

What an absolute honor it was to visit with President Ronald Reagan when we reached Washington, D.C.

I told the President, "I hope, in some small way, I have been an inspiration to you."

Do you know what he said? Well, he didn't say anything; he just teared up. I guess that's how he came up with my nickname, "Mr. Inspiration."

Most people haven't had to fight for our freedom. For those of us who have had to fight for it, life has a flavor the protected don't often comprehend or fully understand. I go around smiling every day because I enjoy being alive. I enjoy that God has a specific plan for my life, and to continue to fulfill that plan just brings a very special joy to my heart.

Of course, I have challenges. I have a ton of challenges, but the Word of God strengthens my faith. In Proverbs chapter 30, verse five, it says, *"Every word of God is pure: he is a shield unto those that put their trust in him."* In my everyday living, as a general rule of thumb I'm a pretty happy guy because AOA is *always* better than DOA. *Always.*

ABOUT THE CONTRIBUTOR

Born and raised in Milwaukee, Wisconsin, Bob Wieland attended the University of Wisconsin. As a talented baseball player, he was negotiating a deal with the Philadelphia Phillies when instead he was drafted into the Army.

Once serving, Bob chose to become a combat medic. In June of 1969, in the middle of the jungles of Vietnam, Bob was serving with 1st Platoon Alpha Company, 2nd of the 14th battalion, 25th infantry division, on a search and destroy mission. He and his squad were told to go into an enemy stronghold, a place called the Ho Bo Woods (with the reputation of being the third most dangerous area in Vietnam), and turn the place into a parking lot. Much to their surprise, it was their *own* company that was ambushed instead.

Before he knew it, there were explosives going off, men getting injured and killed, and everyone was yelling and screaming for help. Running up to assist his fallen comrades, Bob stepped on and detonated an 82 mm mortar, a round designed to destroy tanks. When he hit that booby trap, as Bob describes it, his legs went one way, and his life went in another direction.

Bob, who has always refused to quit, inspires and encourages others to do the same. When he began his recovery, he could hardly lift five pounds, but after intensive rehabilitation he moved to California and began lifting weights and competing with the world's best *able-bodied athletes*. Eight years later, he would break the official world record in the bench press at the United States Power Lifting Championships.

Bob's love for sports continued throughout his life as he moved from completing one extreme goal to the next, no matter how long it took him. In 1981, Bob got the idea to walk across America on his arms while raising money for Vietnam War veterans. In 1982, Bob departed on his cross country journey, from Knott's Berry Farm in California, to Washington, D.C., which took him three years, eight months and six days to complete.

Toward the end of his journey, Bob was invited to the White House by President Reagan. There, in the Oval Office, President Reagan gave him the title, "Mr. Inspiration." After meeting with the president on May 14th, 1986, Bob and his comrades joined together again for a very significant visit to the Vietnam Memorial. Bob Wieland was one of 15 soldiers in America honored as one of the Grand Marshalls for the unveiling of the Vietnam Memorial.

Since then, Bob has biked across America and back, competed in numerous triathlons, and become the only double amputee to complete the rugged Iron Man Triathlon in Kona, Hawaii, without the use of a wheelchair. Bob later enrolled at California State University in Los

Angeles, majoring in physical education with a secondary interest in exercise physiology.

In 1989, he joined the staff of the Green Bay Packers as a strength and flexibility coach. The NFLPA named Bob Wieland, "The Most Courageous Man in America," and the Vietnam Veteran Foundation honored him with the title, "National Vietnam Veteran of the Year."

Bob Wieland is also the spokesperson for the Los Angeles Unified School District. This school district consists of approximately 800,000 students, is comprised of 4,000 schools, and offers over 50 programs per year.

As a keynote speaker throughout the country, Bob Wieland continues to inspire, motivate and touch the lives of many. To find out more, visit bobwieland.net or contact Winning at the Race of Life © at (626) 292-2258.

You can read more of his amazing testimony in Bob's book, *One Step at a Time: The Remarkable True Story of Bob Wieland.*

CHAPTER 28

MY JOURNEY FROM CORRUPTION TO REDEMPTION

Nizar Terzian

For I know the thoughts that I think toward you, saith the Lord, thoughts of peace, and not of evil, to give you an expected end (Jeremiah 29:11, KJV).

Introduction

My name is Nizar Terzian. My wife is Emma Boghossian and we have three wonderful boys, Arsen, 18, Arees, 14, and Masees, 9. We are originally from Armenia and we worked and lived in many cities before we landed and settled in Canada on July 25, 2006. We emigrated from United Arab Emirates where we had worked for many years in Dubai and Abu Dhabi.

I was born again in 1995 and since then, every time we move to a new city, our first priority is to find a church. We visited many churches in Canada when we first arrived.

I remember there was this one in North York, the usher at the door warmly greeted us saying, "Emma and Nizar, we saw your testimony on TV. You are the one who tried to kill his father twice."

I immediately thought, *Probably it's better not to share that part of my testimony if that is what people will remember.*

But yes, I did try to kill my father twice. For that very evil act and many others, as you will read later, I should have been killed or at least jailed. But God had another plan for my life, and here is my story.

Childhood

I was born in Baghdad on July 4, 1970, the first child to my parents. I have one sister and one brother. My mom was a doctor and my father was a senior architect. He designed many landmarks including a cathedral and a few palaces for the Iraqi president at the time, Saddam Hussein.

I saw Saddam a few times. I sat on his lap when I was little boy.

As a family, we traveled a lot and we had almost everything. My dad raised me to be a strong man and independent individual, to make my own decisions and be responsible, but at the same time he was obsessed with controlling everything and everyone around him. That, of course, included me. My dad was always right, even when he knew he was wrong.

Teenage Years

My childhood was a delight until I hit teenage years when my father realized I am not a little boy anymore. That innocent father-son relationship turned to be the worst nightmare for both of us.

He wanted to keep controlling my life. He thought he should know who I talked to, where I went, what I did. He listened to my phone calls, read my daily journals and searched my room every day to the point that I locked my bedroom. He even questioned my friends about me, and that was very embarrassing for me at the time.

Eventually, 12 to 13 years of a good father-son relationship was damaged for his lack of trust and obsession to control. At 14, we stopped communicating altogether. We couldn't talk for five minutes without triggering a fight. Sometimes, months would pass without even saying a greeting to each other although we lived in the same house.

I started smoking at 12. At 15, I started gambling and carrying a gun. When I turned 17, I played Russian roulette and probably committed every sin you could imagine except killing someone with my own hands. I was a playboy. I smuggled illegal trades, including weapons. And, yes, twice I put a gun to my father's head and my mom's tears were the only reason I didn't shoot him.

On a bright note, and with all that going in my life, I was an A+ student, a talented soccer player and a person who had a big heart to help anyone in need.

The First Turning Point

The car accident happened when I turned 16. I was driving my father's car, which was a gift from Saddam Hussein to my father after he finished building one of his palaces in Baghdad, and got into a very serious accident. His car was destroyed.

I was driving on a highway and, for some reason, a tourist bus in front of me decided to make a U-turn. I couldn't stop my car and ended up underneath the bus. I towed the car home only to face my angry father; of course, he was informed.

I approached him to apologize and explain what had happened but he never looked at me.

He started swearing, pointing at the car and saying, "You will fix it!" Then he went inside.

Probably, that was the time I most needed my father's support, maybe a hug or at least look at me and check if I am still in one piece. None of that happened.

My mother was standing in a corner and crying. She knew what was coming next.

I left home and decided to do anything to fix that car. I started working after school and nights. I worked as a taxi driver. I bought and sold stuff in scrap yards, or any small business that could generate money. The taxi driver was an interesting job because I met so many different kinds of people.

One time I had a drunk passenger who said, "This is a free ride boy; you better know that," but he paid five times the fare when I dropped him off.

Anyway, in spite of all those struggles in my life, I finished high school with a 98% average — third out of my fellow graduates — and went to the University of Architecture.

For many years, home was like a motel for me: the place where I least wanted to go. I lived mostly outside, with friends or on my own. The path I was walking exposed me to so many good, bad, dangerous and adventurous venues in life. I got to know so many people from different walks of life, from the President's son to VIPs to the simple laborers on the street. I could get you out of jail with a phone call, or send you in with one!

My life was different than most of my peers. I was working very hard, partying very hard, gambling, smoking, drinking and dating girls, but there was one secret habit that I kept doing almost every night: I had a little green Bible under my pillow which I read every night, though I never remembered one single verse.

The Second Turning Point

In 1992, the whole economy crashed after the war (Desert Storm). My businesses were going down and many negative things happened in my life. Brothers of one of my girlfriends threatened to kill me if I didn't convert to their religion and marry their sister. My best friend was killed by the secret police. Everything was a complete mess, and I can see now that was my rock bottom.

Did I think of suicide? Yes, I did, but I didn't buy that idea because it wouldn't help. I am not a loser and would never be one. I've always believed, "quitters don't win and winners don't quit." I like to face challenges and win. So I kept going and fighting the odds.

It was at that point of desperation when I met Emma.

Emma's parents and mine knew each other well from the Armenian community. Her father was a general in the army and one of the best surgeons in the country. For me, I had heard of Emma but we had never met in person before.

The first time we talked was when Emma called me one day trying to be the peacemaker for one of my ex-girlfriends. She asked if that girl and I could reconcile. I remember telling her that it was none of her business and I hung up the phone. But she called once more asking to give my ex one last chance. I agreed.

How God Used Emma & the Pentecostal Church in Jordan

I didn't usually attend family-oriented social events, but Emma invited me to one of those events to meet my ex. I decided to go with one thing on my mind: send a clear message to my ex — "it was over."

I didn't know anyone in that ballroom, so I ended up spending the whole time with Emma. For some reason, I told Emma what I was going through and a little bit about my struggles. Her reaction was a surprise to me. It was the first time I didn't hear back any condemning words. She didn't preach to me; she just listened.

She had heard a lot about this nasty guy, "Nizar." Some people even told her it's safer for her to stay away from me.

But she listened to my story and then said, "If you want, I can pray for you, and there is a Church in Jordan that can pray for you, too. Why don't you give God a chance?"

Those words were very strange to my ears. All I'd heard until that day were discouraging and condemning comments. Negativity was clouding my entire life. No one ever told me, "Give God a chance," or, "I can pray for you." On the other hand, those strange words were "sweet" to my ears as well, because I'd tried almost everything in my life — money, power, connections, partying and drugs, but I never had one peaceful day. I had so much yet I always felt empty.

So I said, "I will give Emma's God a chance. Let's see what this God can do."

Over the following days, a few things unexpectedly and miraculously changed. I felt the intervention of a supernatural power in many areas of my life in a way that I had never experienced before. I felt the hands of God surrounding me, keeping me safe from those who were after my life, and I could sleep in peace for the first time. The fear of the unknown diminished. At that point, I instantly knew that was Emma's God.

Emma's God was the one fighting on my behalf as it says in Exodus 14:14, *"The Lord shall fight for you, and ye shall hold your peace."* That very day I decided two things: 1) My lifestyle must change (and it did), and 2) Emma would be my wife (and it happened).

The Wedding & Escaping from Iraq

Emma and I knew it was a miracle, and our relationship was getting stronger and closer. We got to know each other in more depth over the next few months. We became engaged in November 1993, and I should confess the following eight months of engagement were probably one of the most challenging times in my life.

I wasn't yet born-again though I was struggling to unplug myself from my past, from everything and everyone I knew. I was trying to be a better person but that was mission-impossible without a divine power, the help of the Holy Spirit.

Anyway, both of us knew we were on the right path. Hundreds of Godly men and women in that church in Jordan were praying for us. Their lead Pastors were in consistent contact with us, especially with Emma, pouring Godly wisdom, prayers and encouragement into us as we were taking slow but steady steps toward our marriage and future plans.

If there is one word to define this period, it is *"iron sharpeneth iron; so a man sharpeneth the countenance of his friend"* (Proverbs 27:17). Both Emma and I have strong personalities and strong opinions; although we share the same Armenian Orthodox background, we lived in two different environments. Our determination to overcome all challenges and obstacles before us and "give God a chance" allowed us to move forward.

We marked August 25 for our wedding and started planning for our big day. For me, I could see my life moving in the right direction; we were building trust in each other and drawing our future dreams.

August 25 was the big day and it finally arrived, but it wasn't less challenging. Emma and I were fighting on the phone and we almost called it off. Then the photographer called before noon apologizing that he couldn't make it because his cousin had passed away. To top it up, one of my dreams was to get married in a classic car; I'd arranged a 1934 Rolls Royce and it was stolen on our wedding day.

For the wedding reception itself, I had to arrange for bodyguards because there were two attempts on my life the weeks before our wedding and I was still receiving those threats. We had over 700 guests and it must be safe. In spite of all those challenges, the day was a blast for everyone and everything went smoothly. This was another sign for me that Emma's God was still working!

Immediately after our wedding, we decided we must leave the country. I used my contacts to get a fake passport because my name was on the blacklist for many reasons. We got that passport after a few months and drove almost 18 hours to Jordan.

At the border we faced another challenge. The immigration officer stared at me and it seemed like he recognized me.

I turned to Emma and said, "Probably we are done," but just as he approached us he got called to the operations room, and we rushed quickly to get the exit stamps on our passports and move out.

Arriving in Jordan & Visiting the Church for the First Time

The next morning we arrived to Amman, Jordan, very exhausted but extremely happy that we had made the journey. Pastor Sam was the first person to greet us at our new residence. (He is the lead Pastor of the Pentecostal church that was praying for us.) We had a very peaceful time together and he spared no time in praying for our future, and giving thanks to "Emma's God" for our safe travel.

We settled down in Amman for a couple of days and then Emma asked if we could visit that church and thank them for all their prayers.

I said, "Okay," so we showed up the following Sunday.

It was the first time for me to be in a Pentecostal church. I was looking around to figure out what was happening--people lifting their hands, laying their hands on one another, praising and worshipping on the other side...

The whole thing was new to me and I told Emma, "These are bunch of crazy people; I am out."

She said nothing and off we left.

Visiting the Church a Second Time

We started looking for jobs over the next two weeks, and meeting friends and family, but there was a gentle voice in my ears all the time saying, *"Go back to that church."*

I told Emma, "Let's visit them again. I know those people were praying for us the last couple of years and it wasn't nice that we left without even thanking them."

So we went to the church the following Sunday. Pastor Sam was preaching about the prodigal son. He said things about my life even Emma didn't know at the time, and I was questioning, *How on earth does he know all this stuff?*

Toward the end of his service he asked if anyone wanted to invite Jesus to change their life. All I know was that I was crying at the altar for the next few hours.

Twenty-four years of corruption were redeemed that very minute! I left church that day a new creation. All old things were gone and I was a new person (2 Corinthians 5:17). I knew it and I felt it. It was the best feeling with abundant joy that no words can explain.

On that day, I started remembering what I had read years ago from that little green book, The Bible. My memory was sort of restored. That is why I always believe there is no good or bad time to read the Bible, the living Word of God.

I remember my first prayer that day was, "God, I am a sinner; forgive me." Then I prayed, "God, I forgive my father and my family for everything they did to me. I forgive everyone who hurt me in any way, and I also forgive myself for my foolishness."

That very prayer allowed me to move on and be the person I am today. That very prayer allowed God to use me and my family. Now, 21 years after the day I was born-again, it is so clear to me how the devil trained me to be a loser but God raised me up to be a warrior!

I was born-again in May 1995, a new Christian on fire with a great joy in my heart and a fully energized spirit. I approached Pastor Sam asking him to allow me to volunteer in a ministry.

He thought for a minute and said, "Yes, we need someone to help in the kids' zone."

Well, that was not something I wanted because kids were probably the only things that I couldn't stand at that time. They are very noisy and very demanding and I didn't have time for kids.

I asked the Pastor, "Please, won't give me something else?"

With a smile, Pastor Sam replied, "Probably that is exactly where you should start."

I obeyed his instruction. We started our ministry in that church with the kids department, making photocopies and arranging the rooms for the ministry.

It was not for a long time after we started with the kids that God allowed us to get more involved in other ministries at the church. Soon we were leading the kids' ministry. Through the next few years, we got involved in leading with the youth groups, the counselling ministry, prayer cells, and then God opened doors for us to reach out to non-Christians in many restricted areas and train leaders. Since then, our slogan is, *"As for me and my house, we will serve the Lord"* (Joshua 24:15b).

Over the last 21 years we have had many challenges and we have faced giant mountains. We did walk in the valley of the shadow of death a few times (Psalm 23:4a), but we looked at every challenge as an opportunity to see God's hands at work. Our attitude has always been, *Let's see what God will do this time.*

We always dwell on these words:

If God be for us, who can be against us?
(Romans 8:31)

*Nay, in all these things we are more than conquerors through
him that loved us.*
(Romans 8:37)

I can do all things through Christ which strengtheneth me.
(Philippians 4:13)

There was a challenging time in our lives when we could not afford to buy basic items, but we were honest with our tithes and offerings. I remember how God honored that and we used to find cash in our garbage bins or the pockets on our coats.

In 1996, we moved to Dubai through another miraculous intervention by God. It was almost impossible to get a work permit at that time but God arranged it for us. We worked and ministered in Dubai until 2006 when we came to Canada where the first priority for us was to find a church.

Throughout our journey, we learned that "family" is the enemy's first target. We've learned that family is God's idea, it's not a manmade thing. That is why the enemy is trying viciously to degenerate and redefine the family, to make it a manmade puppet, so it can be easily messed up and destroyed.

Today, we need stronger families, built on the rock that is Jesus, more than any time in the past. For that reason, I have decided to dedicate the last chapter of my testimony to address the modern family.

A Word to All Parents

- Colossians 3:21 says, *"Fathers, provoke not your children to anger, lest they be discouraged."* Cheer your child on. Encourage them. If you don't do it, the enemy will take advantage of this great opportunity and will do it for you. Your children are your most valuable investment in this life, not your stocks or your RRSP, etc.

- Speak truth into your children's lives. Proverbs 18:21 says, *"Death and life are in the power of the tongue: and they that love it shall eat the fruit thereof."* Be very careful of what you speak into your children's lives. Every time I went home I could hear my father swearing and cursing at me, "You are a loser," or, "You will never be anything." No wonder my biggest fear growing up was I wouldn't find a job!

- Every time you swear and curse your child (or anyone else in the same sense) you give the enemy ammunition to fight them. Every time you tell your child, "You are a loser," the devil shouts, "Amen"! Please don't do that. Speak truth into your children's lives. Pray over them and claim, "My child will come back; my child will be successful." Tell the enemy he will never, ever get your children.

- The Bible say in Proverbs 22:6, *"Train up a child in the way he should go: and when he is old, he will not depart from it."* One of the greatest problems we have in society today is many of us are not raising our boys to be men nor raising our girls to be women; they are raising them to be anything but!

- Leave behind sweet memories. I have great childhood memories, and miserable ones after that. What memories you are leaving for your child?

- The biggest need for your child is a peaceful house and someone to talk to. Your house should be their safe haven, and you need to be the person they want to talk to. What you sow is what you reap. This is a basic rule in life. Seeds of hatred can never grow flowers of love. Proverbs 11:29, *"He that troubleth his own house shall inherit the wind: and the fool shall be servant to the wise of heart."* Please stop troubling your own house. They asked a teenage boy once, "Why did you mess up your life?" He said, "It was the best way to hurt my parents and get their attention!"

I missed a lot in my life, so I decided my own house will be different. It will the safe haven for my children. It will be the place where they find peace and Emma and I will be the ones whom they would talk to first.

A Word to All Children

- Exodus 20:12 says, *"Honor thy father and thy mother: that thy days may be long upon the land which the Lord thy God giveth thee."* Rest assured your parents love you, but they are human and they make mistakes. Jesus obeyed and respected His parents, and He set the example for us to follow. Remember, you don't have your parents forever, so cherish every minute with them. Treat them, every day, like it's the last time you may see them. Honor them so you will have a blessed life.

- Ephesians 6:12 says, *"For we wrestle not against flesh and blood, but against principalities, against powers, against the rulers of the darkness of this world, against spiritual wickedness in high places."* This battle starts here in the mind, and to win the battle of the mind you need to have a mindset for battle. We should know that we are all struggling with an enemy who has thousands of years of experience. The only way to win this battle is to have God on your side and be saturated with His words.

- Hosea 4:6 says, *"My people are destroyed for lack of knowledge: because thou hast rejected knowledge, I will also reject thee, that thou shalt be no priest to me: seeing thou has forgotten the law of thy God, I will also forget thy children."* Besides the knowledge from social media, we need spiritual knowledge, Biblical knowledge and education. Entertainment is good, but it doesn't teach us how to fight and win a spiritual battle.

- Proverbs 6:27 says, *"Can a man take fire in his bosom, and his clothes not be burned?"* Do not be deceived: you could be saved by grace, and praise God for that, but sin has consequences on your life. Yes, God is merciful, but He is equally just.

- 1 Corinthians 15:33 says, *"Be not deceived: evil communications corrupts good manners."* Your friends tell more about you then your resume. Who are your friends? Who do you spend time with, share your stories with and get advice from? Do they draw you nearer to the cross, or away?

- God's words in Jeremiah 29:11 says, *"For I know the thoughts that I think toward you, saith the Lord, thoughts of peace, and not of evil, to give you an expected end."*

You are not a mistake, you are not a number and you are not a loser. If the enemy is training you to be one, make no mistake that God wants you to rise up and know how much He loves you. All His plans for you are to prosper you!

In a closing comment, I want all readers to know that I am praying for you, even before this book is printed. My prayers for you are in two directions: salvation and forgiveness.

One day I will stand before God's throne and the devil, the accuser, will shout, "Nizar is guilty and must go to Hell!"

But Jesus, my Redeemer, will say, "I paid the price for him. Nizar is as white as snow and cleared to enter my kingdom."

The Bible confirms numerous times that we are all sinners and need God's grace. I received that grace 21 years ago. What about you? Who will stand up for you on that day?

If you are not sure, please pray these words with me, "God, I am a sinner; forgive me. Jesus, I ask you to live in my heart and change me."

Trust that God will do miracles in your life. Trust that your sins have been forgiven and you are a new person in Christ. Welcome! You are now in the family of Jesus Christ!

You cannot experience the full extent of the joy and the peace Jesus promised if you are holding anything against anyone. Unforgiveness will always hold you back. It hinders God's plan in your life. Forgiveness is not memory loss, it is pain-free memories. Forgiveness brings healing, so I invite you to pray for and forgive any person who hurt you in anyway. It could be your family, like in my case, or it could be your child, spouse or colleague. It could be a teammate or neighbor, maybe a boss, or even an ex-spouse or your siblings.

I pray God will bless your life abundantly and break all the chains and bondages that are holding you back and hindering God's plans for your life. The only true hope we have is in the cross of Jesus. The only redeemer we have is Jesus Christ. The only redemption for us is in his blood.

Take a step in faith. Give God a chance. He will never disappoint you.

ABOUT THE CONTRIBUTOR

Nizar Terzian was born in Baghdad on July 4, 1970, the first child to his parents. He has one sister and one brother. Originally from Armenia, his mother was a doctor and his father was a senior architect to the President.

Nizar graduated with an honor degree from high school in 1988 and studied at the University of Architecture. Married in 1994 to Emma Boghossian, they have three boys. They lived in many cities over the last 22 years, but settled in Canada in 2006.

Currently, he works full time in Toronto while Emma is the Director of the Christian Education department at their local church. They both are blessed to have the opportunity to partner together and serve as a team in ministering to their community.

CHAPTER 29

THE REVELATION

Carolyn Fields

That if thou shalt confess with thy mouth the Lord Jesus, and shalt believe in thine heart that God hath raised him from the dead, thou shalt be saved. For with the heart man believeth unto righteousness; and with the mouth confession is made unto salvation
(Romans 10:9-10, KJV).

Daydreaming had become a frequent means of escaping my abusive home situation. I would often let myself drift off into a gentle, relaxing sleep during the day. On one particular day I experienced a very unusual dream — a startling dream — not a relaxing dream.

The atmosphere was filled with the angry roar of thunder and the violent pelting of hail. That dark sky was torn open by lightning. As my daughter, Ne Ne (Nailah), and I were watching this surreal scene with the gathered onlookers, Jesus and His angels and the saints descended. The anointing of the Glory of the Lord was so tangible. Both conviction and great love were poured upon us.

Ne Ne, drawn by His presence, moved closer and closer towards Him. He stretched out His hand in welcome toward her. She looked back at me and then waited expectantly for Jesus to beckon me forward also. He faced me with tears in His eyes, and then looked directly into her eyes and shook His head with the answer. I could not go.

This unexpected, negative response sent me head first into a panic attack. With my heart racing, I was jolted awake. I was terrified that I could not go to be with Jesus and with my daughter. My shaky fingers dialed for an ambulance. I was hyperventilating.

God already knew who would be sent to treat me. He had arranged for a young, Christian lady to minister to me. She, too, had suffered from panic attacks at one time. Reaching out to Jesus had put an end to her terrifying episodes. She shared with me how much Jesus loves us and wants to be a central part of our lives.

Following that encounter, I began to have more visions in which Jesus told me just how much He loved me. In response, I decided to join Florence, a wonderful Christian woman I knew, in worship at a local Baptist church. Florence and her friends had been praying for me regularly.

Years before, Florence had told me how much Jesus loved me and wanted me to live and be with Him for eternity. She took me to church so that I would be saved. However, I could not understand the concept of salvation. Now, I earnestly sought salvation and eagerly agreed to be baptized in water.

While cooling down at home after the baptism, I had another vision. In my vision I saw Jesus, Moses, Abraham and Elijah in the clouds above. The power of the Holy Ghost poured down on me from the cloud on which Jesus was standing. The powerful presence of God was the strongest which I had ever felt. This experience spurred me on to seek a closer relationship with God.

I had little knowledge of the Word of God so I assumed since I was baptized, and was going to church on a regular basis, that I was saved. I soon learned that my assumption was incorrect.

A preacher on the 700 Club on television got my attention when he said, "There is a young lady watching me right now. You go to a Baptist church and you got baptized and received the right hand of fellowship. If you died today, you would not be with Jesus." He went on to say, "No one can come to the Father except through Jesus Christ."

I was stunned with his revelation. Then he proceeded to state that I could be saved, right at that moment, as explained in Romans 10: 9 & 10, *"That if thou shalt confess with thy mouth the Lord Jesus, and shalt believe in thine heart that God hath raised him from the dead, thou shalt be saved. For with the heart man believeth unto righteousness; and with the mouth confession is made unto salvation."* I prayed that prayer along with him that night. From that turning point onward, God became even more active in my life. I was now truly His.

God continued to direct my path. Ne Ne was asked be a model for a local hair stylist at a hair show in New York City. I accompanied her to her appointment regarding the details of the job offer. I had a very uneasy feeling about this offer. These negative feelings were reinforced after I met two other co-workers from Barbados who were also going to the show in New York. Their joking conversation made me uncomfortable because they were telling Ne Ne how to put "roots" on her husband in order to keep him from cheating on her.

I advised my daughter not to take this job. She agreed with me, but after I left, the owner of the salon convinced her that she would just need to stay at the show long enough until her hair was styled. Then she would return home.

My stress was mounting, especially after I visited a School of the Prophets in New York City. A prophetess there said, "I see a fire that came and took them away from you. God is going to give you beauty for ashes." I asked the Lord what this warning meant and if it was for someone else, not me. When I returned to my hotel room, the Lord gave a disturbing answer.

I dreamed that Ne Ne and I were in a large crowded house. A terrible sense of impending disaster settled upon me. I tried, in vain, to warn everyone. They would not listen. Leading the way out, I rushed out the door with my daughter following close behind me. When I turned around to check on her progress, I saw her beautiful face, pressed in panic on the other side of the door's window. I watched helplessly as a giant foot came down on the house, crushing it.

More warnings nagged at me but I reasoned that I was just being an overprotective mother. Ne Ne didn't feel at all well on the day she was to be picked up for the show. She wanted to cancel but knew that she had agreed to model. She was reluctant to let others down.

I wanted to scream, "Don't go," but the scream would not come out. Oh, how I regret that I had not screamed loudly.

The next day a policeman knocked on my door with devastating news. There had been an accident. One passenger in a car had died but he didn't yet know if it was my Ne Ne. My mother and aunt went to identify the body. I was unable to go.

As I sat waiting and trembling, I saw the accident unfold before me. Everyone in the car had fallen asleep. Ne Ne woke up and frantically got the driver's attention. She unfastened her seat belt and reached over the driver to help control the steering wheel. The car smashed into a guardrail and flipped over, hitting a tree.

Without a seat belt, Ne Ne had no natural chance for survival; but she did have a choice. The Lord showed me her being revived twice. She went straight to the Lord and He let her decide if she wanted to stay with Him or to come back to earth. She chose to stay with Him in heaven. Her physical body died of multiple concussions.

Gary, a friend of mine who was a state policeman, called to give me the details of the accident and, specifically, how my daughter's quick actions saved the lives of the others in the vehicle. The survivors of that horrific accident did not know the Lord as Savior.

God is the loving God who waits patiently to reveal to each one of us that we must recognize and confess we are sinners, and that the great price to wash our sins away has been paid by the sacrifice of His perfect son, Jesus, upon the Cross of Calvary. Due to God's immeasurable love, whether we are saved or not, He watches over us and nudges us onto the narrow path which leads, not to damnation, but to eternal life with Him.

Sometimes nudges come in the form of dreams and sometimes God uses other people to give us a nudge. Jesus loves me so much that He had someone literally identify with me, personally, on T.V. He didn't want to have to tell me that I couldn't be with Him throughout eternity, but He did because He loves me.

He loved me enough to let me have the vision that I couldn't go with my daughter and with Him so that I'd come to understand what I needed to do in my heart to be saved. He revealed Himself to me and baptized me with His wonderful Holy Spirit.

Watch for those nudges in your own lives. Make sure that the direction which you are being shown lines up with the Word of God, and respond to His guidance. You shall not be disappointed for God is love and He wants the best for you, His child, the one whom He created.

ABOUT THE CONTRIBUTOR

Apostle Carolyn Fields is the founder of Higher Dimensions School of the Prophets Academy, which is located at 2048 Chestnut Street, in Harrisburg, Pennsylvania 17104. Higher Dimensions (of God's Holy Fire Ministries) has been in existence since April 7, 1998, and School of the Prophets started in 2002. Ken was saved in 2000, married Carolyn two years later, and has played music for the church.

For contact purposes, including more about the School of the Prophets Academy courses and programs, please call: (717)315-4294, (717)261-5920, or visit them on the web at:
www.schoolfortheprophets.com

CHAPTER 30

OUT WITH THE OLD AND IN WITH THE NEW

Anaiah Kirk

Therefore if any man be in Christ, he is a new creature: old things are passed away; behold, all things are become new (2 Corinthians 5:17, KJV).

In 2003 at the age of 18, I thought I was on top of the world. I was about to embark on a career as a professional competitive freestyle skier allowing me to travel the world and live an exciting lifestyle. However, in the winter of 2004, everything changed.

As a result of two serious head injuries I lost my job and my girlfriend, and was forced to quit doing what I lived for: skiing. At the lowest point of my life, I found something I wasn't looking for and achieved something I didn't realize I wanted — a relationship with Jesus Christ.

God began to make Himself a reality to me, which led me to let go of my old lifestyle and embrace a new one. I chose to start a relationship with God. Soon after that I had a life-changing encounter that erased all my doubts about Him. I realized that knowing Him and His will for me was the life I always wanted.

When I was fourteen years old, my life was perfect. I had my family, health, friends, sports and a solid faith in God. That was before my life was flipped upside down.

Growing up, I knew my father and mother had their ups and downs just like any married couple. But in the fall of 1998, I came home from a Wednesday night church service and went upstairs to my room. I heard my parents arguing. It was the last night my mother and father slept under the same roof.

The next morning my mom left the house. For the first time in my life I saw my dad cry. At first I hoped the split would be temporary. As weeks turned into months and months turned into seasons, I knew their marriage was over. Still, I felt compelled to try and do something to fix it.

I became a mediator between my mother and father. As I tried to mediate between them, I learned about things they'd done to each other and the struggles they shared. Also during this time I learned that my mother had feelings for another man while married to my father. The more I learned about my parent's relationship and their struggles, the more I questioned the beliefs that had been instilled in me such as true love, trust and faith in relationships.

I struggled with the idea of church and God. *If God created the church to uplift people and help heal them, then why did church and God seem to be splitting my family apart?*

Before long, I came to see a new reality. Love was not what I thought it should be. My family was no longer a family. Church wasn't good for a person. It now seemed like a structured dictatorship. As for God…why would a loving God allow so much hurt? *Was there even a God?*

I gradually lost my belief that God really cared. As my faith dwindled, I struggled more in school. I began to believe that my parents' divorce was a result of their disagreement on how to raise me, making me ultimately responsible for the break-up. Tears flowed so much for so long, my heart finally dried up. My heart callused over and grew bitter.

I struggled with the Christian faith. I'd grown up learning about loving your neighbor and even your enemy. In Church I heard people talk about "esteeming the other person above yourself" and "laying your life down for others." I *heard* so many good things, but I saw the opposite happening all around me. I felt those who called themselves Christians were hypocrites.

During the winter of my fourteenth birthday I went on a ski trip with my father to Lake Tahoe. I had grown up skiing occasionally, but when I went to Tahoe that winter, a freestyle skiing movement was in its early stages. Now, it's an Olympic sport. I was immediately drawn to the skiers I saw doing flips and spins. That same weekend, I went home and bought twin tip skis and a season pass to my local ski resort.

For me, skiing was a perfect sport. I didn't have to rely on anybody but myself to excel. I could enjoy the beauty of the mountains without any interruption of school or people. Most importantly, skiing allowed me to get away from home and forget about the troubles in my life.

On my sixteenth birthday, my parents were in such a bad legal battle over their divorce that they forgot about my birthday until later that night.

Two days later I had to take Amos, my golden retriever, to the vet to be put to sleep. He was painfully dying from cancer. I'd had him since I was 10 years old. He loved to hike, swim and play. When my parents were going through their divorce, Amos was always by my side. He slept by my bed from the night he show up at my doorstep until the morning we put him to sleep. He was my best friend. And I took him to die.

I didn't think life could get any worse. I was wrong.

The next week I was driving to visit my brother at college. My friend David's mom passed me with her sister and niece in the car with her. I waved, and a moment later pulled over to get gas.

Twenty five minutes later, I saw that a car had gone off the road into a ditch. I considered pulling over to see if I could help but the car didn't seem to be in very bad shape. I figured everyone was okay and I might cause an accident myself if I stopped. I continued to my brother's dorm.

I was hanging out in my brother's room with some of his friends when my cell phone rang. My father told me David's mom had been killed in a car accident. I was consumed with guilt. If I had pulled over, maybe I could have saved her life...my best friend's mother's life.

That night I drank until I passed out.

I continued to lose all faith in God. *How could He let my parents divorce? How could He allow my dog to die? My friend's mother to die? If God was so good, then why was everything around me so bad?*

For the next two years I put on a front to my family, my school and my church. I pretended I was fine so everyone would leave me alone. But I wanted out of this life.

During my senior year of high school, I started winning major skiing competitions and traveling. I was finally breaking away from my life at home, breaking away from family, church and God. My senior year in high school was spent on the road competing. Two months after graduation, I packed my bags never to return home again. I was finally out! No family, no God.

My dreams began to come true. I was putting myself through college, skiing and competing. I had a girlfriend who I thought was my first love. For the first time since I was fourteen, I was happy. That was all about to end.

Within one week, everything that made me happy was again taken from me. Due to two concessions within three days (the seventh concussion of my career) I was advised to stop skiing. After an emergency trip to Stanford University, I was advised I could go into a coma if I hit my head again. I was forced out of contracts to ski the world and pursue my dreams. I was forced to quit skiing.

The same night I returned from Stanford Hospital, I was informed by a friend that my girlfriend was cheating on me while I was out of town. In disbelief, I drove over nine hours home to find her in bed with another man. My heart broke. Seeing her in bed with another man reminded me of my mother's infidelity; a stab to my heart.

As I walked away from her home at 2:30 a.m. in the middle of a snow storm, I realized my life would never be the same. I would never finish my dreams of skiing professionally. I would never marry this girl and I wouldn't be able to finish college until my conditions healed. *If* they healed.

As I neared the third story balcony to my apartment, I fell to my knees. Never had I cried internally. My soul was broken. My heart was broken. I was done with this life. I stood up and looked over the balcony. The thought of suicide came to mind. It was so sudden and so powerful I had to get away from the balcony.

Inside my freezing, one-bedroom apartment, I lit a candle and broke down crying. Still crying, I looked up and saw a Bible above my refrigerator. The candle lit up the gold words, "Holy Bible." I stared at the Bible, wondering who put it there.

"I don't believe in You," I said, "but if You are there, You have one chance to speak to me. If You don't, I'll never open this book again."

I opened the book and for the first time in my life, He--through the Bible--spoke directly to me. I opened to Hosea 1:2. The Lord told me not to marry an adulterous woman. I wanted to be with my girlfriend forever, even after what she had just done to me. God was saying no.

I then opened the Bible randomly to Exodus 20:5. God was telling me He was a jealous God. He was jealous for me and wanted me to stop giving my attentions to this world. He wanted me to give them to Him.

Amazed that He had just spoken directly to me through His Word, I again randomly opened the Bible and landed on Luke 15:7. *"I say unto you, that likewise joy shall be in heaven over one sinner that repenteth, more than over ninety and nine just persons, which need no repentance."*

Repent? *Repent from what?* Lord, if You're speaking to me, what do You want me to repent from?

I continued reading and soon came to the parable known as the prodigal son. In that parable, the rich man's son left his house, spent all of his inheritance and ended up living with pigs in order to eat their food. After realizing he had nothing left, the son returned home afraid his father would not accept him back. But when he returned, he was not only welcomed back home, he was completely restored, just as if he had never left and sinned.

The father in the parable said, *"It was meet that we should make merry, and be glad: for this thy brother was dead, and is alive again; and was lost, and is found"* (Luke 15:32).

As I read this parable I got teary-eyed. I knew the Lord was calling me home, but I didn't want to go.

Over the next few days I thought on all that happened. *Could it be God was real? Was he really calling me home or was this coincidence?*

Not wanting to go home, I decided I would try to go to Church in my ski town, Mammoth Lakes. While driving to church, I decided I would stay in Mammoth and go home after I saved enough money to buy a newer car. As those words fell off my lips, my phone rang. The caller was my aunt.

"Anaiah," she said, "I don't want you living out there anymore. If you come home, I'll give you the car that's in my garage."

I told her I would call her back and let her know. Then I pulled over in disbelief. After catching my breath and my thoughts, I turned my car around and started packing my stuff. I was going home.

The following Wednesday night I attended church. It was the same church I was raised in. The same church my father and brother still devoutly attended. I drove into the parking lot with mixed emotions. I was excited about seeing everyone again, but I also felt embarrassed.

People here thought I was going to be a professional skier, and here I was, back a square one. As I stepped into the foyer, I received numerous greetings and hugs. As much as I appreciated everyone's love, I still hadn't decided whether I would move back to Mammoth once my head injuries healed.

I walked into the main building hoping I would feel something spiritual, but I felt absolutely nothing. I just sat in the back row and listened to the music. After worship time, a man stood at the pulpit and preached about the prodigal son. Everything he said confirmed the decision I made to come home.

I knew the Lord had spoken to me through His Word, through my aunt and through the preacher. I was definitely where the Lord wanted me to be, but from my past experiences, I couldn't trust Him. That is, if He really was real.

For over a year I struggled with the decision I had made to return home. I continued to go to church, started dating a new girlfriend and re-enrolled in a local junior college with new career ideas. But time and time again I couldn't shake the mistrust in God. I couldn't let go of my past experiences. I contemplated quitting school and moving back to Mammoth and re-turning to skiing. I didn't want to make any rash decisions.

A few years earlier I would have done whatever my feelings told me to do. Now I was afraid God might have a plan for my life. If He was real.

Scared and uncertain about my future, I went for a drive to clear my head. My phone rang and my friend invited me to a Bible study at Mike's house. Little did I know, my life was about to change forever.

For the first 15 minutes we talked about prayer, showing the love of Christ to others, and trying to live good lives. Then Mike brought up the topic of being in and creating the presence of God, or "manifesting" His presence. I asked him what he meant by that expression.

"Have you ever been in church, worshiping God and you feel His presence?" he asked.

I was reminded of a time when I was a child. I had felt His presence at a Summer Church camp retreat. It was so strong it was hard for me to walk.

"That was the presence of God," Mike said. "When we truly love God, He dwells within us everywhere, all the time."

"But how do we manifest the power of God?" I asked.

He compared it to a flower that drops seeds. Those seeds then become flowers of the same species. Jesus chose us and we are to become just like him, imitating His very life.

Everything in me wanted to live a life that reflected Jesus' character. He was wise, loving and kind, but He was also a strong man who lived what He believed, not compromising, even to the point of His own death. I wanted to live this way. *But how?* I figured I had a long way to go before I could manifest the presence of the Lord in my life.

Other people in the group voiced opinions and read from scripture. While they were talking, I felt an intense heat on the right side of my body from the top of my head to the bottoms of my feet. Out of the corner of my eye, I saw Mike with his arms stretched out and his hands open toward me. When I faced him, he dropped his arms and acted like he hadn't done nothing unusual.

I thought, *What a weirdo.*

A minute or so later, my entire body became hot as if a warm robe had been thrown over it. Mike had his arm stretched out toward me with his hands wide open again. This time, when I looked his way, he didn't drop his arm. As they remained up and outstretched, I felt God's love and presence surround me. I made eye contact with Mike and his arms lowered.

"Anaiah," he said, "God's very presence is here, and in His presence is love. He wants you to know He loves you and will never let you go. You are His. Bought by his blood."

My soul broke. I buried my head between my legs, fighting tears. There was complete silence in the room and I heard a voice say, "Be still and know that I am God."

Overwhelmed by Gods presence, I screamed out in my mind, *I am tired of compromising. And I'm tired of having doubts about You and Your plans for my life. I'm sick of worrying about my future and what career to go into. I want to forgive the people who have hurt me. I don't want to play these stupid games. I want a relationship with You. I want whatever You have for me. I want Your will. I want Your presence in my life. Please, don't leave me. Change me, or let me go!*

A man from the group put his hand on my shoulder.

"Anaiah," he said, "I don't know what's going through your mind right now, but the Lord is here. He wants to heal your broken heart and show you His love. If you give yourself to Him, you won't have to worry about your future or about what job you'll have. You will be able to show love and forgiveness even to those who may not deserve it, because God has shown you love and forgiveness. Just be still and let God work in your heart."

Hearing him say out loud the words that had been going through my head amazed me. I was overcome by the presence of the Lord. It was so heavy on me, I collapsed face down on the floor. As I lay there, I handed every part of my life over to God: my goals, my dreams, my aspirations...my past, my present, my future. I told God everything I had was His.

The moment I said these words, I experienced something that is almost impossible to describe. I lay on the floor with my eyes closed and saw what appeared to be flashes of light. It was like looking into a strobe light.

As I looked into it, each flash brought back a memory of God which began to restore my faith in Him. One flash was a memory of me laying on the church floor at the age of two watching my mother praise and dance in church; even then I must have recognized the presence of the Lord. Another was a memory of me worshiping God at Junior Church. Another flash jolted a memory of learning about King David's tabernacle in the wilderness.

With each flash came a restoration of my faith, mind and heart. It was like God was cleaning out the viruses that plagued my life while He downloaded a better, restored system.

After about an hour I tried to stand up, but was so weak I had to sit down. As I sat, I realized I had just met with God and was never going to be the same again. Like Moses encountering the burning bush of God, I had encountered God. I was changed. For the first time in my life God was no longer a mythical idea, but a real, loving Being who had just saved my life.

Looking back on that day, I have seen God's continued grace in my life. At times, I wondered if the changes I had experienced, if the presence I had experienced, would die down and leave me where I was before. I'm here to tell you what I found to be truth. Jesus Christ is Lord. He has and continues to love and change my life for the better. This life I am living is a life I would never change.

Since handing my life over to Christ at Mike's house over 12 years ago my life has not been peachy. It's full of ups and downs, happiness and sadness, moments of great confidence and moments of uncertainty. However, I can't imagine living without the Creator. I will never be able to stay away from the pursuit of His presence.

Revelations 3:20 says, *"Behold, I stand at the door, and knock: if any man hear my voice, and open the door, I will come in to him, and will sup with him, and he with me."* Since the day I was born, God's knocking has been on my heart. Since the day you were born, God's knocking has been the heartbeat of your life.

Daily, He knocks, giving you another day to live, another chance to respond to Him. The tug that is on your heart and the unfulfilled areas in your life will never go away until you open the door to Jesus Christ.

Before I opened to door to Him, I was hungry for answers, peace, hope, fulfillment and purpose in this life. But when I opened my life to Jesus Christ, I found everything I had been looking for. It was just like Revelations 3:20 stated. Jesus came into my life and He dined with me. He fed my soul and provided life to me now and eternally.

ABOUT THE CONTRIBUTOR

Anaiah Kirk was born in October 1984, in Tuolumne County, California, and grew up in small town Mi-Wuk Village, which is located just outside Yosemite National Park. Living at the footsteps of Yosemite and the Sierra Nevada Mountain Range, Anaiah naturally spent his time outdoors backpacking, skiing and fishing.

In his teens, Anaiah pursued skiing professionally until two devastating injuries ended his career and forced him to go back to college. He obtained a bachelor's degree in Criminal Law and started a career as a Juvenile Probation Officer. Transitioning to the Department Of Corrections and Rehabilitation, he works as Supervising Correctional Counselor II.

Anaiah married his high school sweetheart, Aimee, and they have two young children. Although he has a busy life, Anaiah has written one book, *The Life I Always Wanted*. It's a book to inspire a generation of young men and women searching for meaning in their lives, meaning that can only be found with a relationship with Jesus Christ.

He is also currently working on his second book which he hopes to release in 2016 or 2017. That book is to guide young men in their fight for sexual purity. After battling with sexual addictions and pornography, Anaiah was able to overcome his struggles. His detailed strategies are outlined in his next book. It is Anaiah's true heart's desire to share this second story, a message which has changed his life and the lives of those he has discipled in this arena already.

You can obtain his book at:

www.thelifeIalwayswanted.com

anaiahkirk.com

or on Amazon.com

CHAPTER 31

FACE TO FACE WITH JESUS

Dr. Sherry Anne Lints

And that he died for all, that they which live should not henceforth live unto themselves, but unto him which died for them, and rose again.
(2 Corinthians 5:15, KJV).

The question has been asked of me many times, "When did Jesus Christ become more than just a name to you?"

Truthfully, I don't remember Him ever being *just a name* to me. My mother has vivid memories of me loving Jesus as a child. When I was a mere six years old, I wrote a poem about Jesus in school and would talk about Him and would even talk *to* Him.

As far as I knew, I always loved Him, always knew Him — surely, I must have known Him, *right*? After all, didn't I do all the right things?

I went to religious education classes. I attended church regularly. I wore my pretty Sunday dress with white bobby socks and black patent leather shoes. I sat, bowed and kneeled. I prayed, confessed and communed. Yet, sadly, I was soon to learn that I knew *of* Him, but, no, I didn't really *know* Him — until one painful day when I met Him face to face.

To understand the circumstances leading me to this pivotal moment, allow me to first explain what my growing-up experience was like. Between my two parents there were five divorces. Out of that came nine half-brothers and sisters, five step-brothers and sisters, as well as my brother and myself. Therefore, my upbringing was, shall we say, tumultuous at best.

Love meant intense discipline, followed by vicious cycles of tearing down and building back up, only there was no time to build back up before the next storm would hit again. Self-worth did not exist and family members all needed to search for various ways to make meaning out of chaos. Some chose alcohol, some chose sex, some chose violence and rage, but all played the game — all were actors in this drama that repeated itself daily. All wore masks.

For some reason, and maybe it is because of His sovereign hand on my life, I did not turn to these "bad vices." I was going to be a "good girl." I would go to church and pray that I would "do right by God." I decided I would not smoke or drink, and I vowed that I would not have sex outside of marriage. This, I figured, would make God very happy with me and then at least one person would love me and not be angry with me, so I thought.

Unable to please or change my parents who were trapped in alcoholism and abuse at home, I became an extreme over-achiever in school, striving my way to the top. This was in spite of the fact that, at the age of five, it was discovered by the school nurse that I had a hearing and speech impairment.

Little did I know that I was becoming addicted to man's accolades and to my drug of choice: pride. I had trophies in everything from fishing to bowling to pageants — complete with tiaras and sashes —to full scholarships and a whole lot of newspaper publicity. I couldn't get enough. I was the poster child for perfectionism, not that I even knew what that meant at the time. I was gloating with success and I seemed to have it all.

Sure enough, this standard of excellence drove me right into a nervous breakdown during my first trimester of chiropractic college. I couldn't achieve the grades that I was used to in high school and undergraduate college. I was overwhelmed by the poor acoustics of the large auditoriums, and the school was not set up for the disabled. I was so used to being a big fish in a little pond, and now I was nothing but a little fish in a very large pond. I was scared and confused and my ego was becoming bruised.

Shortly after, I lost my first and only serious relationship — a man I loved and who I thought loved me. At that point I was convinced that I was unlovable and began to believe all those lies I heard as a child (that I was no good, that I was a mistake, etc.). I wondered how I could be worth anything if my parents didn't love me, my family didn't love me, my boyfriend didn't love me, my school didn't love me — if I didn't love me?

I felt there was no purpose for my existence and therefore no hope for me. I wanted to throw in the towel. I threatened the Lord that I was going to end it all unless He could give me one good reason not to. I lay on the floor kicking and screaming, begging Him for help, asking Him for any sign that He was real or even heard my prayer.

It was at that moment that I literally saw the bloodstained face of Christ, as He hung on a cross with a crown of thorns piercing His brow, lift His battered head to say, "I *died* for you; will you *live* for Me?"

I cannot even begin to express what a freeing moment that was for me. I immediately got up from the floor and onto my knees and began to thank God for saving my life, for dying that I might have life and have it more abundantly (John 10:10). I did not need to do *anything* to please Him; He already loved me and chose to die for me to pay the price for any sin that I ever could and ever would commit.

He paid the price for all the times I would fall short of His perfect will for my life, even when I thought I was doing everything right and didn't know that I wasn't. He gave His life as a sacrifice for me so that I could be reconciled to the Heavenly Father. I could never make right all the wrong things that I've done, but Jesus covered it once and for all by His death, by the giving of His life for mine.

The Bible says, *"For the wages of sin is death; but the gift of God is eternal life through Jesus Christ our Lord."* (Rom. 6:23). Jesus paid that price for me — and you. Thanks be to God.

From this point on, I began to internalize the concept that Christ died to give *me* life and that I needed to die to *myself* and the sin of pride. I needed to turn it all over to Him and live for Him, not me.

Through the workbook, *Search for Significance,* I realized that I did not need to earn Christ's love and that He already loved me even before I ever got a single A+ or trophy in school.

According to Ephesians 1:4-6, God chose me before the foundation of the world; He accepted and adopted me before I ever knew Him or loved Him.

For the first time, I had a deep spiritual awakening in Christ. I saw the depths of my own sin and how very much I, in all my perfectionism, needed a Savior. I was not God, but He was. I now *knew* who He was and who I was not. I began to pick up the pieces of my broken, torn life. I asked God to show me how I could best be used to show His glory and goodness to others who are lost and hurting and still trying to do it by themselves.

Christ never commanded us to "go it alone," but rather, through Him we can achieve all things--to reveal His image and bring glory to His name — to build His kingdom and not ours for the betterment of mankind.

In the 10 years that followed, I've been awe-struck watching God unfold a number of lifelong dreams before my eyes. You see, I have always wanted to be a singer and I have also always wanted to be in a movie. I used to sing into a little one-dollar hairbrush as a young girl pretending that I was Whitney Houston, and told myself that one day I would be on a tour bus.

When I started attending a full gospel church as a teenager, a spiritual mother recognized a gift of music in me and introduced me to Christian music, specifically gospel, and more specifically, the Gaithers. At 17, I did my first church solo and have been singing for churches and other events ever since.

As I watched the singing desire start to become fulfilled, I began to pray more earnestly for an opportunity to be in a movie, especially a Christian movie. Through a series of God-orchestrated events I made contact with Kelly's Filmworks, and in 2008, the same year I made my first CD, I appeared in my first movie.

I have seen the fulfillment of my longing to be on tour buses as I've enjoyed visiting a number of artist's tour buses in the last few years, either as a friend or to pay a doctor visit. I have since appeared in another film as well as a music video. I have written and continue to write community passion plays, and have seen the salvation of unsaved family members and friends.

My prayer is that I would continue to grow daily in relationship with the Heavenly Father, the Son, and the Holy Spirit and in the knowledge of God's Word. I ask that He would use my abilities, disabilities and challenges to inspire hope among all people of all walks of life.

I share my life story to tell you that God *does* have a plan, even when you don't see it or you didn't come from the best of circumstances. I've heard it said, "When you are at the end of your rope, you are not at the end of your hope."

God hears you and He loves you. He has not forsaken you and will not leave you (Hebrews 13:5). Turn to Him, lean on Him and trust in Him — *and Him alone.*

I conclude this testimony with one of my favorite Scripture verses encouraging us that God truly knows our heart's desires, and He is certain to bring His will to pass in His way and in His time, for His word says, *"He hath made every thing beautiful in his time"* (Ecc. 3:11a).

ABOUT THE CONTRIBUTOR

Sherry Anne Lints, Doctor of Chiropractic, singer, speaker, actress, writer and fitness trainer was born with a bilateral hearing and speech impairment. She appeared in the films, *"Clancy"* and *"The Perfect Gift,"* and was a special guest on both *TBN* and *100 Huntley Street* in Ontario, Canada.

She is a contributing author for the book, *Modern-Day Miracles,* and has released four full length CDs. She has opened for many Gaither Homecoming Artists including The Hoppers, The Booth Brothers, The Collingsworth Family, The Martins and Gordon Mote. Sherry Anne can be heard across the country and has charted nationally on the Southern Gospel Top 80 Chart as seen in *Singing News magazine.*

Additionally, Sherry Anne is a *Singing News* TOP TEN Nominee for Favorite New Artist.

Sherry Anne shares a powerful testimony of overcoming. Frequently speaking for elementary schools, colleges, conferences, seminars, woman's retreats, youth programs, churches and other events, it is Sherry Anne's true desire to minister worldwide with the message of God's unconditional love and forgiveness.

For more information, visit: www.SherryAnne.com

"Whether therefore ye eat, or drink, or whatsoever ye do, do all to the glory of God."
(1 Corinthians 10:31, KJV).

CHAPTER 32

GOD'S ABUNDANT LOVE AND MERCY

Rosanne Quinlan

Trust in the Lord with all thine heart; and lean not unto thine own understanding. In all thy ways acknowledge him, and he shall direct thy paths.
(Proverbs 3:5-6, KJV).

The Surprise

It all started at the tender age of seven when my loving, German grandfather, whom we named Pa, called up the farmhouse stairs from the cozy kitchen below to wake me out of a sound sleep. I remember sleeping under layers of warm blankets with a kitten to keep me company.

Why is Pa rousing me? I thought to myself. I jumped out of bed to feel the cold floor meet my feet and descended the drafty stairs with the kitten scurrying behind me. When I finally reached the warmth of the wood stove at the base of the staircase, I noticed a curious little black box on the corner of the kitchen table. With pipe in hand, my grandfather motioned for me to open this odd-shaped object. To my surprise and delight, it was a half-sized violin.

Soon I was taking lessons and thriving at it. I practiced very hard every day. I loved my violin teacher. He was like a father to me — the father I so craved and wanted to please.

As a child, I had a profound awareness of the "spiritual" and I especially loved Jesus. Born into a big, Catholic family, going to church on Sunday was like spreading butter on bread—we always did it. God was a large part of life. My mother played a big role in encouraging all six of her children to be the best we could be.

God's Liquid Love

In 1979, I was reborn in Christ. Ironically, a few months earlier I had just given birth to my first child, a darling baby girl whom we named Mary Theresa. I went into post-partem depression, had to be hospitalized and was subsequently diagnosed as manic depressive.

I remember that I saw before me these terrifying beings with distorted faces. I now know that they were demons. There were six of them and horrifying to look at.

As these fiends continued to mock me, I cried out with all of my heart, "Jesus, if you're real, please help me!"

In the next moment heaven and earth became one as the real presence of Jesus illuminated the darkness and dispelled the demons. Instantly, the terror was gone.

His light was like nothing I had ever experienced in this earthly plane. His presence was like liquid love which surrounded and consumed every fiber of my being. I felt as if He lifted me up and cradled me in His strong arms as one would cradle a baby. I was completely enveloped in Jesus' radiant love. This was the first of many divine encounters with my Lord and Savior.

Fifteen months later, my beautiful baby boy, Christopher, was born. As a stay-at-home mom I was happy and loved my little family. However, the manic depression persisted and I found myself in and out of hospital for several years. I still loved playing my violin and over the years I continued to play at various churches in the area.

The Fragrance

I found myself smoking up to two and a half packs of cigarettes a day. It was 1983 and as a young mother I had tried several times to quit, but to no avail. I knew I had to do something when I noticed the wallpaper in my kitchen turning brown from nicotine stains.

My poor children, I thought.

I was consumed by guilt because they were forced to breathe in their mom's second-hand smoke, but I felt that I was powerless to do anything about it. Nevertheless, as I inhaled another cigarette I prayed and sought the Lord's forgiveness early one Sunday evening.

"Lord," I prayed, "please forgive me for ever taking up smoking. How can the Holy Spirit live inside of me when I'm so dirty inside? I can't quit. Please help!"

Later that evening I attended a prayer meeting at my church with some Charismatic Catholics. As I was encircled and prayed over, a very strong fragrance of peppermint enveloped me. Next, I felt an invisible presence blow powerfully into my mouth. Independent of my own breathing, this fragrance travelled down my throat, through my esophagus and circled around inside my lungs, travelling back out of my mouth.

Then, I saw emblazoned in light directly in front of me the words "You are healed."

I was overcome by tears of joy washing away years of struggle and guilt, the bondage miraculously broken in an instant. The healing was so complete that I had absolutely no desire for a cigarette, even to this day.

Drug Free

Two weeks after my mother died in 1986 I experienced the love and mercy of God through another divine encounter. I had had a very vivid and terrifying nightmare that I was becoming mentally ill again. The dream jolted me awake. I found myself crying out to Jesus once again in desperation.

Slowly, His illuminating light gently enveloped my bedroom once more. Jesus was at my side and touched my shoulder. Instantly, His love poured all over me — that same love that I had experienced several years earlier when I first encountered Christ. Since then, and for the last 30 years, I have been medication free by the powerful intervention of Jesus Christ. I am completely healed. Praise God!

Depths of Despair

The following spring while I was in prayer, the whole kitchen suddenly lit up with the presence of the Holy Spirit. He instructed me to pursue a music degree in September at McMaster University in Hamilton, Ontario. For the next few years I studied part time so I could be home to care for my children, which was always my primary concern. Nonetheless, there had been a deep yearning to one day obtain a music degree.

It seemed, however, that the closer my walk became with Jesus, the unhappier my marriage became. As a result, I started seeking day counselling at a women's shelter in Hamilton.

In 1991, half way through a music-degree program, my husband left. Without ever receiving any support payments from him, I was instantly plunged into poverty.

In the ensuing years, learning to rely on God to a much greater degree, I saw many miracles of provision when we had nothing: groceries appearing on my porch, a second-hand car provided for me, even money given to me at the bank when the account was empty through what I believe to be angelic intervention.

The most excruciatingly painful time of my life was in 1994 when the children's father convinced them to live with him. I was left with $10,000 from the sale of the house, which I lived on for the next nine months. Homeless, I moved from one siblings' home to another until I could finish teachers' college and acquire a fulltime teaching position.

That year the school boards were hardly hiring at all. Finally down to my last $100, I was truly in the depths of despair.

Answered Prayer

In August that year I remember getting on my knees and begging God for a miracle. Then I got the call — a position as a music teacher at a local school. They wanted me for September.

A couple of years later, after what seemed like an eternity, both my children returned to live with me. For a while our abode was a leaky, one-bedroom basement apartment. Nonetheless, I was overjoyed because my children were back.

Pursuit of Excellence

In 2000 I received a word from the Lord to play the violin excellently for Him. With this mandate from heaven, and given a burning passion to match, I often pondered how I could fulfill this. My children, now young adults, had moved out to pursue higher education themselves. Alone as a fulltime teacher with little to no spare time to practice my violin, how could I possibly accomplish this heavenly assignment?

Two years later, a friend and I found ourselves in front of a little Baptist church in Dundas, Ontario. There we joined hands and prayed that the Lord would make a way for me to continue my violin studies.

The Family Secret

School was out. It was March Break 2003 and I was looking for a house to buy. It was very important to me since I had lost my home when the marriage collapsed. Alone in my real estate agent's car the Lord spoke these audible words, "Wait for me. I'll show you were I want you to live." Elation matched my excitement.

The following May my elderly father, still a widower, was having a lot of health problems. He needed assistance and asked me if I would move in with him and be his fulltime caregiver.

Dad was paranoid schizophrenic. As a result I was never very close to my father, but always craved that loving affection that I saw other little girls get from their daddies. I now know that my father was not capable of giving me the love and affection I needed growing up. At the time though, I was left with a lot of bitterness and anger toward my dad; but God had a plan — a plan of restoration and forgiveness. I said no to Dad that day.

I was so angry with God that I yelled at Him all the way home, "What is this? Is this some kind of practical joke? If this is really You, You'd better give me a confirmation!"

Having no knowledge of what happened between my father and myself, the next morning my sister phoned early and woke me. She told me that the previous night she'd had a very strange dream that I went to live with our father. This was my confirmation.

Taking a leave of absence without pay from teaching, where I had a salary with benefits, was probably the scariest thing I've ever done. It made no earthly sense. Even my friends advised against going to live with my father; but I knew that this was God's will, so I had to trust Him.

One year turned into almost nine and a half years. The Lord blessed me abundantly for my obedience to Him. God opened a door for me to continue my pursuit of excellence with the violin by providing a very accomplished, eastern-European violin instructor whom I saw for a ten-year period.

But more importantly, I was able to forgive my earthly father as well as my former husband, and my heart was healed. Better still, I was learning to get to know my heavenly Father, whom I now wanted to please.

Evangelizing the Nations

A few years after my father's passing I was introduced to a choir and orchestra whose whole mission is to evangelize. Through the baton of their talented director, this group of Spirit-filled believers brings the good news of Jesus Christ to the nations. Consequently, over the past several years my violin has taken me around the world.

God turns all things to good for those who love Him (Romans 8:28). My life has been a testament to this. Even though we all go through trials and sometimes great difficulties, God will use those situations for His Glory if we let him. Thank you, heavenly Father, for Your abundant love and mercy.

ABOUT THE CONTRIBUTOR

Rosanne Quinlan resides in Burlington, Ontario, Canada. She is the mother of Mary Theresa and Christopher, and the grandmother of Julien and Eliot. Rosanne has taught music in the Greater Toronto/Hamilton school boards and currently operates two thriving violin studios in the Burlington, Ontario area.

She has performed in several symphony orchestras and holds both a Bachelor of Music and a Bachelor of Education degree. Rosanne is currently pursuing an A.R.C.T. violin diploma through the Royal Conservatory of Music in Toronto, Canada.

PART V

Neither is there salvation in any other:
for there is none other name under heaven
given among men, whereby we must be saved
(Acts 4:12, KJV).

CHAPTER 33

THE MIRACLE ROSE

as written by Rose Hackenberg, Javetta Saunders and Dr. Jerry Horner

And it shall come to pass, that whosoever shall call on the name of the Lord shall be saved
(Acts 2:21, KJV).

To share my testimony and to speak about the greatness and the mercies of God, what He can do in everybody's life, is such an incredible, high honor. If people could only hear about the name of Jesus. And you, dear reader, God created you and designed for you a plan for this life on earth. He knew where you were born and in which family you would grow up because He put you into that family.

Saying all of this, I grew up near Munich, Germany, with seven other siblings. My mother was a very devout Catholic. Throughout my childhood growing up, I had many sad and hard things happen to me. As a result, early on, I started to rebel.

I lost most of my interest in completing the business school which I was attending at the time as a direct reaction to being molested and raped on numerous occasions and over a long span of time of abuse from neighbors, friends and even one family member. I felt such shame, guilt and condemnation. I could not focus on accomplishing anything because of what had happened to me. My self-worth had plummeted to an all-time low.

I pulled out of the business school that I had been attending and instead I focused on leaving my small town, in an attempt to try and leave the deep sense of internal shame behind me.

Thankfully, one of my bothers lived in Zurich, Switzerland, so I decided to move there. I worked in an office and had a German boss. She was thankful to have me working for her, and I was thankful to have a job.

After about a year of working and living in Zurich, I got "acquainted" with the nightlife, which was the "high life" of clubs, or so I thought at the time. I began to meet some female professional dancers. This was just the beginning and these steps brought me to a place in Konstanz/Bodensee Lake. More specifically, it brought me to a particular high profile night club where I quickly determined that I had met my "Mr. Wonderful."

In little time we became lovers and he over-talked me and pressed me into prostitution. To fulfill my dream as quickly as possible and "his dream for me," which was a "lady's boutique," he told me that this was the wisest and fastest way to make a lot of money. The "lady's boutique," for me, was when the real highway to hell started. After many and repeated dramas and hard times in that lifestyle, I was completely and utterly devastated and literally hopeless.

So many things happened that I know now could have easily cost me my life if it had not been, upon retrospection, for the total and complete hand of the Lord on my life. These, and many more moments where the hand of God was miraculously upon my life, are all detailed in the book which the Lord arranged for me to complete for His total glory.

Throughout my life I found myself running like a lost sheep into immense mountains of fear, depression, alcoholism, addictions, hopelessness and utter despair. I was lost in the wilderness of this world without God.

It was in that moment of desperation that I remember crying out to God.

I said, "If there is a God in Heaven, please help me to get out of this lifestyle" and *that* is when God Himself became my game changer.

To even escape that lifestyle is a total and complete miracle from God! It was mere weeks after that prayer, after nine *years* of that life, that the Lord began to supernaturally arrange for me to immigrate to the United States of America. Even when it seemed impossible, God had a way, His way, and a most masterful purpose in mind.

After being denied immigration to the United States of America by government officials, the Lord talked to my spirit and told me clearly to go back to that government office. This time the Lord instructed me to go at lunchtime.

When I walked in this daunting office there was no one there except one lone worker present. I stated my case and, through what I believe could only have been an angel placed there for me that day, I walked out of that office with the unheard of — a four year work visa to the United States.

This was absolutely incredible and cause for great joy and celebration in my heart. I knew that I knew that I *knew* that God had miraculously answered my humble prayer of the heart.

Next, God opened the doors for a family to assist in bringing me to Los Angeles, California. I was in the United States of America after only three and a half months. Because God moved, everything went so quickly. I steadily improved in the English language during this time and God not only gave me employment as a waitress but He arranged for me to go back to high school — Hollywood high school.

The struggle at the time was that I was still an alcoholic. I was also a very heavy smoker and under so many bondages, which could have been an early death. God in his amazing grace and mercy gave me the opportunity to hear His word over television and I got saved through the 700 CLUB program.

Knowing full well that I was a complete alcoholic, and while in the midst of also battling other physical symptoms throughout my body, I learned from the doctors that I had liver cancer. *How, many times,* I thought, *have I cried out for deliverance from so many things?*

I was so ashamed about my drinking and here it was that Easter time was coming. I clung onto the Lord through this process but was just so deeply ashamed. I went with a German friend to a sunrise church service. I was so hungry for God but at the same time I was extremely embarrassed about the drinking and the eating disorder I fought. On the night of Easter Sunday service, I literally poured my heart out to God and pleaded with Him for His help.

I remembered a preacher saying that if you don't know how to pray, just take hold of the name of Jesus. That is what I did. I needed help in my situation and I was at the point of recognizing that. So I took hold of the name of Jesus and I decided to believe what that preacher had said.

It was so worth it to press in because I had a visitation from Jesus, and He healed me after that prayer which I detail about in my book. After that encounter, I connected with a well-known church in Los Angeles and a great woman of God who was one of the Prophets of that church, who later became my mentor.

I experienced great things during this time of wonderful friendship and training, and I grew steadily in my faith and in the "Bible language." Many healings and miracles were happening wherever the Lord was leading me to go and where I worked.

The next opportunity that the Lord had for me was a challenge — to move to the east coast of Florida. This took a big leap of faith for me. This was a God-sized move!

There, God fulfilled a promise that my mentor and I had believed for: my mentor was married in Lakeland, Florida, and after six months in the state of Florida I, too, was married into a beautiful, faith-filled marriage.

Not long after being married, my husband felt a call to evangelism. He had a dream to be a Pastor. It was a joy but at the same time it was a steep learning curve to accomplish this kind of work for the Lord. It was hands-on training. My husband went to the Church of God training school, and I was in the Holy Ghost school. Many great miracles were happening and the gifts of the Spirit were there in operation. We even had a revival and were blessed with a prayer team from the Brownsville Worldwide Revival. Yes, God gave us many blessings.

My husband and I were assigned to Panama City to a great church with great potential. But then, something happened — an attack from satan who came as an angel of light. After that, my husband requested a divorce. My entire world broke down.

Through a long period of depression God gave me another visitation and, again, it took time but my heart was healing. My new path, by God's magnificent grace and strength, was laid out for me. Soon I was ministering in various places and was being used in deliverance and the healing of broken hearts. God had used me mightily and turned things around for His glory.

Then came the time that my longtime friend, Javetta Saunders, whom I had met by divine appointment years back in Los Angeles, came to me and said, "The Lord is dealing with me to help you to write your book."

Years before, I'd ministered to her and spoke many times into her life and we had a wonderful friendship in the Lord. She knew what God had done in my life and she brought me, through her influence, to minister on worldwide television and to share my book as a testimony. That book, *The Miracle Rose,* is the story of God's glory and my being transformed by the power of God. To God's glory, the foreword was even written by Reinhard Bonnke and endorsements were supplied by the Lord from many great people of God.

Dear One reading today, I am praying that the story of how I came to believe in God and how I came to accept Him into my life will awaken a "God interest" in you. I pray, dear friend, that you will call on Him today.

You don't have to understand everything. I didn't either but I just believed and called on the name of Jesus. The Bible says in Romans 10:13, *"For whosoever shall call upon the name of the Lord shall be saved."* That was my experience.

But now, I would like to humbly ask you, "Would you walk with me to the throne room of God in Jesus' Name and receive Him as your personal Savior and Lord into your life?" This is my greatest honor to lead you into this prayer.

If you would like to have Jesus cleanse and change your life for the better and to walk with Him in a fresh start day by day, please say with me, "Here am I, Jesus. I want to know You and I desire Your help. Please forgive me of any and every sin of the past. Yes, I do know that I have sinned.

"I thank you that You have forgiven me and cleansed me from the stain of all of my sins, and You have washed me clean with Your precious blood which You shed for me on Calvary. I believe that You died for me and rose again as the Bible has said. I thank you for coming into my heart, and for giving me a new life in You that I have desired so much."

Beloved, if you have said this prayer and have committed your life to Jesus today, you are a Christian and a new believer in Him. Your sins are washed away and cast into the sea, never to be remembered again. You are a new creation. Thank Jesus for saving you and delivering you today.

Now, since you are a child of God, tell someone. It will help strengthen your faith and you will reaffirm your trust in Jesus and the prayer that you have just prayed with me.

I would also like to say to you today, if I may, that I know the power of Jesus to break the bonds of addictions or whatever your needs may be. If you are in a struggle of any kind and you want to be free, you can take some steps for your deliverance if you identify and renounce all addictions and practices that have enslaved you. Those addictions may be alcoholism, pornography, smoking, gambling or some other indulgence, or even an attitude such as greed, jealousy, envy, pride, unforgiveness or some other destructive habit.

God will cleanse you even if it has been the occult, witchcraft, fortune-telling, the horoscope, New Age and related, He will forgive you of all of your sins and cleanse you of all that. Your past has been forgiven by the blood of the Lamb.

God miraculously delivered me with the help of His people and through the power of His Word, which I had to act upon by walking with Jesus. Ask the Lord to lead you into a Holy Spirit-filled church. There is so much more waiting for you to receive there.

God's love is leading you, helping you into a greater life, into a God-fulfilled, satisfying life which you could never have known before. God has now become your heavenly Father, and through Jesus Christ His only Son you became His beloved one. He will lead you and guide you into all truth. You became exactly what Jesus was speaking of in John 3:3-8. You have entered into the Kingdom of God by being born again into this new life.

Thank you, my dear friend, for giving your life to the Lord. And by the way, as you have given your life to the Lord all of heaven just stopped for you, yes, just for you — for one person — who is giving their life to Jesus. All the angels of the Lord have just rejoiced over you and the greatest thing of all is this fact: your name is written in the Lamb's Book of Life.

Great things are in store for you now because God is bringing you forth for *your* designed destiny. I am truly a miracle and you can be, too, because God's love is reaching out to you, and my love and prayers are for you, also. I was an empty vessel whom Jesus filled with His love and goodness. He will do this for you if you ask Him to and allow Him to.

Trust Him today, won't you? It will be eternally worth it and you'll be glad that you did.

ABOUT THE CONTRIBUTOR

Rose Hackenberg resides in Dothan, Alabama, and attends New Vision, her home church. From there she does evangelistic work, leads prayer meetings praying for the United States of America and is active in full-time ministry for the Lord. Rose's ministry was birthed out of God delivering her from a lifestyle of prostitution and God giving her a brand new beginning as an evangelist preaching for the Lord.

Rose's testimony is an example of how God can, and does, make a way when there truly seems to be no earthly way out.

Rose Hackenberg's amazing book entitled, *The Miracle Rose,* by Rose Hackenberg, Javetta Saunders and Dr. Jerry Horner, was endorsed by Miles Monroe, Rev. Dr. Pat Robertson, Freeda Bowers and the late Donna Douglas (known as Ellie Mae Clampett on *The Beverly Hill Billies*), and her book's foreword was written by Evangelist Reinhard Bonnke. Her incredible book is available at Barnes and Noble and most other book retailers worldwide.

CHAPTER 34

CHILD OF WOE

Rev. Maury Blair

God is our refuge and strength, a very present help in trouble
(Psalm 46:1, KJV).

It was so hard for me as a child to understand why my stepfather hated me so much. All I knew was that I was not part of the family and I was unwanted.

One of my older half brothers told me often how he remembers the first day I was brought into our home. I was a little baby lying on the living room floor and he was all excited. I was his new little brother and he sat there looking down at me. Suddenly, the door opened and in walked his uncle, who had adopted him and his brother and sister. My brother told me he was in shock as my new stepfather broke into a rage, walked over and kicked me against the wall. I lay unconscious on the floor.

My stepfather then turned, cursed and yelled for my mother; he wanted to know what this "black bastard" was doing in his house.

My brother picked me up, thinking I was dead.

When my eyes opened and I began to cry, he rocked me and said to me, "Maury, it isn't going to be good for you to live in our house because my new dad hates you already."

This was the start of more than thirteen years of severe abuse in my life. I was under constant pressure by the predator, my stepfather, as he cursed and beat me and deprived me of any peace during my childhood. As all child abuse victims do, I took the shame and the blame for all of my mom's suffering as she refused to give me up.

I remember lying in bed on Friday nights, buried under my brothers' bodies so he wouldn't see me when he came back drunk from the bar and came upstairs looking for me. He would then make my mother sit at the table downstairs in the kitchen, drink his beer and curse her for bringing that "ugly black bastard" into his home.

I would listen to him cursing mom and hear my mother's crying and I thought, *If I wasn't here, he wouldn't be cursing her,* and that if I could die he would treat her better. *I must find a way to die.* I stood on bridges looking down at the water but couldn't bring myself to jump. Then I thought of going up on the big train bridge and if I couldn't face the train I would have to jump. Either way, I would die, and he would treat mom better.

I used to climb up a tree at the back of our house and hide among the leaves when he would come out looking for me; in all those years he never once looked up into the tree and saw me there. If he had, I probably would have jumped in a panic and died.

Being a child, I started to believe what my stepfather said about me. I conjured up this image of myself as the most fowl human being on the planet.

Mom sent us to Sunday school and church on Sunday mornings so he could sleep in because he had a hangover. We were "holy terrors" in that church and nearly drove the preachers insane. We smoked up in the washrooms, crawled under the pews while the preacher was preaching and tied men's shoelaces together--and then ran for our lives at the end of the service! I will never forget how they put up with us and loved us.

They knew mom was a backslidden Pentecostal preacher who was married to this violent alcoholic man in the community, but they still really cared about us. I would hear in Sunday school that Jesus loved me and died for me. Then, I would go home and get cursed and beaten.

My first revelation of God's personal love for me came right in my home. I was upstairs in the bedroom watching the flood surging by our home (because we lived right on the river bank in Paris, Ontario) and one of my younger half bothers came up to watch with me. What a sight it was as the raging water and chunks of ice swirled by our home!

I realized that my stepfather was home and I said to my half brother, "He's here, he's here!"

My brother asked, "Who's here?"

"The Old Man," I said (that's what we called him, "the Old Man").

"No, he's not home yet," my brother said.

All of a sudden, the Old Man charged into the room cursing. He grabbed me by the throat, raised the window, and held me out over the raging water threatening to drop me. My mother heard the commotion from downstairs.

She came up with the anointing of God on her and told him, "In the name of Jesus," to bring me in and put me down.

Looking into my stepfather's face I saw a look of fear I had never seen before; he was afraid of Jesus. He put me down and walked out of the room with his head down. I knew, from that day on, the Lord had His eye on me.

My stepfather became very ill when I was almost 14 years of age and he didn't bother me anymore. He was too sick. When I was 15, I had to quit school and get a job to help my mom raise his five children. He got sicker and sicker. Three years later, when he was in the hospital at death's door, he wanted to see me. I finally gave in and went to see him.

He had two requests: the first was, would I change my name? (He wanted to give me the family name.) I refused the offer. Second, he asked if I would continue to help mom raise his kids. I said I would, and then left to have a coffee and a cigarette. When I came back, he was dead.

About a year later, I was 19 and we were living in poverty in a condemned shack down by the river. My paycheck was all the income we had. My mom handed me a book one day, written by Dr. Norman

Vincent Peale, entitled, *Stay Alive All Your Life*. I read that book all alone in the back room where I slept, and God entered my life by the Holy Spirit.

That was the start of my journey to become a survivor of severe child abuse. I am so thankful that Jesus found me and changed my life; and that the local church, where we had caused so much trouble, welcomed us into the family of God. It took God, time and people to heal my broken life. You can read the entire story in my book, *Child of Woe*.

If I could, would I want to turn the clock back and start my life all over and have a wonderful dad and a loving mom and be brought up in the church with lots of friends and not live in poverty like my family did? To have safety and security all through my childhood? Would I like to go back and change my history?

No thanks. I wouldn't change any of the horror or pain because of the wonderful experience I have today in Christ, as a result of His healing in me through the Holy Spirit's marvelous work. I grew up without a real dad, but I have one now — Abba Father, He's my Father!

I was directing Teen Challenge, ministering with our staff and team, and sharing my story with a group of the residents when one of them interrupted me and said, "Hey, Maury, you're one of us!"

That caused me to realize so many of the addicts and alcoholics we were ministering to had backgrounds so much like mine, and that had a great influence on me telling my story.

I have often said that my story is my mother's story; her wrong choices and her mistakes which led us both into years of pain and abuse. My mom came back to the Lord and He used her to minister, to preach and to teach in our local church before she died at the age of 64.

I am so thankful that the Lord doesn't give up on us.

ABOUT THE CONTRIBUTOR

Maury Blair is the Founding Director of Breakthrough Ministries. For over 20 years he was involved in directing the ministry of Teen Challenge in two Canadian cities; Toronto, Ontario, and Vancouver, British Columbia. Maury and his wife, Beverly, have two daughters and five granddaughters — all gifts from God!

His book, *Child of Woe,* has been translated into Spanish, German, Thai, Russian and Polish. It has opened doors for him to share the message of hope in Jesus in prisons, schools, detention centers, "child abuse" conferences, and churches in Iceland, Puerto Rico, England, Thailand, Australia, Russia and Siberia, Poland and all across Canada and the United States.

The theme of his ministry is simple: "Your past does not have to destroy your future. There is help available, but you must deal with it now. If you leave it, you will face it later and it will affect every relationship in your life. God cares about your pain and rejection, and so do we."

You can contact Maury by e-mail at btmaury@sentex.net or you can go to his Breakthrough website at www.breakthroughnet.com and see his *Child of Woe* movie trailer, which was previewed at the Phoenix International Christian Film Festival in Phoenix, Arizona, in August 2010. It won first prize at the festival for a movie trailer. Chris Atkins is presently working on a short version movie of *Child of Woe.* You can order the book by contacting Maury directly.

He has a radio outreach through Loud Cry Radio. The station broadcasts his messages all over the world.

He also has a *Child of Woe* Facebook page where you can watch his interviews on YouTube as well. The ministry has had visitors to their Breakthrough website from all over Canada and the United States and from 51 other countries of the world. Maury is so thankful to God for the privilege of serving Him!

CHAPTER 35

THE FREE GIFT

Jim Barbarossa

Repent: for the kingdom of heaven is at hand
(Matthew 4:17b, KJV).

Many years ago my wife and I settled down to raise a family. My wife met some great people at the church where we were married and I believe this was the start of my receiving the "free gift" that I want to tell you about.

Over the years our family grew. We had four wonderful children, a fantastic marriage, financial success and many good friends. Sounds good, doesn't it? Even though it was good, I had many questions:

- Why am I here?
- What is life about?
- Is it possible to live just to die?
- What good is financial success when we must die?
- Why do it?
- Why even be here?
- Why do I feel so confused?
- What is the answer?
- Why, when I have so much, do I have a feeling of emptiness?

For 19 years I strongly believed that my family was the only thing that mattered and I set out to provide for my family with everything the world had to offer. Almost everything I did was geared to provide for my family and generations of family to come.

Also during this period of time, I searched high and low, trying many things to fill the emptiness or void I felt — playing softball with the guys and drinking after the games, playing racquetball and drinking after the games, buying campers, snowmobiles, new cars, houses, etc. I tried working extra hours to make more money, buying more worldly possessions, starting a business, investing in and buying real estate, etc. All of these things gave me a very short-lived pleasure or happiness that would not last. It would leave as quickly as it came.

Fortunately for my family, while I was providing for their worldly lives, my wife, Carla, was building a foundation for our eternal lives.

I have always believed there was a God, and I would occasionally pray when things were so far out of my control that I could not fix them. A few things come to mind that caused me to pray: like when my daughter was only weeks old and we had to put her in the hospital and I feared for her life; also, when my son lay in the hospital with a staph infection; and when my wife was very sick with an infection in her blood system and the doctor told me that my wife only had a 50/50 chance of survival.

The most recent time was when a friend called for our support when his father was very ill. Carla went to help our friend while I stayed home with the kids.

As I lay there in bed that morning, I told God that I felt my friend's father was still needed in this world, and that there was much good he could do by teaching God's Word to people like me who still needed help. I asked God to please save my friend's father and to give him the opportunity to help others like myself. In return, I promised to try to follow his path, starting with attending church that coming Sunday.

The following Sunday I attended church with my wife and it was a very peaceful feeling. The people at church all seemed so happy and full of life that it made me want to return the next Sunday.

As the service was ending on my second visit, I felt very relaxed and was in no hurry to leave. After searching for the answers to my earlier questions, I came to the conclusion that we could not possibly live just to die. There was no other answer or reasoning to my problems and questions other than believing in God and having enough faith to accept His Son, Jesus Christ, in my life; so I did.

The love I saw in all the people "hit me," and it was like nothing else I have ever felt in my life. At that time I was not sure if it was Jesus filling the empty place in my heart or just all the love of the people reaching out to me, but whatever it was, I hoped it would never stop. And if I could have one prayer answered, it would be that all God's people have the opportunity to share the same experiences that I have come to enjoy, need and want.

Looking back, I know that the Lord was with me every step of the way. The path He was leading me down was to teach me about the values of the world and temporary happiness, versus complete and total joy and the values of the Lord.

The Lord blessed me and my family by enabling us to make the right decisions on what I called my "gut feeling," but now I know it was my inner spirit leading me to worldly prosperity so that I would someday be able to testify that the things of the world are temporary and that worldly happiness will slip away very quickly.

Even though I was blessed with prosperity before being blessed as a Christian, being a Christians means more to me than anything the world has to offer. Recently, my wife and I were approached by a lady we did not know and she asked us to pray for her heart problems. She said she could see that we were Christians. Being recognized as a Christian was one of the best moments in my life.

In 1990, I had to quit my job of almost 20 years due to a rare blood disease. The doctors did not know what caused it, and said they could do nothing for me. In January 1994, the Lord told me He was going to heal me of that rare blood disease. In March 1994, I took the same blood test that had led to the diagnosis of the rare disease. This time the results were negative. My blood had been cleansed by the Blood of my Savior. By His stripes I was healed (see 1 Peter 2:24). Praise God.

Up to this point, everything you have read occurred 20 years ago. Today, I am still healed. My blood is normal. To the glory of God I have shared this story of God's healing power all over the world. God has called and sent me as an equipping evangelist to the Body of Christ (the Church) to speak into and bring change in four specific areas:

1. To identify, release, and establish the Ephesians 4 gift of the equipping evangelist in churches around the world.

2. To call the 97 percent of Christians who refuse to share their faith to repentance and then to train and equip them to witness for Christ.

3. To raise up and equip an army of shofar blowers (the ram's horn originally used by the Israelites and blown through as a horn) around the world.

4. To teach Christians how to handle their finances according to God's plan, not the world's plan.

At the writing of this book, Carla and I have been married 42 years. We have four children and 12 grandchildren.

If you have any questions or problems like I had, don't try to weather the storm on your own; come in out of the rain and let the Son of God, Jesus, meet your every need. Let Him lead you and guide you, through the Holy Spirit, from now to eternity. Since I accepted Jesus as my Savior the empty place in my heart has been permanently filled with the love of Jesus Christ, the Holy Spirit, and God our Father.

God can meet your every need, and will, if you do your part. I urge you to read God's Word daily, pray daily, praise the Lord's name daily and go to church every time the door is open.

"If ye abide in me, and my words abide in you, ye shall ask
what ye will, and it shall be done unto you"
(John 15:7, KJV).

ABOUT THE CONTRIBUTOR

Jim and Carla Barbarossa are Apostolic Equipping Evangelists, and are the founders of Step by Step Ministries. God has called Jim and Carla to "Prophecy to the Dry Bones"; to reach the nine out of 10 Christians that never witness and teach them how, while at the same time releasing and raising up the gift of the Ephesians Chapter 4 Equipping Evangelist in the local church.

Their evangelism training materials and outreach tools won first place in contests advertised by Charisma Magazine in May of 2007. Their evangelism outreach tools and training materials are now being used in over 107 nations of the world resulting in over 50 new churches being planted and over 500,000 souls coming to Jesus in the last 7 years. Their evangelism tools and training materials have been made in the Spanish language, and Jim and Carla are presently establishing outreaches and scheduling Pastors and Leaders Conferences in Peru, South America.

On January 1, 2012, Jim and Carla launched "Indiana Regional Unity Gathering." You can see more at this link: http://www.step-by-step.org/regionalunity.htm.

In 1996, God called, appointed and anointed Jim Barbarossa to teach on blowing the shofar from a biblical Christian perspective. Since then, Jim has been asked to blow the shofar to start conferences all over the world. As Jim sounds the ancient Hebrew instrument of repentance, praise, worship and warfare, it's as if we enter into the Holy of Holies and the deliverance and salvations follow.

As Carla Barbarossa worships the Lord in dance, the awesome holy presence of God is ushered in. Tears stream down the faces of many as they experience the bondage-breaking, yoke-destroying Shalom (Peace) of God.

Jim and Carla are the founders of TheShofarman.com. God has commissioned them to supply shofars to God's end time army of Shofar Sounders around the world, preparing the way for the end time harvest and the coming of the Lord.

Jim is an entrepreneur, businessman and author who has been blessed with a powerful testimony and loves to teach by example. Carla is a true worshiper who has the gift and anointing to bring people into the Father's presence through worship and dance. Jim and Carla's desire is to help you find God's will for your life, while at the same time perfecting you to do the work of the ministry.

God has given Jim a revelation on tithes, offerings and finances. During February and March of 2008, God instructed him to do five minute teachings on tithes and offerings in his home church for a period of eight weeks. The end result was that tithes and offerings doubled! People quit overspending and started saving part of what they earned. Jim believes these principles can be applied in every church.

Jim's testimony was in the August 1997 F.G.B.M.F. (Full Gospel Business Men's Fellowship International) *Voice* magazine, of which he is a member.

Jim and Carla have been happily married for 42 years. They have four children and 12 grandchildren. For more information you can visit their websites at:
www.step-by-step.org and www.theshofarman.com, e-mail: jim@step-by-step.org or call (219)762-7589.

CHAPTER 36

CROWN OF THORNS MIRACLE

Brad Ferguson

For who hath despised the day of small things?
(Zechariah 4:10a, KJV)

"Two thousand years ago a remarkable man walked this earth who revolutionized human nature. He was called the Prince of Peace. He taught men truth that can set them free. And He preached a gospel of love. Yet He told us not to seek after peace, freedom or love. He said, "Seek ye first the kingdom of God and His righteousness." He promised that if we did so, we should then attain the only lasting peace, freedom and love."

The place was our town's civic coliseum. The occasion was the 1972 graduation ceremony of one of our city's high schools. I was a sophomore college student there to watch my new girlfriend, who had graduated early and was attending college with me, walk across the stage and accept her diploma with the rest of her class.

The words quoted above signaled the end of the address from the valedictorian of Tascosa High School. Full of pomp, excitement and poignancy for the students and their parents, the graduation ceremony was tedious for those like me who had few emotional ties to seven hundred and fifty kids graduating from the high school which was the chief rival of my alma mater. Yet, the valedictorian had grabbed my attention, partly with her listing of the Vietnam War era social and political troubles we were all living through but primarily with her unexpected offering that Jesus was the answer to those problems.

I had been raised in church but was really just a nominal Christian. Maybe that was why such a public and thinly disguised proclamation of the Savior grabbed me so strongly that I never forgot it.

My parents divorced a couple of years later. My girlfriend broke up with me soon after that. Though I didn't take it well, I don't blame her. I had become bitter and had no rudder. I was close to graduating college but was depressed enough that I didn't attend my graduation ceremony when it came around. I had gotten back into martial arts and eventually became a black belt, something that had become the main sense of purpose in my life.

I decided to visit my best friend from high school who had moved to Oklahoma. He had become a Christian and was meeting regularly with a Navigators Bible study group. I had grown up attending church so discussions about Jesus and the Bible were not foreign to me, though you didn't have to be a real Christian to be a member in good standing at that church.

But this time, talking to my friend who had actually been studying the Bible, things seemed different. He was different than he used to be and the atmosphere in his home was different from anything I had known before.

When it came time for me to return home, he drove me some miles to the nearest bus station where I could catch a ride back to Amarillo. The drive took place before sunrise. Motoring through the flat countryside with an unobstructed view of the stars in the black sky, I began feeling something that I don't think I had ever felt before. It was something that seemed to be imbedded in that night sky but not tied to it. I was afraid that I was leaving something important, something bigger and grander, more secure and more meaningful than anything I had ever known.

I was afraid that if I went back home, I would become disconnected from whatever it was. We talked about it and my friend told me that it had to do with the Holy Spirit and that He was also there in Amarillo. He told me he would get me in touch with someone from the Navigators in Amarillo, and that studying the Bible with them would keep what I was feeling at that moment alive.

I did get in touch with that person with the Navigators. He was a dentist who mentored several new Christians. He met with me several times and helped give me a biblical foundation to stand on. I again started attending the church I grew up in and became friends with some biblically oriented Christians my age. We had wonderful times studying Scripture and fellowshipping together.

After some months I decided I wanted to go to seminary. The church I had grown up in, and that my friends and I were attending, gave me a small scholarship to attend their seminary at Texas Christian University. It didn't take me long to wrestle in my spirit because I believed the Holy Spirit was leading me on to where I was truly meant to attend.

I had met some fellow believers from the Baptist seminary a few miles away while they were on our campus witnessing to students at TCU. They could see that spiritually I was one of them. I joined their fellowship and began attending their church. That will always stand out in my mind as one of the most spiritually formative periods of my life.

In addition, staying in student housing, my roommate was a man in his 40's who was from India. He was a strong believer who had left his family behind for a time in order to get a seminary degree. He was another spiritual anchor for me.

He told me stories of a revival that had broken out in his church in India, St. Mary's church, *Niranam*, which was established by St. Thomas in AD 52. At age 16, he gave himself to the ministry. At age 18, Jesus appeared to him one night and called on him to honor the commitment he had made at age 16 to go to the mission field. He tried to reason with the Lord that he should go to college and learn to help support his family. Jesus was firm about needing him on the mission field.

My future roommate agreed to go with great enthusiasm. Afterward, though, he found he was unable to get out of bed, but for several weeks during his sleep he was shown many places in India where people needed to hear the Gospel. After the story about his experience with Jesus got out, people from his church began gathering at his house in the evenings to pray. Revival broke out in their town and surrounding villages, and after 30 days he found he could walk again.

He went straight to find people to minister to who lived in a depth of poverty we cannot even imagine.

It was 1979. By now, I was a genuine spirit-filled Christian.

"They laid Him in a grave and told us He was dead. But He rose again to prove that He had crushed the serpent's head. He has given life to us through the power of His death And in His resurrection won the final victory. Sing alleluia to the worthy Lamb. Who was slain and died for us, but rose again to reign."
(from Easter Praise)

A very tough, brawling drug dealer who was on his way to prison, and who had been led to the Lord by members of the church, had requested another song I'd written be played at the last service he attended before being transported to his new concrete and steel room. A deputy sheriff led James into the church and later took him away to jail. The song James wanted to hear one last time was a ballad he felt reflected his lost, rough life. Unknown to anyone, it also started the birthing of a relationship that had gestated for years, and which *Easter Praise* a few weeks later would give breath to.

A Christian band named Jeremiah's Commission had just performed at Trinity Fellowship, the small church I was a part of in Amarillo. They played a song I had recently written called *Easter Praise*. Shortly after Jeremiah's Commission finished *Easter Praise* and the congregation was dismissed, a good friend caught me in the church parking lot. She wanted to introduce me to a lovely young visitor to the church named Debbie.

Debbie had heard the song James had requested a few weeks earlier, but after "*Easter Praise*" she found my friend and asked, "Who is this Brad Ferguson who wrote these songs I keep hearing?"

"Oh, Brad?" my friend said as if I were family. "I'll introduce you."

Debbie confessed to me later that when she saw me, I was wearing the ugliest sweater she had ever seen. She also said that at our introduction, something inside her leaped with joy or recognition.

Debbie and I began spending time together, mainly talking. We are both introverts (she more than I), but we can be very talkative when it comes to discussing ideas. She had her Master's degree in English literature, and one evening as I was asking about her thesis on C. S. Lewis, she mentioned something from the address she made at her high school graduation. She had been valedictorian. I hadn't known that before and found it very interesting.

I told her I'd like to hear her speech if she had it handy. She found a copy of it on one of several neatly organized book shelves and began reading it to me. The further she read, the more I realized this was the valedictory address I had heard and been impressed with seven years earlier at my then-girlfriend's graduation.

Debbie and I were both caught off guard. This prior connection seemed like a "coincidence" of astounding proportions. Although our relationship was still new, and we weren't certain what implications to place upon our encounter from seven years before, we believed it was significant.

When Debbie and I met, I was not only between relationships but also between jobs. I soon took another "between job" as a study hall aide at the high school I had graduated from 10 years earlier. It wasn't the kind of job anyone makes a career of, but bringing order to a previously disorderly place brought "thank you's" from more than one serious student.

Although I was unaware of it, God was also bringing order into my life. In my pre-Christian days, I had a short-lived job making jewelry. I soon learned that the school had a jewelry-making class. I got to know the football coach who taught the class and he told me that if I had any jewelry I needed to cast, he would cast if for me while casting projects for students.

Christmas was just around the corner and I set about making a pendant for Debbie.

On Christmas day, Debbie was stunned as she held the beautiful pendant I'd fashioned for her in her hands. She had seen a few pictures of my work but she only had a passing knowledge of the time I'd spent making jewelry. That part of my life, the part before I really came to

Christ, seemed far away and insignificant. But it was not insignificant to God. As she gazed at her Christmas present, Debbie suggested that maybe I was supposed to make jewelry for a living.

The idea had never really occurred to me. If I made jewelry now, I wanted to make Christian jewelry. I wanted my faith in Jesus to be reflected in everything I did.

Seeing what I could do, Debbie sat down and excitedly sketched a design on a piece of paper, handed it to me, and asked if I could make a pendant that looked like her drawing. I studied her sketch and replied that I had never made anything like it before but that I would try. The next day I set my simple wax sculpting tools on my study hall desk and, surprisingly quickly, sculpted the master model of our original Crown of Thorns pendant.

I know there was something more than my hand at work in the sculpting process. When I first thought I was finished I had what seemed to me a clever idea: put thirty-nine thorns on the pendant to symbolize the traditional number of lashes Jesus received when he was scourged.

I started counting to see how many thorns I needed to add or remove to bring the number to 39. I counted again because I must have made a mistake.

I counted a third time.

It already had exactly thirty-nine thorns.

I could hardly wait to get off work and take it to Debbie for her approval. She was very impressed. It was exactly what she had pictured in her mind. She did not notice the number of thorns on the pendant and was amazed when I told her my story about the thorns. We were both convinced that God had guided my hands in the sculpting process.

After the Crown of Thorns pendant was cast and polished, we noticed more unplanned symbolism. The pendant was a circle that intersected with itself seven times. The circle represents eternity; seven is the biblical number for perfection and completion. Thus, our Crown of Thorns pendant symbolizes God's eternal gift to us, the perfect and complete atonement for our sins that Jesus made through His suffering and the shedding of His blood.

Wow. We didn't plan any of that, but we are convinced that He did.

Something in me had attached itself to Debbie because of her proclamation at a high school graduation ceremony that Jesus was the answer to our troubles. Seven years later (perfection and completion), something in her attached itself to me because of my proclamations of Jesus in song. A picture placed in her mind and the movement and skill placed in my hands, when brought together at the proper time, brought about a powerful symbol of God's love for sinners and His victory over sin.

At the end of the semester, I quit the study hall job and started my Christian jewelry business, Samaritan Arts Jewelry. I set up a small workshop in a corner of a room in the house I grew up in. There were many trials in my effort to get established, and it took 20 years for me to begin to understand the difficulties of owning and running a business.

Even though I had a degree in psychology, I was in my 40's before I figured out that I was an artist by nature. It took me a while to say that openly because I had always thought of artists as...*kooky*. It took me even longer to realize that artists are seldom the most gifted businessmen.

Although many people in our church kept urging Debbie and me to get married, it was seven years after we met before we felt directed, or released, by God to marry. We had the longest wedding ceremony anyone we knew could remember, and after our honeymoon Debbie and I set up house together. I continued to struggle financially, and sometimes my attention was divided between my business and pro-life work.

Sometimes the struggle seemed to be too great. Nevertheless, God provided.

We would remember the way in which God used us to bring our Crown of Thorns pendant into existence. We would remember the early days when a dying woman sent her son to buy a Crown of Thorns pendant so that she could wear it when she was buried. Or the woman who told me that she lay dying in a hospital bed (which doctors said she'd never get out of) and a friend gave her one of our Crown of Thorns. Whenever she felt it, she remembered *"by whose stripes ye were healed"* (1 Peter 2:24b). She rose from that bed with a beautiful testimony of healing.

We would remember missionaries who wore a Crown of Thorns because they served in countries where wearing a cross could get them killed. We'd remember the cancer patients who bought the pendant because of the testimony of a worker at the local cancer center who always wears a Crown of Thorns. Nor will we ever forget the nonbeliever who bought one on the spot after reading the story about the first one I made because he knew someone "who needed something like that." We know many people have heard the Gospel of Jesus' death for sinners because they were curious about one of our Crown of Thorns pendants or rings someone was wearing.

God brought us together as we heard the other proclaim the gospel. He enabled me to fashion the picture from Debbie's mind into His Crown. He wove unplanned symbolism into that small sculpture as I sculpted it. He has chosen to use that Crown of Thorns to again proclaim His Gospel through those who wear it.

I have to say, "Praise God," for the way He weaves His call to forgiveness and salvation into the everyday things used by people who follow Jesus. But isn't it usually in everyday things and moments which seem small to us that we communicate and pass on the love of God and the reality of salvation to others?

ABOUT THE CONTRIBUTOR

Brad and Debbie Ferguson started Samaritan Arts® Jewelry in 1980. There they design and make their well-known Crown of Thorns™ jewelry, Signet Purity Rings™ and True Love Waits® rings for young people, Christian wedding rings and other Christian jewelry. They serve the people of their local area from their store — voted the "Best Designer Jewelry" of Amarillo — located at 2427 Interstate 40 West, Amarillo, Texas 79109, and their customers around the world via their website, www.SamaritanArts.com.

CHAPTER 37

ENDURE TO THE FINISH LINE

Chris "Fireman" Brown

I returned, and saw under the sun, that the race is not to the swift
(Ecclesiastes 9:11a, KJV).

Many in the international track and field world and in my native country know me as Chris "The Fireman" Brown. I am also called "Eternal One," "Lion," "Evergreen," "Father Time" and "Old Campaigner." However, I was born Christopher D. Brown on October 15, 1978, in Wemyss Bight, Eleuthera, Bahamas, also known as a Family Island or Outer Island, known for its pineapples.

I began my running streak at the early age of seven, naturally following in the footsteps of my parents and older siblings (two of whom were local track standouts). Running track in Eleuthera was quite typical of many kids at that age. Although I was far from typical, I wasn't the best on the island nor in my settlement, let alone the country. It took a while for me to become aware of this being my gift from God.

My talent was being noticed and admired by many in the community. I advanced and began competing in national competitions at the high school level. These competitions afforded me opportunities to perform in the nation's capital of New Providence, Nassau, as well as in a variety of Pan American nations.

Keep in mind that where I came from, I did not have access to a track or proper facilities for training, so the streets, grass track, sand and beach was it. In spite of that and by the grace of God, I went on to establish and maintain the national record in the 800-meter. This was the event I initially focused on prior to my transition to the 400-meter.

While at Preston Aubrey High School, during my senior year (1996) I developed an attractive athletic profile. I was poised to receive one of the many scholarships being offered by a school visiting from the United States. However, the person in charge of collecting the group of senior athletes (including me) to meet with the college recruiter intentionally changed the meeting time without notifying two athletes; I was one of them.

Heartbroken, my eyes filled with tears. That was very hard to comprehend and digest at the age of 17.

At the time, I wondered *why* that happened to me. Still developing my relationship with God, I wondered why He would *let* that happen to me. I thought I'd missed out on what would be my only opportunity to pursue my newly-realized dream of running for a university in the nearby U.S.

After coping with the disappointment from that devastating blow, through the encouragement of my coach, Mr. Michael Coakley, and my Mother who believed in me, I moved to Nassau and voluntarily repeated my senior year in order to make myself available to college recruiters once again. That part of my journey was a real test of my young faith, a faith instilled in me at an early age.

It took a lot for me to go back and start something I had already completed. As God would have it, as it was in Eleuthera, it was in Nassau; again, I was a track standout, this time at R. M. Bailey High School. Through my perseverance and determination, the sacrifices and hard work paid off. Top U.S. colleges and Division I universities began approaching me from all corners and angles with scholarship offers.

God was opening new doors for me.

I decided on Southern University at New Orleans-SUNO in New Orleans, Louisiana, where I competed in track for a year. Then I transferred to Norfolk State University in Norfolk, Virginia, where I continued to be a track standout.

During my college track career, I established school records that still stand. I also made my first national team (Bahamas) which resulted in a 4 x 400m Gold medal at the CAC Games in Barbados. I participated in a host of international competitions representing my country and, most notably, became a first-time Olympian, participating in the 2000 Summer Olympic Games in Sydney, Australia.

After reflecting on where I came from, I could see how God had blessed me. My faith grew stronger.

In 2003, I transitioned into track professionally. In the time that followed, I participated in my second Olympic games (Athens, Greece, 2004), World Outdoor & Indoor Championships (Silver/Bronze medalist), Pan American Games (Double Gold medalist) and a host of other elite meets. One of my most outstanding achievements was marked when I broke the Bahamas' National Record in the men's 400m at the Golden League Meet in Oslo, Norway, on June 6, 2008. I ran a superb time of 44.40. Additionally, I placed fourth in the men's 400m finals in Beijing with a time of 44.45, and anchored Team Bahamas' men's 4 x 400m relay to a Silver medal in my third Summer Olympic Games (Beijing, China).

Following the 2008 season, I was inducted into my University's and Conference's Hall of Fame, Norfolk State University and MEAC, respectively (2009). Then I went on to win the Gold medal in the 400m at the World Indoor Championships in Qatar. Most significantly, I participated in my fourth Olympic Games in London, England (2012) in which I placed fourth in the men's 400m finals and captained the men's 4 x 400m relay team to a Gold medal. This was history-making for the country of the Bahamas, as well as for the international world, breaking a long-standing United States' record in the event.

April 2013 witnessed me wearing the new hat of "meet organizer" when I presented the Inaugural Chris Brown Bahamas Invitational (CBBI) track and field meet. This idea was a vision given to me by God where elite and junior athletes showcased their talent on Bahamian soil. Through much prayer and works of faith, He brought it to fruition.

In 2014, I continued my work as an athlete and went on to win my fifth consecutive medal at the IAAF World Indoor Championships, this time in Poland. I brought home a Silver medal, running a personal best time in my indoor career as well as for any quarter-miler aged 35, again making history for the Bahamas and worldwide.

I was also chosen as a featured athlete by the IAAF (International Amateur Athletics Federation). That meant a group of international journalists conducted a "Day-in-the-Life of Chris Brown" project in both Nassau and Eleuthera. I was completely honored by this selection and blessed to be able to share my humble beginnings along with the places that contributed to making me who I am.

While in Eleuthera, with the help of Adidas, I made a significant donation of track shoes to the young South Eleuthera track athletes. They still sometimes run without shoes as I did as a youngster. It was a proud moment for me to give back.

Other highlights include my performances at the IAAF Bahamas World Relays in Nassau (2014 and 2015) and our history making performance at the 2016 IAAF World Indoor Championships in Portland, Oregon. There, I anchored the 4x4 team to a Silver Medal, the country's first in this competition.

I continue to work hard on and off the track using the talent God blessed me with while consistently working on my craft. I am said to be one of the top-ranked and well-respected quarter-milers in the world. Currently I am preparing for the 2016 Summer Olympic Games in Rio de Janeiro, Brazil, in August, all the while reminding everyone that, "age ain't nothing but a number!"

God has blessed me beyond measure. When I reflect on myself as the "little kid" from Wemyss Bight, Eleuthera, Bahamas, who had no idea this would be the journey I would take, I am humbled. I thought the only door for opportunity had closed, but God opened several more. He afforded me the opportunity to travel the world, meet new people and impact lives. As my relationship with God has progressed, I have learned to remain obedient to Him and to put all faith and trust in Him.

As my mother taught me, "What *God* has for me *is* for me."

This has been my mantra. I say to those who have experienced road blocks, hurdles and obstacles in life to never give up, fight harder, push harder and believe in God. Believe God that what *is* for you *will* be for you. Two biblical verses I stand on are, *"The stone which the builders refused is become the head stone of the corner"* (Psalms 118:22, KJV) and *"...The race is not to the swift, nor the battle to the strong..."* (Ecclesiastes 9:11, KJV) but to him who endures until the end.

Described as a blessed, consistent, fierce and tenacious athlete, I am also extremely blessed to be a husband to my wife, Faith, and father to two daughters, Emerald and Zorah, and newest addition, son, Shiloh.

ABOUT THE CONTRIBUTOR

Chris 'Fireman' Brown — 5-time Olympian, 3-time Olympic Medalist, 9-time World Indoor/Outdoor Championships Medalist, Pan American Games Double Gold Medalist, Commonwealth Games Medalist, and 2-time Hall of Famer and graduate of Norfolk State University shares his unexpected journey to becoming a professional track and field athlete and the influence of God's divine power.

Chris represents his country of the Bahamas and specializes in the men's 400m and 4 x 4 relay. He has been ranked throughout the years as one of the best quarter-milers in the world, many noting his consistency, longevity and ability to overcome adversity.

Chris can be followed on Twitter: @Da_RunnerBrown and visited on his website: www.chrisbrowntherunner.com

You may also visit Chris's track and field invitational (Chris Brown Bahamas Invitational) on Twitter: @BahamasInv and its website at: www.bahamasinvitational.com

Chris' Fireman' Brown Olympic Gold Medalist, 2012
World Indoor Champion, 2010
Two-Time Hall of Famer, 2009
www.chrisbrowntherunner.com

CHAPTER 38

"END OF THE LINE, GUYS" GOD SAVES HIS ANOINTED ONES

Rev. Donald M. Hackbardt

*Now know I that the Lord saveth his anointed; he will hear him
from his holy heaven with the saving strength of his right hand*
(Psalm 20:6, KJV).

It was late spring 1969 when I strapped my 22-year-old frame
securely into the cramped "sling" position on the UH-1 "Huey"
helicopter. I was one of two door gunners on that chopper trained to
handle the powerful weapon known as the M60 machine gun. Should
anything go wrong, we were the crew's last bastion of hope.

On this, my first mission, I began by asking the Chief Warrant
Officer if I could pray for God's protection. I stared at my scripture
verse taped to the inside of the chopper's door opening: *"I will lift up
mine eyes unto the hills, from whence cometh my help. My help cometh
from the Lord, which made heaven and earth"* (Psalm 121:1-2).

The mission was simple: fly from our base camp to a certain
location on the Ho Chi Minh trail deep within southern Laos, landing
one mile or so ahead of a large North Vietnamese Regular troop
movement. There, we would drop our "cargo" of three Air Force
Intelligence Officers; they were set to rendezvous with a Special Forces
unit already on the ground to call in B-52 air strikes against the enemy.

As any good soldier knows, no mission is ever easy. As we neared
our target, the chopper pilot's voice crackled through our helmets.

"End of the line, guys," he said.

He had no way of knowing how true that statement was. As the Huey descended, it became clear that something was very wrong. Instead of being greeted by a unit of Green Berets, we were setting down smack dab in the midst of an entire battalion of North Vietnamese Regular troops. In a split second, the tense voice of the Chief Warrant Officer filled the aircraft.

"Abort! Bad Intel! Abort!"

But it was too late. A barrage of furious AK-47 fire pierced every nook and cranny of our Huey. With no armor, the bullets cut through the helicopter like a warm knife through butter.

In the storm of gunfire, the enemy managed to shoot off our tail rotor, leaving the pilots helpless to control the doomed chopper. We were now in a 150-foot tailspin to the ground below. After whirling through the thick, hot air for what seemed to be an eternity, we crash landed on a levy separating two large rice patties.

There we were. Approximately a thousand or more of the enemy surrounded our four man crew and three Air Force Intelligence Officers. All that stood between us and them was me, our 2nd door gunner, and our M60s.

I should have been scared to death, yet, as I instinctively fixed my sights on the enemy's helmets while they crouched behind the levy to our west, I remained calm. You see, as I stared toward them, my eyes also saw God's word taped to my door and I remembered my prayer. I knew God was with me and would sustain me.

Then all hell broke loose. "Get on the floor right now!" I screamed to the pilots and Air Force Officers as 7.62mm AK-47 rounds again ripped through the aircraft, killing the door gunner covering my rear. A second later, the co-pilot took a bullet in the neck as the plexiglass front window shattered.

Blood was everywhere. The Huey crumbled around us.

With each passing second, the enemy attempted to position themselves closer, tightening their noose around our perilous position.

A sense of terror set in among the remaining pilot and three Air Force officers. In the relentless and deafening hail of gunfire, God kept my mind focused on Him, His promises *("...My help cometh from the Lord, which made heaven and earth")*, and of course, the enemy.

Bullets struck me and my lead layered vests (one was tied to the back of my "sling") from nearly every angle. Even with the lead armored vests, each piece of flaming lead felt like a hammer blow to my gut.

If the situation wasn't bad enough, now a platoon of North Vietnamese Regulars approached from the waters behind us.

Seeing this, I unleashed a hail of gunfire on the enemy in front of me.

BOOM! BOOM! BOOM! BOOM! BOOM! BOOM! BOOM! BOOM! BOOM! ...release trigger.... repeat.... making sure the M60 barrel didn't overheat.

Seconds felt like minutes.

Platoon after platoon charged our location.

I screamed to the Air Force officers, "You know our position. Call in air support and just burn 'em'!" before jumping to the rear gunner position to fire on and kill the enemy approaching in the water behind us.

In the heat of the moment, the officers gave our closest support aircraft the correct coordinates.

Just when I thought I wouldn't be able to hold the enemy off anymore, I saw the most beautiful sight of my life — two F-4 Phantom jets streaked low through the sky, dropping their payloads of Napalm that tumbled like huge fireballs on the remaining enemy forces in front of us. A tense half hour or so later, a rescue helicopter emerged through the thick smoke and carnage.

Salvation had arrived in more ways than one. God had rescued me (already a believer), the Chief Warrant Officer and the three Air Force officers from this fiery trial. From that day forward, during each rotation of duty, everyone I flew with became "believers" and Bible readers. They personally witnessed God's deliverance and protection and I believe they wanted to trust the Lord as I did.

We never again entered the skies without me repeating Psalm 121: 1-2. I'd pray with the crew and intelligence officers, "Lord, the mountains are the challenges we might face today from the enemy. Where does our help come from? It comes from you. We pray for your protection in Jesus' name. Amen."

Just as I needed the spiritual armor that God's word provided me as a door gunner in the rice patties of Laos (and, by the way, throughout the course of my life), today's soldiers need God's word in the mountains of Afghanistan, Iraq, Syria and other danger zones across the world.

The enemy and location may be different, but the challenges and fears are the same. Can you imagine experiencing the combat situation I just described without being a "believer" in Jesus, and knowing the comfort and confidence that God's Word provides? Not knowing whether a Taliban fighter with an RPG is waiting around the next corner to shoot your chopper out of the sky? Or fearing that the man walking by your patrol is a suicide bomber waiting to detonate his explosives?

The truth is that only God knows. He comforted me in Laos and He wants to do the same for our soldiers in trouble spots around the world, just as he wants to do for each of you reading this. That way when you or our brave troops pass through their own daily challenges, or the fiery furnace of combat, they can be confident in knowing that their *"...help comes from the LORD, the maker of heaven and earth"* (Psalm 121:1-2).

ABOUT THE CONTRIBUTOR

Rev. Donald M. Hackbardt, the CEO/Executive Director of God's Word to the Nations Mission Society since May 1992, is recognized for showing dedication, leadership and excellence in Bible translation, effective communication, and outreach strategies.

Rev. Hackbardt is a 1973 graduate of the University of Michigan and, later, one of IBM's top salesmen before he entered the ministry in 1982. He frequently travels and speaks to religious groups about biblical outreach strategies. In addition, he also receives invitations to speak at the conventions of a variety of vocations outside the Church about the importance of "The Ageless Challenge: Effective Communication," inasmuch as the topic relates to both success in communicating God's mission, as well as financial success in the business world.

The highlight of his career began in May 1992 when he was selected to lead a translation project that ultimately produced "*GOD'S WORD®*," an exceptional new translation of God's saving, life-changing message that uses clear, natural English and not "theological jargon."

Born April, 13, 1947, Rev. Hackbardt grew up in Highland, Michigan. He was married to Linda (Daymon) Hackbardt on July 18, 1970, nearly 46 years ago, following his return from SE Asia and her later participation in the "1970 Miss Michigan Pageant." They have two grown sons, Nathan, (age 45) and Alex, (age 42). They have all lived in the Jacksonville, Florida area since December 2000.

For more information about the nonprofit 501(c)(3) religious organization, God's Word to the Nations Mission Society, visit http://www.godsword.org or call Rev. Hackbardt at (904) 716-3436 to talk to him.

CHAPTER 39

TRANSCENDED BY THE GOD OF PSALM 40

Donna Martonfi

He brought me up also out of a horrible pit, out of the miry clay, and set my feet upon a rock, and established my goings. (Psalm 40:2, KJV).

During my entire life I had *hoped* there was a God in heaven. I never dreamed I would find the answer while still alive on planet earth.

However, at the age of 19, I had given birth to a baby girl who had spina bifida. She was only expected to live a few days at the most.

Staring at the empty crib beside my bed was unbearable. I went into the living room and screamed out at God, not in anger, but out of a broken heart.

Full of pain and sorrow, I said, "What have I ever done to You to deserve this?"

I heard a majestic voice emanate immediately from every part of the room--from the carpet, the curtains, the coffee table — so that the entire room was encompassed with this thunderous and yet so very gentle voice. I didn't have to ask, "Who is this?" It was undeniably obvious it was God Himself.

"I did not do this to you," He stated, "but I will repay you. I will send you twin boys."

I jumped off the sofa and ran into the bedroom to wake my husband up, yelling, "Get up! Get up! God is in the living room! We're going to have twins!"

My husband had been born and raised in a communist country which instilled in him there was no God, just like there was no Santa Claus nor tooth fairy. He could not fathom how people in North America could actually believe in an invisible, supernatural being, yet he very cautiously approached the living room and peeked in.

"It's okay, Donna," he said. "Everything is going to be all right. We'll get you some tranquilizers. Please, come lie down."

Lie down? You don't talk to God and then go lie down.

I called everyone I knew. It was three o'clock in the morning but I called my mother, my mother-in-law, my friends and even some coworkers babbling about God being in my living room. Their response was all the same.

"You need to go lie down. You need to get some tranquilizers. Everything's going to be okay."

I couldn't make them understand so I eventually gave up; but I never let go of the promise God gave me. My little girl, Diana, lived to be almost eight months old and died on July 16th, at 11:35 at night. The following year, to the very day of July 16th, at exactly 11:35 p.m., my twin boys were born according to God's word.

I called everyone back and said, "I told you so!" It had no impact. So, continuing on my merry way and focusing on my new, happy, all-consuming little family, I didn't give God a second thought either.

About six years later, I had a supernatural experience with God once again. I actually thought the boys and I had possibly been hit by a car and that we were somewhere between heaven and earth. The entire episode lasted about eight hours. Space does not permit me to tell the whole story in such a short article, but you can read about the entire experience in my book, *Uphill Climb,* or on my website: www.psalm40ministries.com.

After that profoundly surreal encounter, I was afraid people might think I was out of my mind so I literally told God to go away, leave me alone and not to bother me anymore. I told Him I would deal with Him after I died. Of course, not realizing at the time that *at that point* it would be too late.

I began a career in real estate and for many of the agents, the thing to do on Friday afternoons was to visit some very well-known and very expensive psychics in Toronto. Regrettably, and without realizing the horrible implications and unwanted doors these encounters would open, I entered a frightening stage in my life that caused my husband and me to actually fear for our lives and the lives of our children. It became worse and worse until it culminated in an experience a few years later that should have sent us running out the front door, except we thought it would be to no avail as the poltergeist would simply follow us.

One night while discussing how we were certain something very "evil" was after us, our kitchen cupboard slammed open. A ceramic cooking pot, which was situated at the *bottom* of a pile of plastic bowls, shot straight out about 12 feet without disturbing the bowls piled on top of it. Then, with a loud and thunderous bang, the pot shattered into a trillion pieces directly above our heads. A second later, there wasn't so much as a chunk or tiny particle to pick up, only a powdery residue. We were startled, yet so used to phenomenon like this happening on a regular basis that we just got up and went to bed without even cleaning up the mess. We didn't know where to turn for help.

It just so happened that the very next evening I was presenting an offer with a very attractive and obviously intelligent real estate agent. She kept talking about Jesus, even though she didn't look "corny." She was all excited because she was going to be baptized on Sunday by being fully immersed in water. I had never heard of such a thing and was determined to witness this remarkable event.

It turned out to be more than remarkable. When I walked into the church I felt as if my hair, which was down to my waist, shot out in every direction and stuck straight up in the air. Simultaneously, it seemed as if wave after wave of electrical current was sweeping up and down my body. I became electrified. I even suspected that the carpet had been plugged into an electrical outlet.

This time I determined I wasn't going to say anything about it possibly being the very presence of God. Wasn't I surprised when *both* my sons commented that we just had to come back because they "sensed God in this place."

Since they validated what I had already been deducing, I then surveyed the church and noticed something I had never seen before in my life. I saw people "worshipping" God. They were immersed in God. Their faces actually glowed with the tangible "love" of God all over them. Naturally, I decided to come back just one more time and check it out.

It was my divine appointment. The visiting evangelist preached the entire message directly to me and wouldn't take his eyes off of me. It was as if he knew all about me and the struggle and terror our family had gone through the past couple of years. I didn't know what to think. *Were these people all psychics? Could he read my mind? How could he possibly know these things?*

He kept asking me to put my hand up but I refused. I glared at him and shook my head "no." I actually sat on my fingertips so my hand wouldn't go up all by itself. I didn't know what to expect.

His name was Keith Parks and he said, "The Holy Spirit pointed you out to me when I walked across the altar of this church and the Lord wants to give you a miracle."

I thought, *I don't want a miracle. I just want the devil to get off my back.*

Then, he actually threatened to come down and get me, so I put up my hand to stop him. That's when it felt like an angel just picked me up by the scruff of my shirt and I floated to the front of the altar. I then felt like a deluge of black filth was gushing out of me and at the same time like a torrent of rushing water was pouring in to replace the sin and filth that was pouring out.

At that moment, all fear was removed from me. I actually sensed it leave. Fear had been a huge part of my entire life. I was afraid of dogs; I was afraid of water; I was claustrophobic. To sum things up, I was afraid of my own shadow.

I was raised "on and by" fear, but at that moment, down at that altar, it had completely lifted. I later tested it on the largest dog I could find and, to everyone's astonishment, I even jumped into the six foot end of a swimming pool and did aquatic ballet!

My life changed so dramatically that day. All the hocus pocus and ominous events stopped immediately. It was like somebody had pulled a curtain and we had stepped into an entirely new life. I was so totally different that my husband became determined to come and find out what I was involved in.

He walked into the church an atheist, but walked out "born again" and renewed by the power of Christ. He said it was like God had taken a great big, huge fist and hit him straight between the eyebrows.

Our relationship with the Lord grew stronger each day, and He became as real as any human being I could touch or feel. We've experienced, and continue to experience, countless miracles and "God encounters" over the years.

Ultimately, my prayer is that everybody would come to the place where God would become an integral part of their lives as well. I am certain that they would never regret making the decision to follow Jesus. A passage in the Bible totally summarizes our transformation and it is Psalm 40:2-5:

He brought me up also out of a horrible pit,
out of the miry clay,
and set my feet upon a rock,
and established my goings.
And he hath put a new song in my mouth,
even praise unto our God:
many shall see it, and fear,
and shall trust in the Lord.
Blessed is that man that maketh the Lord his trust,
and respecteth not the proud, nor such as turn aside to lies.
Many, O Lord my God, are thy wonderful works
which thou hast done,
and thy thoughts which are to usward:
they cannot be reckoned up in order unto thee:
if I would declare and speak of them,
they are more than can be numbered.

Before I conclude, I need to interject an important element into my testimony. After that night in my living room, I spent many years wondering why God had said, "I did not do this to you." One day, He reminded me of an incident that happened when I was pregnant with my daughter.

A coworker had taken out an Ouija Board and we very innocently asked it if I was going to have a boy or a girl since there was no ultrasound back then. The thing began to move all by itself. It spelled out that my baby had a "bad heard." We didn't know if it meant "heart" or "head," but we knew beyond a shadow of a doubt that we had tapped into something very dark and dangerous.

I had no idea that God clearly warns us to have nothing to do with the occultic realm or we would suffer consequences. I did suffer the consequences of my foolishness and it cost the life of my precious baby. I know this because one evening, God vividly and in great detail revealed that this was the reason behind her affliction.

Another scripture in the Bible, Hosea 4:6a, says, *"My people are destroyed for lack of knowledge,"* even though our Heavenly Father does not want even one to perish. Instead, He tells us *"that whosoever believeth in him should not perish, but have everlasting life"* (John 3:16b).

The decision to perish or not to perish is yours. Here and now, God is asking you to make a choice. This is the most important decision of your entire life.

My prayer is that you will see what God has done for me and put your trust in Him.

ABOUT THE CONTRIBUTOR

Donna is ordained with the Canadian Assemblies of God and has been in ministry since 1996 when she founded Psalm 40 Ministries. For many years she hosted live, call-in television programs in both the United States and Canada, and has been privileged to be interviewed and share her amazing story many times on other Christian broadcasts.

She is a passionate and gifted public speaker and a truly riveting writer. More than 100 of her articles have been published in city newspapers in both Florida and South Carolina. She has penned four books which are available in most bookstores or you can order them through Amazon.com. All of her stories will encourage you to believe God for the impossible and to live your life to the fullest in that supernatural realm that is available to you on a daily basis.

You can visit her website at: www.psalm40ministries.com

CHAPTER 40

ONE TICKET TO HEAVEN, PLEASE

Rev. Dr. Mark Virkler

Then Peter said unto them, Repent, and be baptized every one of you in the name of Jesus Christ for the remission of sins, and ye shall receive the gift of the Holy Ghost
(Acts 2:38, KJV).

Born Again at Age 15 — When I Joined Fundamentalism

I was lying in bed, trying to fall asleep and a thought kept going through my mind, *If you died tonight, you are not prepared to go to Heaven.* Little did I know that this flowing thought was actually the voice of the Holy Spirit calling me into God's kingdom. I couldn't shake it, so I got up and went downstairs to tell my parents I wanted to be saved. They drove me to the minister's home where he explained the plan of salvation and prayed with me. That night, my life was forever changed.

The church I joined at age 15 believed that anyone who was not a member of that denomination was not a Christian or going to Heaven. Wow. I was saved into a church which practiced intense judgmentalism. Talk about a rocky beginning.

My Early Experiences — No Holy Spirit

My first Bible included marginal notes that taught dispensationalism, which includes the belief that the gifts of the Holy

Spirit are not for today. Liberals, on the other hand, teach demythalization, which is the belief that the miracles Jesus did were mere myths and need to be stripped away. Both ends of the doctrinal spectrum marginalize the role of the Holy Spirit.

I led people to the Lord with no mention of the Holy Spirit and no expectation that they would necessarily experience anything when they were saved. They were just guaranteed Heaven if they said the right words.

Learning to Experience the Holy Spirit Took Me 25 Years

- Five years into my Christian experience I received the gift of speaking in tongues.

- Ten years in, I learned to recognize the voice of the Holy Spirit.

- Fifteen years in, I learned to cast out demons.

- After 20 years, I learned to interpret dreams.

- After being born again 25 years, I learned to lay hands on the sick and see them recover.

My 25-year process can be shortened. New Christians can move in the power of the Holy Spirit immediately, and if they do, all Heaven will break forth in their lives, so we have created a website called *Born of the Spirit* (www.bornofthespirit.today).

How Central is the Holy Spirit in the Salvation Process

A young man from Asia emailed me his two-way journaling, where one writes out God's dialogue with them. I saw demonic interference in the journaling and suggested he read over our salvation blog to make sure he was saved. However, it was my older version — how I used to present the salvation message. He read it, followed the steps it outlined for salvation, and then let me know he felt nothing happened.

Well, that is not what I was hoping for! I believe the Spirit bears witness in our hearts that we are children of God (Rom. 8:16), so I expect people to feel something. Not that I always believed this. I used to believe feelings were soulish and you didn't need to feel anything when you experienced salvation. I believed you accepted salvation by faith, based on the facts of Scripture, thus ruling out any heart sensations.

Cigarettes? Really?

The young man's next suggestion was that he felt he needed to give up cigarettes before he could be saved. I asked him if he felt the Lord told him that.

He said, "No."

My inner conclusion was that he didn't need to give up cigarettes in order to be saved; that was something God could work out with him at a later time. *Was there something wrong with my salvation article?*

I decided I should review what I had written to see what I'd said that made him think he needed to give up cigarettes first. I read it and discovered that three of the first four steps I had listed were: acknowledging, repenting of and forsaking your sins — and this was all before you invited Jesus Christ or the Holy Spirit into your heart.

Wow! That would make the overcoming of my sins a striving of my flesh, rather than a work of the Holy Spirit. The biblical definition of this is a "dead work", something I do by the flesh rather than by the strength of the Spirit (Jn. 6:63). Dead works need to be repented of (Heb. 6:1-2). Okay, now I was sure my salvation blog definitely needed to be rewritten.

What does the Bible say about salvation? It says, *"Repent ye, and believe the gospel"* (Mk. 1:15b). Of course, that verse doesn't tell what I am repenting of or what the gospel is that I now believe in; I needed to explore further to see if I could find the answers to these two critically important questions.

Are Sins Dealt with Before or After Salvation?

I discovered that many verses speak of putting off sins *after* being saved, and that this is accomplished by the transforming power of the Holy Spirit within us (Rom. 8:9-14; 2 Cor. 3:18; Gal. 5:16-25; Eph. 4:22-32; 1 Jn. 1:5-10; 2 Pet. 1:2-11).

So What Is It, Then, That We Repent Of?

I came to the conclusion that we repent for believing satan's big lie, introduced in the Garden of Eden, that *you* can *know* (Genesis 3:4-5). Satan suggested that it's all about me and what I think to be true. "You" became the false god of humanism; "know" became the false god of rationalism. All other sins in my life are an outworking of this one big lie and these two false gods. Other sins will fall away once satan's big lie is dealt with.

Salvation begins then with me renouncing satan's lie of independent living and turning back to God's original intent, which was that I live out of daily walks with Him in the cool of the day (Genesis 3:8), or "dependent" living, living and walking by the Spirit (Galatians 5:25). Sins of my flesh will be overcome by the power of the Spirit within me (Romans 8:13). I will not be overcoming them with the strength of my flesh, as the efforts of the flesh profit nothing (John 6:63).

We Preach the Gospel of What?

Now for the second part of Mark 1:15b, *"Repent ye, and believe the gospel."* What is the gospel that I am asked to believe in? I concluded that it is the "Gospel of the Kingdom", not the "gospel of salvation". I noticed that the gospel of salvation is only mentioned once (Eph.1:13), while Gospel of the Kingdom is mentioned six times (Matthew 4:23; Matthew 9:35; Matthew 24:14; Mark 1:15; Luke 16:16; and Acts 8:12).

Out of these seven times, we are never commanded to preach the gospel of salvation. Four times the Bible says Jesus preached the Gospel of the Kingdom (Matt. 4:23; Matt. 9:35; Mk. 1:15; Lk. 16:16), once that Phillip preached the Gospel of the Kingdom (Acts 8:12) and once it states that the end will come after the Gospel of the Kingdom has been preached to the whole world (Matt. 24:14), which seems to quite clearly mean that we are supposed to be preaching the Gospel of the Kingdom.

I understand this to mean that we align ourselves with Jesus the King who demonstrated "Kingdom" power by taking authority over disease, sickness and death. He cast out demons. He healed the sick.

Then He commissioned and empowered us to do the same. This is the gospel I preach. Repent of living separated from the King, and come experience Kingdom power!

What Was the Climax of Peter's Altar Call?

Finally, we get to the altar call. What is the promise at the end of our salvation message? Peter concluded his first gospel presentation with these words, "...*Repent, and be baptized every one of you in the name of Jesus Christ for the remission of sins, and ye shall receive the gift of the Holy Ghost"* (Acts 2:38). Wow! Just a bit different from my close which had always been, "You will go to Heaven when you die."

Amazing Things Happen When You Honor the Holy Spirit

The climax of the salvation experience is that one receives the Holy Spirit. He joins Himself to our spirit and flows effortlessly out through us, transforming us through God's awesome healing power.

I have seen many healed as I pray for them. One older gentleman was instantly healed of all arthritis in his pain-ridden legs as a result of healing prayer. I have cast demons out of thousands of people and seen their lives transformed and illnesses disappear. I have had demons cast out of me, and my inner turmoil was released and a 15-year recurring, tormenting dream vanished instantly.

I receive dreams of counsel and guidance from God on a weekly basis. These have provided healing and direction for my life over the last 35 years. When I am on the wrong path, I have a warning dream. When I am sinking, I have a dream of falling. When I am doing well, I have a dream of soaring.

Once, my wife went to bed angry and God gave her a dream of an angry bull being invited into her home where he knocked the glasses off her face and crushed them, meaning that when one allows anger in, they can no longer see things clearly. The imagery and counsel in dreams is endless and breathtaking.

I now energize my spirit by speaking in tongues. I have experienced healing of a persistently stiff neck by forgiving and releasing a person who had offended me. I have honored the health laws I discovered in the Bible and at age 64 I am healthier than I was at age 30. I have not needed to visit a doctor since I began following God's health laws 24 years ago.

As you can see, this Gospel (good news) of the Kingdom offers blessings which enhance every area of my life. Peace, joy, laughter, health, healing and happiness are mine. I am experiencing a better marriage than I ever had in my younger years. I have wonderful relationships with my children and grandchildren. I experience financial blessing. My bills are paid. Really, what more could a person ask for? And yes, I have received eternal life also.

I invite you to embrace the good news of the Kingdom. Repent for living independent from your Creator and welcome God as your King, allowing His blessings to transform every area of your life.

ABOUT THE CONTRIBUTOR

Mark is a trailblazer and a "how-to" guy — practical, biblical, spiritual and hilarious enough to have many people tell him that he should be a stand-up comedian. Everyone thoroughly enjoys his training approach as he draws you into an interactive learning experience of communion with God.

Dr. Virkler has written more than 50 books in the areas of spiritual intimacy and growth. His best-selling series on how to hear God's voice has sold over 250,000 copies. He is the founder of Communion With God Ministries (www.CWGMinistries.org) and Christian Leadership University (www.CLUOnline.com), an online university where the voice of God is at the center of every learning experience.

Mark has taught on developing intimacy with God and spiritual healing for more than 30 years on six continents. The message has been translated into over 40 languages, and he has helped to establish more than 250 church-centered Bible schools around the world.

CONCLUSION

Aren't you rejoicing in these 40 incredible short stories that you've just read?

In closing, I want to give glory to God, and to share with you that there have been so many instances of God's divine intervention, and such amazing God-encounters in my life, that I simply couldn't imagine my life without the Lord now. It isn't possible. God is so incredible, and He truly does love all of His creation. That includes you!

God has such a great and wonderful plan for your life. He is just waiting for you to tap into it. What would you think if you could have your very own "Salvation encounter," or "God encounter"? God is waiting just for you. He wants you to come to Him, though — in truth and in sincerity of heart and mind.

If you are being drawn by God right now, I ask you to consider not only what it would look like being with Him in Heaven one day, but how incredible it would be to live an active Christian life — like our testimony contributors in this book? How fascinating would this be to you?

Living this kind of life is entirely possible, but it is ultimately up to you to decide if this is for you. If the Christian life is sounding more interesting by the moment, then I believe the Lord is calling you to experience this Christian walk. Would you like to make this decision right now?

If so, I've included below some words from a friend of mine, Mark Virkler, President of Communion With God Ministries. He would be honored to walk you through your next step in this Christian walk — dedicating your life to the Lord Jesus Christ, and starting out by saying the Sinner's Prayer.

If you would like to take this next step of faith, I greatly encourage you to do so. This prayer is very simple. If you sincerely believe this in your heart, and profess your confession with your mouth to another, you are saved, my friend.

As with Mark's testimony, "One Ticket to Heaven, Please," you will, indeed, be assured of your Salvation in Christ. If you died today, you know that you would, in fact, go to this very real place named, "Heaven." So, I gladly refer you to Mark Virkler to lead you into Salvation, and to add some incredible teaching along the way.

Here is Mark's walk through the Sinner's Prayer, [1] with some added information for you with permission from his website www.bornofthespirit.today. It is an excellent website for both seeking and new believers who wish to explore Christianity and grow in their journey with the Lord.

I sincerely hope that you will repeat this prayer. Let it really sink into your spirit. You will feel refreshed, invigorated and more alive than ever before as you say the following words:

***

I REPENT for being master of my own life and living separate from God.

"And saying, The time is fulfilled, and the kingdom of God is at hand: repent ye, and believe the Gospel"
(Mark 1:15).

To repent means you change your mind. I repent of satan's big lie in the Garden of Eden, when he said, *"...your eyes shall be opened, and ye shall be as gods, knowing good and evil"* (Gen. 3:5b). His suggestion was that instead of taking daily walks with God in the cool of the day, and hearing from God and receiving His wisdom, we could figure things out ourselves. Satan suggested independent living (out of self), rather than dependent living (out of the Holy Spirit).

Jesus came to restore relationship: Jesus, of course, modeled the original design of the Garden when He said, *"...The Son can do nothing of himself, but what he seeth the Father do"* (Jn. 5:19, 20, 30; 8:28, 29, 38). No more striving with my own strength: The first foundation stone in the Christian life is to repent from my own strivings which the Bible calls dead works (Heb. 6:1, 2). A dead work is a work which originates with self rather than God. It is a work which follows satan's suggestion to live out of MY initiative. This is the FOUNDATIONAL SIN, out of which all other sins flow.

So if at the point of salvation, we deal with this one foundational sin, this will restore us to a relationship with our Heavenly Father. We can once again live out of His voice and receive His power. Once fellowship with God is restored, other sins will get cleaned up. Indeed, evidence that one has repented of this foundational sin and been born again is that these other sins are disappearing (1 Pet. 2:1-2; Acts 26:20; Heb. 5:9; 1 Cor. 3:15; 1 Cor. 5:5; Titus 2:11-14; 2 Thess. 2:13).

With your spiritual eyes fixed on Jesus, pray this prayer: *Jesus, I change my mind about You. You are the Son of God and You are God. You came into this world to show us the way we are to live and to provide eternal life to those who would accept You.*

I CONFESS with my mouth that Jesus is Lord and BELIEVE in my heart that God raised Him from the dead

> *"That if thou shalt confess with thy mouth the Lord Jesus, and shalt believe in thine heart that God hath raised him from the dead, thou shalt be saved"*
> (Romans 10:9).

> *"For God so loved the world, that he gave his only begotten Son, that whosoever believeth in him should not perish, but have everlasting life"*
> (John 3:16).

With your eyes fixed on Jesus, pray this prayer aloud: I confess with my mouth that You, Jesus, are Lord, the Ruler over all. You are the Christ, the Son of God. I believe in my heart that God raised You from the dead and You are alive forevermore, seated on Your throne in heaven next to the Father. The heavenly hosts worship before Your throne. I believe Your blood that was shed on the cross washes away all my sin.

Deepen the experience: You may want to repeat the above a couple of times, slowly, reverently and emotionally while seeing each scene as you speak it. This allows these truths to sink deeply into your heart and spirit.

I RECEIVE You, Jesus, as my Lord and my Savior.

> *"He came unto his own, and his own received him not. But as many as received him, to them gave he power to become the sons of God, even to them that believe on his name"*
> (John 1:11, 12).

With the eyes of your heart fixed on Jesus, pray this prayer: I receive You as my personal Lord, King and Commander. I invite You into my life as the Lord and Ruler of my life. I no longer choose to be in charge of my life. I give it to You.

I invite You, Jesus, to have first place in my heart and my life. I ask for Your cleansing blood that was shed on the cross to come now and wash down over all my sins. Come make me clean. Restore me to a right relationship as a child of my heavenly Father. Thank You, Lord, for Your cleansing blood! I stand clean and white in Your presence. I put on Your robe of righteousness which You are handing to me. Thank You, Lord.

Pause in His presence: Now tune to flow and watch Jesus come and wash away your sins, cleansing you, and placing His garment of pure white upon you, covering you with His righteousness. What does it feel like, wearing the garment of Christ's righteousness?

I WELCOME You, Holy Spirit, into my life to rescue and empower me and to restore me to intimacy with my heavenly Father.

"...And ye shall receive the gift of the Holy Ghost"

(Acts 2:38b).

"But if the Spirit of him that raised up Jesus from the dead dwell in you, he that raised up Christ from the dead shall also quicken your mortal bodies by his Spirit that dwelleth in you"

(Romans 8:11).

Pray this prayer as you watch the Holy Spirit enter into your heart:

Holy Spirit, I welcome You into my heart, my soul and my body. Come, enter me now. Take up residence within me. Be the Source of power in my life. Be the Source of my life. I choose to live and walk by Your leading within. I acknowledge You as the River which flows from the throne of God, and is now flowing within my heart

(Jn. 7:37-39).

Come flow within me. I want to sense Your flow within, and live out of Your flow for the rest of my life. Give life to me now, I pray in Jesus' name. I receive the Holy Spirit. I receive the River of Life. I receive You, Lord Jesus. You are my all and my everything. Thank You, Lord, for saving a sinner such as I was and now equipping me with Your empowering Holy Spirit. What amazing gifts You have given to me!

Now wait quietly in His presence: See the light and energy of the Holy Spirit swirling around within you, changing you, transforming you, enlightening you, empowering you. Is He speaking something to you? Tune to His voice, which is flowing thoughts, and hear what He is saying to you. Respond with, "Yes, Sir," as He is giving you your very first instructions as your new-found Commander and Friend.

***

As Mark has just shared, you are receiving your very first instructions from your new- found "Commander and Friend." Is He speaking something to you? Thank the Lord, and praise the Lord as He pours the gift of His Holy Spirit into you.

Ask the Lord for clarity if you require it. Ask Him to expand upon what He is speaking to your spirit, if you require more explanation. Talk to Him as you would a friend, because He is now your friend, and you can be His friend as well.

The more that you talk to the Lord, the more answers you will begin to receive from Him. Isn't that what we all desire? He promises in His word to fill you with His "goodness,"[2] and "good things."[3] One example of His goodness is His word, another is the gift of Salvation, and yet another is the Holy Spirit. Then there are gifts of the Spirit, and many more blessings in the Lord.

Congratulations! You have tapped into these gifts. I pray that your revelations from the Lord will gradually increase day by day, as you continue to grow in Him and trust in His plans and purposes for your life. You will see that His plans and purposes for your life are nothing short of incredible!

As Mark encourages, "just tune to flow" and watch, wait, and see how the Lord will work, and move in your Spirit, and in your life! Be encouraged! Your spiritual days of illumination and revelation knowledge in the Lord Jesus Christ are just beginning!

I pray that very soon you'll discover the Christian life is the best one of all. Later on when you reflect back over your life, I believe that your heart will be overflowing with such amazing gratitude and peace. You'll be able to say that you've truly been given a life that was extraordinarily fulfilling and astonishingly satisfying in the Lord.

I believe you will truly say, "This Christian life was the best journey that I have ever taken."

Then, my friend, with great assurance and certainty, you will finally be able to say, "One Ticket to Heaven, Please," and you will one day see and know that *your* ticket to Heaven, which has been awaiting you just across the veil, has been at last stamped and officially "accepted"!

With Greatest Agape Love in the Name of Jesus Christ,

Most Sincerely,

~Allison C. Restagno

Christian Author/Speaker

www.moderndaysalvationencounters.com
& www.moderndaymiraclesbook.com

1. *The Four Steps to Salvation and Commentary used by permission and courtesy of Mark Virkler, President of Communion with God Ministries, www.cwgministries.org, and words included from www.bornofthespirit.today*

2. *"For he satisfieth the longing soul, and filleth the hungry soul with goodness"* (Psalm 107:9, KJV).

3. *"Who satisfieth thy mouth with good things; so that thy youth is renewed like the eagle's"* (Psalm 103:5, KJV).

APPENDIX

THE SINNER'S PRAYER

I repent

for trying to be master of my own life. I change my mind about who I want to be in charge of my life. I turn from my useless and unproductive thoughts that I am the center of my universe and choose to believe in the living God who created everything, including me (Acts 14:15). I have lived without a purpose but now I will live to hear and obey You, God (Jn. 5:19, 20, 30).

I confess

with my lips that Jesus is Lord and believe in my heart that God raised Him from the dead. I believe that God so loved the world He sent His only Son, Jesus, to shed His blood to wash away the barrier of sin (Jn. 3:16).

I receive You, Jesus

as MY Lord and Savior (Jn. 1:11, 12).

I welcome You, Holy Spirit,

into my life to rescue and empower me, and to restore me to intimacy with my heavenly Father (Acts 2:38).

This Appendix was used by permission and courtesy of Mark Virkler, President of Communion with God Ministries

(www.cwgministries.org), and www.bornofthespirit.today.

MORE ABOUT ALLISON RESTAGNO

Allison Restagno is a best-selling Christian author. She now has two books in print, *Modern-Day Miracles* and *Modern-Day Salvation Encounters*. She is also an accredited, award-winning music teacher with 25 years of teaching experience, a wife and the mother of a wonderful four-year-old girl.

At the Lord's leading, she has compiled this collection of 40 short salvation stories to encourage, uplift and inspire each Reader to salvation through the Lord Jesus Christ. Having been saved herself at an early age and raised in a wonderful Christian family, Allison has been blessed with the knowledge of Christianity from her childhood years. In the last decade especially, she has been given the opportunity through a series of sovereignly orchestrated miracles to testify about the Lord's saving grace and His amazing supernatural power.

Allison continues to remind her Readers that no matter what the circumstances look like, God is on your side. Just trust the Lord, believe and have faith.

To contact Allison Restagno for a faith-building speaking engagement and hear her powerfully inspiring testimony of God's love and faithfulness, or to order books, please see her ministry websites:

www.moderndaymiraclesbook.com, and
www.moderndaysalvationencounters.com, or email her at
ARestagno@sympatico.ca
She inspires faith and trust in the Lord!

MARGARET HAMPTON
AUTHORITY MEDIA PRESS

Spreading Your Message Far and Wide,

Be Known. Be Seen. Make an Impact.

Raise Funds for Your Charity or Ministry.

Margaret Hampton loves our Lord, and in serving Him, she is devoted to serving her brothers and sisters in Christ. Believing each of us ministers in the workplace, wherever the Lord has planted us, her professional focus now is helping you gain your well-earned public perception as the "authority" in your respective fields, enhancing your reputation and visibility — so your important messages will be received by your constituents, the public and media with heightened credibility and impact. That's why she founded Authority Media Press, and that's why she is assisting with publishing and publicity for *Modern-Day Salvation Encounters.*

You have worked hard and prayed hard to gain valuable knowledge, experience and insights in your field, and to use them for good, whether in charitable or ministry endeavors, or for goods and services that make a meaningful contribution. Now it's time, unselfishly, to boost your public perception as a trusted authority, so you can serve God and man even better with your God-given gifts.

That is what Authority Marketing is all about. Making you a *Best-Selling Author* quickly and with ease, then publicizing your success, is just part of our network's process from which hundreds of professionals, executives, entrepreneurs, coaches, other achievers, ministers and non-profit leaders have benefitted. Our work positions them as the trusted "go-to" expert in their fields or geographic areas to tell their important story. We help them become more quotable in the media and more sought-after as a speaker.

We can tie into that process for you, too, so your ministry, business or charitable endeavors are launched to greater and more visible heights — and effectiveness.

Margaret Hampton brings to you her decades of experience in New York, Washington, Atlanta, and now Florida in executive and consulting positions in diverse industries, with organizations of all sizes, also with ministry initiatives, national health charity board positions, online media, publishing and public relations. An Alcoa Foundation Fellow at Columbia University (M.B.A. – Finance, 1974), Summa Cum Laude with Honors graduate from Florida State University (B.A. – Languages, 1969) where she is in the *Hall of Fame*, Margaret is the recipient of over 13 *Who's Who* and multiple other awards for her accomplishments in business strategy, finance and marketing for both billion-dollar corporations and entrepreneurial businesses. In 1984-1985, she was a contender for a Governor seat on the Federal Reserve Board and was offered the position of Senior Advisor to the U.S. Comptroller of the Currency (the position to which all National Banks reported).

Now she is here to serve you.

Contact: mhampton.cai@gmail.com

CPSIA information can be obtained
at www.ICGtesting.com
Printed in the USA
LVHW081625190620
658572LV00001B/145

9 780995 284302